Learning from West African Experiences in Security Sector Governance

Edited by
Alan Bryden and Fairlie Chappuis

]u[

ubiquity press
London

Published by
Ubiquity Press Ltd.
6 Windmill Street
London W1T 2JB
United Kingdom
www.ubiquitypress.com

Text © The authors 2015

First published 2015

Cover design by Amber MacKay
Front cover image: AlexTanya / Shutterstock
Back cover image: Hans Braxmeier / Pixabay

Printed in the UK by Lightning Source Ltd.
Print and digital versions typeset by Siliconchips Services Ltd.

(Paperback): 978-1-909188-67-9
(PDF): 978-1-909188-68-6
(EPUB): 978-1-909188-69-3
(Kindle): 978-1-909188-70-9

DOI: http://dx.doi.org/10.5334/bau

This work is licensed under the Creative Commons Attribution 4.0 International License. To view a copy of this license, visit http://creativecommons.org/licenses/by/4.0/ or send a letter to Creative Commons, 444 Castro Street, Suite 900, Mountain View, California, 94041, USA. This license allows for copying any part of the work for personal and commercial use, providing author attribution is clearly stated.

The full text of this book has been peer-reviewed to ensure high quality academic standards. For full review policies, see http://www.ubiquitypress.com

Suggested citation: Bryden, A and Chappuis, F (eds.) 2015 *Learning from West African Experiences in Security Sector Governance* . London: Ubiquity Press. DOI: http://dx.doi.org/10.5334/bau. License: CC-BY 4.0

A French translation of this book can be viewed, for free, at: http://dx.doi.org/10.5334/bav

To read the free, open access version of this book online, visit http://dx.doi.org/10.5334/bau or scan this QR code with your mobile device:

Table of Contents

List of Contributors

Emmanuel Remi Aiyede: Senior Lecturer, Department of Political Science, University of Ibadan, Nigeria.

Emmanuel Kwesi Aning: Director of the Faculty of Academic Affairs and Research, Kofi Annan International Peacekeeping Training Centre (KAIPTC), Ghana.

Dominique Bangoura: Professor at the Centre for Diplomatic and Strategic Studies, Paris. Lecturer and researcher, University of Abidjan.

Alan Bryden: Assistant Director and Head of Public-Private Partnerships Division at the Geneva Centre for the Democratic Control of Armed Forces (DCAF)

Lamine Cissé: Former Chief of Staff of the Armed Forces of Senegal, Minister of the Interior of Senegal, former United Nations Special Representative of the Secretary General for West Africa.

Fairlie Chappuis: Programme Manager within the Research Division at the Geneva Centre for the Democratic Control of Armed Forces (DCAF)

T. Debey Sayndee: Associate Professor and Director of the Kofi, Kofi Annan Institute for Conflict Transformation (KAICT), University of Liberia.

Zeïni Moulaye: Foreign Affairs Advisor and former Minister of Transport and Tourism for Mali

Foreword

In September 2015, at the United Nations Sustainable Development Summit, the international community adopted a new global development agenda comprising 17 sustainable development goals (SDGs). From now on, the international framework for development will recognize explicitly the significance of good governance and security for the achievement of sustainable development, notably with SDG 16 on peace, justice and strong institutions.

This step acknowledges the continuum between security and development which experience has confirmed. Indeed, there can be no development without security and vice-versa: the two are inextricably linked. Development contributes to the creation of an enabling environment for security and the rule of law; at the same time, improvements in security establish the conditions for sustainable development.

In their role as security providers, defence and security forces can support the implementation of the international development agenda. Security sector reform (SSR), a process at the crossroads of security, governance and development issues, enables the realization of this potential, given its role in conflict prevention, peacebuilding and long-term development.

For the security sector to contribute meaningfully to development, SSR activities aim to strengthen both the operational effectiveness of security providers and their accountability with regard to the rules and principles of the rule of law. To do this, SSR is one element of a comprehensive approach to promote democratic governance and the re-establishment of the rule of law, which can take several forms. First of all, it is a political process led by national authorities, which, over and above political, security and military institutions, creates buy-in across all segments of society for the purpose of national ownership. The political will of national decision-makers – on which SSR rests – goes hand in hand with the necessity of coordinated support from the wider international community.

Civilian control of defence and security forces and support to mechanisms of democratic oversight – whether formal or reflecting the role of civil society – are equally crucial (relevant ministries, inspectorates, parliaments, non-governmental organizations, the media etc.). Finally, SSR benefits both the security of the state and its citizens (human security) without discrimination.

This volume assembles lessons learned from SSR processes in West Africa, casting into relief key dynamics of security sector governance. It brings together the analysis of experts drawn principally from Africa who, given their personal experience, have participated in or followed closely reform efforts during the periods under consideration.

This study, far from reflecting a standardized approach to SSR, is intended to promote knowledge and understanding that can contribute to ongoing SSR efforts with a view to promoting conflict prevention and resolution and thus supporting development.

This initiative which is supported by the French Ministry of Foreign Affairs and International Development, is part of the wider assistance which France seeks to bring to national SSR processes.

Frédéric Bontems
Director for Development and Global Public Goods
French Ministry of Foreign Affairs and International Development
Directorate General for Global Affairs, Development and Partnerships

Preface

In 2015 the world came together to agree on a roadmap towards a more prosperous and secure future in the form of the sustainable development goals. At the same time, the West African region suffered resurgent threats from terrorism, political instability, democratic reversals, regional health crises and economic hardship. Dysfunctional security sector governance – and the inability of security sector reform (SSR) initiatives to change these dynamics – have played a role in these troubling developments. Indeed, in many places past achievements in security sector governance were called into question as the resilience of the countries under threat appeared to waver.

The Geneva Centre for the Democratic Control of Armed Forces (DCAF) has as its mission to support national actors and the wider international community in promoting democratic security sector governance. In a period when many long-held truths about SSR in Africa are being critically re-examined, we believe it is essential to carefully examine specific reform processes from the perspective of national actors. *Learning from West African Experiences in Security Sector Governance* offers insider perspectives from academics, policy makers and practitioners who have been intimately involved in national processes to design and implement governance-focused reforms in the security sector. The volume deliberately dismisses views of SSR as a series of technical activities in favour of an approach that situates reforms within the context of socio-economic, cultural and political realities that ultimately determine the success or failure of these efforts.

What are the key lessons emerging from this volume? First, there is a need to re-evaluate what we mean by success and failure. Timeframes, approaches and expectations need to be revised to take into account the necessarily gradual, iterative nature of national reform processes. This means that successful reform will need to be understood as a long process of relative progress measured against local and national governance realities, and not as the inflexible application of externally derived models and templates. Second, security sector governance institutions and actors remain under-utilised yet powerful vectors of reform. In particular, this volume shows that parliament and civil society should be far more prominent in SSR programming given the determinant but often neglected role these actors have played in advancing reform agendas. Third, reform approaches have largely failed to recognize the importance of establishing a shared vision for good security sector governance as a foundation for the highly sensitive political process of reform. Aligning expectations, creating shared understandings, and building trust between stakeholders through inclusive dialogue both within and beyond the security forces is a crucially neglected facet of SSR that has often proven decisive in whether reform progresses or stalls.

Looking across these reform contexts, perhaps the most striking observation that can be made is that security decision-making remains in the hands of a very small political and security elite. Indeed, in some cases even talking about security matters is deemed inappropriate by the very actors responsible for security sector oversight and accountability! This must change. Greater dialogue on security matters is the only way that lessons can be shared and learned. We therefore hope that this volume will contribute to the emergence of uniquely South-South perspectives across national and regional actors seeking to apply the principles of good governance in practice. At the same time, for the wider international community the lessons to be learned emphasise above all patience, humility and the primacy of local ownership embodied in an ethos of support rather than imposition.

I would like to join with the volume's editors, Alan Bryden and Fairlie Chappuis, in acknowledging all those that have supported this important research project. First and foremost, this volume has been made possible thanks to the dedication and knowledge of our six chapter authors. I would also like to express my gratitude to the Directorate General for Global Affairs, Development and Partnerships within the French Ministry of Foreign Affairs and International Development for their generous support. In preparing this volume DCAF wishes to thank Margaux Duverney for her constant support in every aspect of the project preparation; Aviva Proville, Salvatore Sagues, Sara Dezalay, Sroda Bedarida-Gaveh and Alexia Casale for copy editing and translation between French and English. Mia Schoeb proved invaluable for her background research; Petra Gurnter for her work in print design and layout; and Tim Wakeford and Frank Hellwig at Ubiquity Press for their patient support for this project. The editors also wish to thank the three peer reviewers who initially contributed their thoughtful and constructive comments on the first draft: Alwin Van Den Boogard, Bruce Baker, and Deniz Kocak.

The views expressed in this volume are those of the authors alone and do not in any way represent the views of the institutions or their representatives involved in this project.

Ambassador Dr. Theodor H. Winkler,
Director
Geneva Centre for the Democratic Control of Armed Forces

Geneva, October 2015

Acronym List

AFL	Armed Forces of Liberia
AU	African Union
BATA	*Bataillon des Troupes aéroportées,* Battalion of Airborne Troops, Guinea
CDS	Chief of Defence Staff
CENI	*Commission électorale nationale indépendante*, Independent National Electoral Commission, Guinea
CNDD	*Conseil national pour la démocratie et le développement*, National Council for Development and Democracy, Guinea
CNDH	*Commission nationale des droits humains*, National Human Rights Commission, Guinea
CNOSCG	*Conseil National des Organisations de la Société Civile Guinéenne*, National Council of Civil Society Organisations of Guinea
CNT	*Conseil national de la transition*, National Transitional Council, Guinea
CONASCIPAL	*Coalition National de la Société Civile pour la Paix et la Lutte contre la Prolifération des Armes Légères*, National Coalition of Civil Society for Peace and the Fight against the Proliferation of Small Arms, Mali
CPA	Comprehensive Peace Agreement, Accra, 18 August 2003, Liberia.
CPP	Convention People's Party, Ghana
DCAF	Geneva Centre for Democratic Control of the Armed Forces
DSF	Defence and Security Forces
ECOWAS	The Economic Community of West African States
EU	European Union
GPS	Ghana Police Service

GRC	Governance Reform Commission, Liberia
ICG-G	International Contact Group for Guinea
IGP	Inspector General of Police, Ghana
LNP	Liberian National Police
MFDC	*Mouvement des Forces démocratiques de Casamance*, Movement of Democratic Forces of Casamance, Senegal
MNS	Ministry of National Security, Liberia
MPRI	Military Professional Resources Incorporated
NBI	National Bureau of Investigations, Liberia
NLC	National Liberation Council, Ghana
NSRIA	National Security Reform and Intelligence Act 2011, Liberia
ONDH	*Observatoire national des droits de l'homme,* National Human Rights Observatory, Guinea
PDG	*Parti démocratique de Guinée*, Democratic Party of Guinea
PGPSP	*Programme de gouvernance partagée de la sécurité et de la paix*, Programme for Shared Governance of Peace and Security, Mali
PP	Progress Party, Ghana
SSR	Security Sector Reform
UN	United Nations
UNDP	United Nations Development Programme
UNMIL	United Nations Mission in Liberia

CHAPTER 1

Introduction: Understanding Security Sector Governance Dynamics in West Africa

Alan Bryden* and Fairlie Chappuis†

*Assistant Director and Head of Public-Private Partnerships Division at the Geneva Centre for the Democratic Control of Armed Forces (DCAF)

†Programme Manager within the Research Division at the Geneva Centre for the Democratic Control of Armed Forces (DCAF)

The promise of good governance for security, development and democracy in West Africa

If the post-cold war era brought new hope for development, security and democracy to the West African region, these hopes seem diminished in the first decade of the new Millennium. The burgeoning Nigerian economy may have shifted the economic centre of the African continent to the West African region, yet economic growth has not met the promise of a better future for a generation of young West Africans deprived of a sound education and relegated to a precarious existence in informal employment. While the pressures of frustrated development have not so far led to violent conflict on the scale seen in the 1990s and early 2000s, these tensions have still contributed to internal crises pitting insurgents, separatists and terrorists (as well as the forces of organized crime) against central state authority. Meanwhile the everyday security crises faced by populations as a result of rising crime and dysfunctional state security provision continue to hold back both the potential for economic development and the deepening of democracy.

While norms of democratic governance seem to have taken root in a number of countries, as reflected in the peaceful and orderly consolidation of

How to cite this book chapter:
Bryden, A and Chappuis, F. 2015. Introduction: Understanding Security Sector Governance Dynamics in West Africa. In: Bryden, A and Chappuis, F (eds.) *Learning from West African Experiences in Security Sector Governance*, Pp. 1–18. London: Ubiquity Press. DOI: http://dx.doi.org/10.5334/bau.a. License: CC-BY 4.0.

democracy in Liberia in 2011, Senegal in 2012, or Nigeria in 2015, reversals in Guinea in 2008, or Mali in 2012 also show that violent competition over the powers of state remains a threatening possibility. A clearer picture of these interrelated challenges is emerging, highlighting the ways that democracy, development and security are intimately interrelated. Thus the experiences of northern Nigeria and Mali as well as Benin, Niger and other states of the region have demonstrated how underdevelopment can cause immediate insecurity and threaten democratic governance. Moreover, these examples also show that what begins as a local, sub-national issue can rapidly escalate, engulfing the political centre of a state but also spilling across borders to become a regional threat. Similarly, instability that stems from elite power struggles at the apex of the state can quickly stall democratic processes, undermining state legitimacy and economic confidence necessary for development: Guinea, Guinea-Bissau and Côte d'Ivoire have all traversed such difficult periods in the first decade of the 2000s.

At a global level this disappointing record has been met with a volley of initiatives. The Millennium Development Goals recognised the relevance of poverty reduction to conflict prevention and these insights were built into international initiatives such as the New Deal for Engagement in Fragile States, which emerged over the following decade including 19 fragile or conflict-affected countries and eventually all OECD donor states (Busan Partnership for Effective Development Co-operation 2011; United Nations 2000; The Paris Declaration on Aid Effectiveness 2005; Accra Agenda for Action 2008; International Dialogue on Peacebuilding and Statebuilding 2011). The World Bank's 2011 World Development Report combined this political momentum towards a more holistic vision with the latest research on democracy, development and security, distilling these insights into an agenda for "security, justice and jobs" through more resilient, more legitimate institutions (World Development Report 2011). In 2015, this agenda has taken a further step forward in making inclusive, accountable institutions an explicit goal of the Sustainable Development Goals and linking this goal to conflict prevention and peace (Sustainable Development Goals 2015).

Governance has become the central concept at this confluence of democracy, development and security. Policy imperatives and scholarly research of development economics, conflict prevention and democracy have thus converged in the claim that the quality of governance can determine the trajectory of national affairs (see for example Halperin et al. 2010; Collier 2007). Seeking to apply these insights in the policy and practice of governance, such research has distilled a set of institutional qualities associated with progress in development, security and democracy under the term 'good governance'. While specific aspects of the good governance agenda vary between contexts and institutions, core elements include: accountability, effectiveness, efficiency, transparency, inclusiveness, equity and rule of law (Shabbir Cheema 2005).

Applying the principles of good governance to the security sector is the goal of security sector reform (SSR). SSR aims to improve security for the state and the population by making security provision, oversight, and management more accountable and more effective within a framework of democratic control, respect for human rights and the rule of law (Bryden and Hänggi 2004; Hänggi 2003; 2004). In particular, applying the principles of good governance to the security sector emphasized the idea that the state could only enhance democracy, development and security if it were concerned not only with matters of national defence and state security but also with human security – freedom from fear for the population (Krause 2006). The concept of human security anchored the agenda for effective and accountable state security provision, management and oversight within a framework of democratic governance, respect for human rights and rule of law.

As a means of strengthening a legitimate state monopoly on the use of force, SSR tends to focus on institutions. North (1990) provided some of the earliest explanations for how institutions can support the delivery of public services, an insight on which Robison and Acemoglu (2012) built by underlining the importance of open-access institutions, while Fukuyama (2013) focuses on the capacity of a government to deliver on public services. If the entire spectrum of public sector institutions have roles to play in providing for democracy, development and security, the part of the state charged specifically with security provision, management and oversight presents special challenges. For this reason, the quality of security sector governance is especially relevant to the current challenges in the West Africa region and it is on these qualities that this volume focuses.

Objectives of this volume

The fact that the quality of security sector governance is crucial to the overall fate of democracy, development and security makes understanding the dynamics of good and bad governance in relation to the process of reform all the more important. This volume focuses on the nature of security sector governance in West Africa through the lens of particular moments and key agents of reform in six states of the region.[1] It presents a collection of vignettes that together tell a larger story about the holistic nature of security sector governance and the dynamics of the reform process in a variety of unique national environments.

This volume differs from typical studies of SSR in that it does not seek to assess reform in its entirety as a longterm macro-national process; nor does it seek to develop an operational analysis of current security challenges. Instead this volume focuses on describing the fundamentally political dynamics of security sector governance and the need to understand these dynamics in the strategy, planning and implementation of SSR. The approach has not been to seek uniformity of analysis but rather to glean insights and perspectives from individuals whose proximity to the local context adds value. The contributors thus offer 'insider' perspectives based on personal background and experience. This has a number of implications. In particular, it is important to note that these accounts are not intended to provide a balanced view that weighs the pros and cons of different perspectives. Rather, they reflect the lived experiences, personal convictions and resulting biases of the contributors.

Security remains a taboo subject in many national contexts in Africa. In order to mobilise potential reform constituencies and build broad-based support for SSR there is a need to demystify the security sector. This requires a deep understanding of context. For this reason, the contributors place great emphasis on the political history that underpins current security sector governance dynamics. The key message is that for national stakeholders (and for external partners that want to support governance-driven SSR) acknowledging the deep historical currents that shape security at the national level is essential to understand opportunities and constraints for reform. These collected narratives are intended to generate practical lessons that can support learning and promote positive change. The fruit of these combined descriptions is thus an analysis of the larger patterns that emerge when these narratives are placed side-by-side, yielding insights for future approaches to SSR that are presented in the conclusion of this volume.

In focusing on micro-dynamics of reform, this volume posits a different understanding of what should constitute success and failure in security sector reform. In particular, this approach is innovative in acknowledging that the significance of specific moments and influential change agents will be fully visible only in retrospect. In the context of on-going political crises and even violent conflict, potentially transformational shifts will often appear isolated, superficial or insignificant. As a result, their potentially transformative character is neglected. Applying an approach that looks at change in a new way finds both successes and failures in unexpected times and places.

In adopting this approach, this volume also corrects a tendency in the literature to idealize conditions for success while neglecting the lessons of failure. Our approach reflects the fact that although examples of positive, transformational change are important, instructive insights also come from examples of reversal, stagnation or failed reform. Some narratives thus describe how reform faltered in a specific instance in the eyes of the local stakeholders. The focus for each chapter was selected in order to draw lessons from countries with diverse trajectories of political development: Ghana, Guinea, Liberia, Mali, Nigeria, and Senegal. This selection covers a range of contexts from democratic transition to consolidation, post-war and situations of democratic reversal. This range offers an instructive basis for comparison that incorporates insights from examples of progress as well as regression.

In sum, the descriptions that constitute the bulk of this volume point to the usefulness of a methodological lens that shifts the focus from macro-national narratives to the micro-dynamics of institutional reform in the immediate political context. Through the eyes and experiences of local actors, this collection analyses the small-scale successes of SSR together with the missed opportunities that have prevented SSR from having more transformational effects. Based on narratives of potentially transformative moments of political reform by eminent national experts with personal experience of these reform processes, this volume shows how SSR efforts influence security sector governance dynamics in significant if limited ways, while drawing concrete and practical insights from these national reform experiences.

Confronting a disappointing record: understanding the challenges of transformational change in West Africa

Despite extensive effort and some progress, establishing more democratic security sector governance is an objective that most African countries find themselves far away from reaching. The complex interactions of history, politics and economics dictate the terms of security sector governance within the unique structural conditions of each national – and subnational – setting. Yet across the region certain shared experiences allow broader patterns to emerge from the descriptions collected in this volume.

Among the most decisive influences on security sector governance are the legacies of colonial and post-colonial statehood. While experiences of colonialism varied, the legacy of an extractive and illegitimate central political authority is a common one across many West African states. In this context the DNA of West Africa's security sector institutions has predisposed them to resource extraction and population control, and these characteristics have carried over into the modern context. Moreover, the experience of extraction and heavy-handed state authority may be the only vision of state security provision that a population and its leaders have ever known. Improving state security provision in such a social context is not a matter of technical reform, training or equipment: it is a matter of rethinking the raison d'être of state security providers from the bottom-up based on a completely new and different vision of what security means and in whose interest it is provided.

While the legacy of colonialism was carried over to West Africa's modern security institutions, these tendencies have been exacerbated by the region's incomplete democratization. As post-independence political regimes embraced patterns of illiberal governance, with extensive external support, they also fostered unresponsive and predatory security sectors focused on regime/state security. A lack of democracy enabled many of these regimes to endure for decades, permitting patterns of predation to become deeply entrenched. Legislatures became beholden to powerful executives and judicial branches became the servants of state power instead of the rule of law. Under these circumstances, few states developed meaningful systems of democratic civilian oversight and national security developed into a domain of influence exclusively reserved for the most powerful political actors and men in uniform.

Even as state security sectors continued to serve the interests of the powers that be, populations took steps to provide for their own security. Commercial security provision became an immediate necessity for those that could afford it, while citizens without such means at their disposal turned to their own devices to protect themselves. Thus it came to be that despite the large and sometimes well-resourced security sectors at the disposal of West African states, the everyday security needs of a majority of the West African population were met by community-based non-state security providers or private security companies.

This context of economic hardship, social inequalities, and political disenfranchisement made fertile ground for armed conflict as social tensions spilt over into crime and political violence. States weakened by ineffective patronage-based political systems lacked the institutional capacity to respond effectively to the challenges with which they were confronted, and institutional and human capacity decayed further in the maelstroms that followed. As the legitimacy of state authority was eaten away by predation and ineffectiveness, the security sector became a further symbol of its illegitimacy as well as the hard edge of state repression.

The emergence of the SSR approach

The SSR discourse emerged in the late 1990s as a response to dysfunctional security sector governance and its consequences. Promoted first by European development agencies, SSR quickly became a pillar of multilateral strategies for crisis prevention, peacebuilding and development for organizations such as the United Nations, the African Union, ECOWAS, the European Union, the World Bank, and the OECD (United Nations Security Council 2014; African Union Commission 2013; Ball 2001; Aning 2004; Council of the European Union 2005; Council of the European Union 2006). While SSR is often perceived as an external agenda imposed on recipient countries, in particular in post-conflict contexts, this perception is inconsistent with the goals, principles and even history of SSR. The reasons for this are both pragmatic and normative. On the pragmatic side of the argument, reform strategies imposed from outside have repeatedly been shown to fail, because they are inappropriate to local context or not rooted in the local governance environment. On the normative side, the principles of good governance are inconsistent with the practice of imposed reform strategies.

Moreover, history has demonstrated that the only sustainable shifts in the terms of security sector governance have occurred in the context of strong national leadership of the reform agenda: examples as diverse as Indonesia during the post-Suharto Reformasi era and South Africa in the post-apartheid transition to democracy demonstrate the efficacy of strong political will for change (Cawthra and Luckham 2003).[2] All of these insights make meaningful leadership and investment in reform by national and local stakeholders essential for sustainable improvement in security sector governance even if reform strategies in practice often leave much to be desired (Nathan 2007; Donais 2008; 2009).

Derived from an understanding of security based on the broader concept of governance, SSR brings together all actors with a stake in security provision, whether as providers, overseers or beneficiaries of security, and regardless of whether state or non-state actors (Chappuis and Hänggi 2013). This governance driven understanding of SSR also accounts for the fact that the holistic SSR concept can involve a broad range of activities from the development of more robust legislative frameworks for security provision, management and oversight, to reforms focused on specific security institutions such as police, military, intelligence or border authorities, as well as particular oversight bodies and functions, such as human rights commissions or ombuds-institutions, parliamentary bodies or the justice sector (OECD–DAC 2007; UN SSR Taskforce 2012; DCAF 2015; United Nations 2008; 2013). Moreover, SSR also recognizes that fact that experiences of security and justice are inherently linked and therefore includes the justice sector. This holistic understanding is the conceptual basis for a comprehensive approach to reform that considers all aspects of who uses force, how and on what authority. Indeed this very point is what makes SSR distinct from other types of security assistance or capacity development – SSR always aspires to improve both accountability and effectiveness. Reform that privileges one aspect in favour of the other would thus be inconsistent with the SSR concept (Chappuis and Hänggi 2009).

SSR began in different states across the region in the early 2000s as a response to the fundamental governance challenges typical of many states in West Africa. In Sierra Leone, Liberia, Guinea-Bissau and Côte d'Ivoire, SSR was variously attempted with significant international support in the context of the recovery from civil war (see respectively, Bryden et al. 2008; Albrecht and Jackson 2009). In Nigeria, Benin, Mali and Ghana, reform was initiated in the context of democratic transitions (see further Bryden and N'Diaye 2011). While SSR is not an agenda specific to Africa, many important cases have taken place there and West African states as well as the regional body ECOWAS have played a key role in developing the concept and practice of SSR. Good governance of the security sector underpins the Protocol relating to the Mechanism for Conflict Prevention Management, Resolution, Peacekeeping and Security (ECOWAS 1999), the Supplementary Protocol on Democracy and Good Governance (ECOWAS 2001), and the Supplementary Act and the Code of Conduct for the Armed Forces and Security Services (ECOWAS 2011) and later the Regional Framework on Security Sector Reform and Governance (ECOWAS 2014; see further, Uzoechina 2014).

The combined regional experience of reform has yielded several insights into typical characteristics of security sector governance in many reform contexts. While our concluding analysis expands in detail on these insights, at this stage it is sufficient to note that political will at the executive level is determinant in progress of reform (or at least disproportionately important). The overbearing influence of the executive in reform processes is linked to the fact that security affairs in general are often treated as a reserved domain over which few civilian politicians have any influence at all. As such securing the endorsement of the security elite for a reform agenda is a sine qua non of progress. The fact that the executive and the security forces maintain a tight hold over the reins of power and over security affairs in turn helps to account for the noticeable pattern of weak legislatures across the region. Whether lacking political authority or human and financial resources to fulfil their democratic mandate, weak legislative control and oversight of security affairs features in every country we examine. In some respects, strong civil society input can compensate for this deficit in formally representative oversight, and vocal and active civil society advocacy for better governance of the security sector is also a typical feature of many West African contexts.

Neglected dimensions of security sector reform

Against the backdrop of the failures in governance characteristic of many political systems across the region, it is unsurprising that SSR has not resulted in transformational change. As Hutchful and Luckham (2010) note, the promise of good security sector governance is very far from the reality in most African contexts and it for this very reason that meaningful SSR requires a radical – transformational – change in the structures of power and governance of many states. This requirement for change in the most fundamental political, historical, and economic structures of governance in order to achieve the goals of good security sector governance has been said to constitute a "uniquely African dimension" of security sector reform, even meriting the term "security sector transformation" (Bryden and Olonisakin 2010).

Yet there is an obvious dissonance between the aspirations of the SSR agenda and the form it inevitably takes: Bryden and Olonisakin explicitly note, "security sector transformation, despite its radical overtones, is likely to be incremental and process-driven" (Bryden and Olonisakin 2010: 22). Despite this fact, current approaches to SSR are predicated on the idea that SSR can make profound changes to the conditions of governance over short time-frames and that the results of such reform strategies, when successful, ought to be obvious. This approach neglects that reality of change as a process, setting unrealistic expectations and emphasizing the least productive aspects of reform. The typical emphasis of many SSR strategies on training and equipping security forces while neglecting issues of democratic governance is a symptom of this problem. A more nuanced approach is needed to understand and assess SSR as an iterative and gradual process.

Acknowledging that SSR is a delicate and incremental process has implications for how we understand and assess the relative contribution SSR makes to democratic governance, peace and development. Taking the iterative nature of transformational SSR seriously requires a shift in focus in order to better recognize and weigh the potential long-term significance of incremental changes in the context of an on-going process. A new optic must be able to incorporate the idea that potentially transformational moments of reform are marked by shifts in the quality of security sector governance that are difficult to recognize as such at the time of their occurrence and may be easily reversed as the process develops in unforeseen directions.

Meaningful signs of change in the structural determinants of governance are small, smaller than approaches to SSR currently allow us to fully appreciate. This leads to neglect of the relative importance of small changes that can lead to long-term shifts, making it impossible to apply a flexible and adapted policy in response to the unfolding SSR process. There is truth to the claim that the goals of SSR are defined by a paradigmatic model of good security sector governance that no society on earth fully reflects. And on this basis, it must be acknowledged that all efforts at reform are found wanting and all measures of change are insufficient when held up against this idealized notion. This tendency to expect too much too soon also means that 'success' in SSR is defined by tangible or visible changes that often prove ephemeral and transitory in practice if they materialize at all. Current understandings of SSR are thus focused on spotting large shifts in outward appearance and overt practices rather than the small changes in norms, attitudes and expectations that may signal steps in the right direction.

Not only are signs of substantive change smaller than expected, they are also more likely to be literally 'invisible'. Current approaches to SSR tend to emphasize visible changes in security provision from physical infrastructure and equipment through to new institutions or systems. This optic emphasizes the formal organizational character of governance which is often only a façade covering up the informal normative basis of security sector governance that defines the real "rules of the game" (North 1990). This point is not unappreciated in approaches to SSR and there have been some innovative attempts to improve on planning, design and assessment methodologies. Most notably these have integrated the dynamics of non-state security and justice provision into actor mapping and reform strategies, and also included more satisfaction and perception based tools in SSR assessments, relying on qualitative methods such as focus groups, interviews and perception surveys (see for example, CENAP/CREDESS-Bdi 2012; Schnabel 2009). While these innovations open intriguing pathways into the question of change in state security provision, too often actual reform strategy remains focused on the institutional impacts of top-down reform programmes.

A further neglected dimension in current approaches to SSR is the effect of exogenous and endogenous shocks. Thus, notwithstanding problems related to bad design, it is also clear that SSR frequently experiences setbacks and full reversals for unrelated reasons. Yet approaches to SSR have so far failed to coherently integrate the fact that SSR may be frequently subject to reversals in transition contexts (Chappuis and Siegle 2015). Considering the frequency with which SSR strategies are beset by endogenous setbacks in the domestic political environment or caught up in the consequences of external shocks, this is a striking exclusion. From a pragmatic point of view, being able to contextualize such setbacks and reversals is a precondition to recognizing possibilities for new openings. This neglected consideration also overemphasizes the relative gravity of reversals and failures, which studies have shown are a common occurrence in democratic transitions and conflict-affected states (see further Halperin et al. 2010; Haggard and Kaufman 1995; Przeworski et al. 2000; Collier 2010; Freunda and Melise Jaud 2013). A progressive view of reform instead requires that gains and losses be understood relative to the local security governance context and not idealized models of statehood that exist nowhere.

Focusing on local conditions of security governance is a further essential element in understanding the transformational potential of reform. In contrast to earlier neglected elements here outlined, the call to focus on local security governance is nothing new to the SSR agenda. Understanding the imperatives of local context as it is composed of local actors, politics, social context and history is essential to reform strategies and further underlines the necessity of local ownership in the SSR agenda. Yet an iterative understanding of SSR requires a much closer reading of local context than SSR specialists have thus far been prepared to make given the inherent limitations of external perspectives on domestic governance dynamics (Schroeder et al. 2013). As a result, the study of SSR processes has been heavily skewed in favour of external analyses of reform contexts that compare superficial changes in security organization or structure with the idealized western model. In order to get beyond the limitations this bias imposes, analyses of reform contexts are required that bring to bear an intimate knowledge of history, social, economic and political context. Local voices, local perspectives can help to correct the bias towards unrealistic expectations that externally driven approaches to SSR have inadvertently created.

Iterative, gradual: reframing the analysis of SSR in West Africa

From this critique of current approaches to SSR follows logically the need to develop an analytical perspective on SSR in West Africa that can capture the potential for iterative and gradual change. In order to properly assess the relative importance of change, a description of the balance of power among various actors within and beyond the security sector is necessary. Such a description must also encompass the structural context within which SSR takes place and which determines security sector governance. This in itself is not a new approach – guidance on SSR always points to the relevance of contextual analysis and actor mapping (see for example, OECD-DAC 2007). In this volume our contributors offer the necessary descriptive elements for such an analysis by focusing on specific moments of change that may reveal something important about the immediate context at stake and the process of reform in general.

Turning first to the structural determinants of security sector governance, the potential for change must be understood against the backdrop of complex interactions between existing political, social, economic and historical trends, which in concert create what Schnabel and Born (2011) define as permissive and non-permissive reform environments. The interweaving of these diverse influences gives rise to the irreducible complexity of governance contexts that defies all but the broadest categorisations. It is precisely because each reform context is highly complex and therefore unique that understanding security sector governance requires an investment in exhaustive description. The complexity of interwoven governance dynamics also provides a rationale for focusing more attention on the micro-patterns of reform since it is at the level of inter-institutional and interpersonal interactions that complexity can yield to useful description. Such description provides a basis for comparative analysis to carefully assess what these patterns of interaction at the micro level might imply for the practice of reform in general and to what extent the findings may or may not be applicable in other contexts.

Where the existing political, economic, social or historical conditions remain stable, there is little room for reform to generate outcomes outside the existing status quo. However, where these structural conditions soften, new outcomes become possible. A typical example of a softening in structural conditions facilitating reform is a case of post-war transition where the influence of traditional power brokers is weakened and new actors have yet to impose themselves: in the uncertainty of the post-war phase new influence can come to the fore. Yet the status quo in an apparently stable situation can also be unexpectedly disrupted when a particular – even apparently insignificant – event catalyses action that can change the underlying situation. In the narratives here presented these dynamics become evident where, for example, a sudden trigger event makes a radical rupture with prior practices possible or even necessary. In the new status quo that emerges following such cathartic episodes, reform may progress or regress; in several of the narratives such trigger events were defining moments in reform processes, setting in motion processes of potentially transformational change. In order to capture the complex dynamics of the structural constraints that define security sector governance in the examples we study, each of our contributors takes the time to recount their own perspective on the most important social, political, economic and historical factors influencing the state's provision of security.

If the structural determinants of security sector governance are the playing field on which political competition over reform plays out, then the moments when competing agendas clash are the defining events in the reform process. These events may be small, even apparently banal changes that come to affect how power is exercised. A decision, a new practice, a policy shift, a change in attitude: such moments of reform can turn out in retrospect to be the foundation for decisive changes that over the long term amount to a transformational effect. At this level of small-scale moments in the reform process, change may come swiftly once the right conditions materialise. Indeed this speed may be matched only by the rapid deterioration that is possible in moments when the status quo destabilizes. Such moments of rapid change create the basis for a new status quo, which will either reinforce and enhance or undermine and prevent progress towards better security sector governance. The continuing succession of such moments defines the overall trajectory of the reform process.

In these decisive moments, specific actors, especially among the power-wielding elites in politics and the security sector, can play a disproportionate role in forcing change for the worse or for the better. Where the status quo remains intact, specific actors may apparently have little room for manoeuvre in influencing the determinants of security sector governance. Yet these conditions can change and sometimes quite quickly, especially when a number of actors come together in a coalition that is sufficient to disrupt the usual practices upholding the dominant status quo. This dynamic has been noted in analyses that point to the relevance of building so-called "inclusive enough" reform coalitions (World Development Report 2011: 120). In the narratives we present here this dynamic was illustrated by the surprising degree of influence that civil society could bring to bear on otherwise insensitive and inflexible regimes. Similarly, the most decisive factor in whether reform would advance or stall was in several examples the positive or negative disposition of top-level leaders in government. Moreover, words alone were often the only instrument these actors used to influence the process one way or another, illustrating the underrated value of dialogue in reshaping security sector governance. To capture this aspect of influence, our contributors pay special attention in their narratives to identifying the champions and spoilers of reform and how their actions defined the crucial moments of the reform process.

If the agency of specific individuals can have a defining influence on the nature of the reform moment, such agency is conditioned by the context within which such individuals operate and will define the room to manoeuvre at their disposal. Yet besides agency, contingency can also be an important driver of change or guarantor of the status quo. Although there is a prevailing tendency to think of reform outcomes as the intended result of planned interventions on the part of specific (too often external) actors, plans may go awry and in complex environments usually do. As a result unintended consequences or accidental interactions can determine the process of reform, its context and outcomes. For this reason a fuller understanding of SSR must make analytical space for contingent, accidental, and unintended effects which often occur at the micro-level. In this volume, authors have traced the logic of reform interventions in each narrative but have also pointed out the many unintended, accidental and contingent effects that decoupled these plans from their intended consequences. This approach has offered nuanced insight into why reforms stalled despite the best efforts of reform champions or advanced in spite of the influence of reform holdouts.

It should be obvious at this point in the discussion that a full account of the reform process requires a profound knowledge of the political, social, economic, and historical context within which it occurs. Not only is it possible that the minutest details of actors or context prove determinant in explaining how reform progresses or not, but perspectives on which details matter most may differ markedly based on knowledge of context. National narratives founded on local expertise and perspectives provides a feel for context that cannot be matched by external specialists, offering potentially new purchase on questions that external analyses have so far failed to adequately account for. This approach is promising because relatively few contributions on SSR in Africa have been authored by experts from the region or nations concerned (see for example Uvin 2009; Malan 2008; Greene and Rynn 2008; Albrecht and Jackson 2009). As a result of this external story-telling, the literature is skewed towards external perspectives on reform that are heavy on technical details and light on political, social and historical context (for important exceptions to this trend, see Bryden and Olonisakin 2010; Bryden and N'Diaye 2011; Bryden et al. 2008).

In contrast, the narratives collected in this volume are the work of a diverse group of individuals drawn from among the research, political and security communities of each country. In describing each context from their own personal point of view, contributors bring to bear all the benefits of direct insider experience as well as a profound knowledge of history, society and politics. These experts have experienced first-hand the processes of reform which they narrate. Their accounts represent personal vignettes in the tradition of thick description, rather than formal analytical case studies in the conventional social science tradition. Their status as national experts themselves embedded in the particular social and political context in which reform unfolds gives them privileged analytical access to perspectives invisible to external points of view, no matter how well versed in subject matter or how familiar with local dynamics. At the same time, this analysis cannot be detached from the authors' own perspectives, experience and predispositions. For all these reasons, these chapters constitute authentically national as well as personal accounts of reform dynamics.

The contributors to this volume focus on the institutional dynamics of security governance and the nature of state security provision. Turning first to institutional dynamics of security governance, it is clear that transformational SSR implies a shift in the balance of power between the relative parties in government; the relationship between the security sector and civilian power; the balance of power between civilian control bodies; and, the dynamics of control and responsiveness between the state and the population. That the governance aspects of reform are laid aside in favour of more short-term, so-called technical reforms is an oft-cited complaint about the formulation of SSR programmes. As a result a number of the narratives collected here focus explicitly on aspects of institutional governance, even though efforts at SSR in these countries are more often associated with ambitious 'train-and-equip' style programmes: for example, T. Debey Sayndee throws new light on the SSR process in Liberia by examining SSR through the lens of legislative developments in a case that is usually treated as an example of police and military reform. Similarly, Emmanuel Kwesi Aning focuses on the little-known example of the revival of the Police Council in Ghana where more attention has tended to centre on the reform of the Ghanaian Police Service itself. Looking at the transition from military to democratic rule in Guinea, Dominique Bangoura describes in detail how reform minded military actors aligned with civilian politicians to rearrange the balance of power – both formal and informal – between the armed forces and a newly elected democratic government.

The second aspect of potentially transformational moments in security sector governance and reform on which our authors focus is the nature of state security provision. From the perspective of good security sector governance, state security provision should address security from the point of view of the population by focusing on the character, accountability, effectiveness and efficiency of organizations charged with the use of force on behalf of the state, as well as how the state meets its responsibility to monitor and control the use of force. These are the aspects of reform that are most likely to reflect short-term changes (though not necessarily positive ones) by the simple fact that the functions of security institutions are most often the entry-point for reforms. In our collection of narratives, E. Remi Aiyede and Zeïni Moulaye show how the poor interface between management, control and performance laid the foundation for the operational failures of the defence forces in Nigeria and Mali respectively. In contrast, General Lamine Cissé offers a personal perspective on how the defence forces in Senegal have in his view escaped politicisation even while facing the dual pressures of an on-going internal insurgency and a delicate consolidation of multiparty democracy. In diverging from alternative accounts of the conflict in Senegal in particular as concerns respect of human rights and treatment of the civilian population, this chapter also illustrates the distance that remains to be bridged between between internal and external perspectives.

An important facet of these narratives is that they do not only consider change for the better. Several contributions document how a potential opening towards reform and improved governance was stalled, stymied or sabotaged by vested interests or accidents of the process: Aiyede details how corruption and vested interests bled momentum from the process of defence reform in Nigeria, while from Mali Moulaye recounts the political manoeuvring that transformed a comprehensive and holistic reform strategy into a dead letter ultimately contributing to the conditions for national crisis which followed in 2012.

The conclusion to this volume presents the lessons to be learned for SSR based on insights from a comparative analysis of these rich descriptions. As such it argues for the relevance of focusing on reform processes as an iterative and gradual evolution in the dynamics of security sector governance. This perspective can reveal developments that may otherwise go unnoticed – both positive and negative – at the national, sub-national and local levels. A detailed explanation of the dynamics of reform can then allow for strategies that are better calibrated to local context while establishing more productive reform priorities. Applying this analytical approach will allow us to draw further lessons from the extensive experiences of the West African region in SSR and to think differently about how to support reforms aimed at improving security sector governance.

Learning from West African experience in security sector governance

In bringing together six eminent experts to describe moments in the long trajectory of their national reform processes, this volume offers a unique take on experiences of reform in each national context. Each of our authors thus focuses on specific moments of policy shift that have led either to a qualitative change in some aspect of security sector management, oversight and control or to a change in the nature of security provision. The approach places particular emphasis on describing how the momentum for or against reform emerged in each unique situation.

Chapter 2 considers the resurrection of the Police Council in Ghana in 1992. Ghana is often cited as a regional example of democratic transformation and improved security sector governance, yet the roots of this transformation remain poorly understood. Filling this gap in the historical record of Ghana's democratic governance, Aning examines the 1992 resurrection of the Police

Council and its patchy track record as an organ for democratic oversight and police management before and since this turning point. Tracing its origins in the first era of Ghana's democratic independence through long periods of neglect under military dictatorship and its eventual resurrection under the constitution of 1992, Chapter 2 demonstrates the usefulness of looking for progress in democratic transformation within the micro-dynamics of a much larger, much longer, reform process.

Chapter 3 looks at the political transition in Guinea. Guinea's long and tortured history of military rule left little hope for the future when a young and inexperienced soldier seized power abruptly in 2008. Yet against this bleak background, a democratic transition has slowly emerged under the guidance of a reform-focused military leader who bridged the civilian-military divide building trust and the basis for a new political era. Focusing on Guinea's delicate political transition during the period of 2009–2010, Bangoura traces Guinea's difficult path back to civilian government and democratic civilian control of the security sector.

Chapter 4 considers the neglected question of legislative governance in Liberia's post-war reform experience. Despite 133 years of unbroken civilian government, one of Africa's oldest independent republics nevertheless suffered from grave democratic deficits in legislative governance throughout its history. Following two decades of military rule and devastating conflict, Sayndee charts the rise of the Liberian legislature and its unprecedented role in establishing an entirely new legislative framework for democratic governance of the security sector in the context of Liberia's long struggle to recover from civil war.

Chapter 5 dissects Mali's record of reform in an era of democratic transition. Slated as the paragon of transformational reform and peaceful conflict prevention in the 1990s, Mali's sudden democratic reversal and subsequent armed conflict surprised many in 2012. Although the state of Mali's security sector has been the subject of much scrutiny since the dramatic events of 2012, Moulaye looks back to earlier attempts at comprehensive SSR in the 2000s, finding the roots of a future crisis in past failures to tackle reserved domains in the defence sector.

Chapter 6 relates the promise of Nigeria's transition to democracy, which seemed to augur a new era of democratic security sector governance. Yet the country's security forces failed to throw off the shackles of dysfunction and corruption leading to dramatic failures in security provision and national defence in the face of a vicious internal insurgency. Against the backdrop of Nigeria's contemporary security challenges, Aiyede explains how Nigerian attempts at SSR over the period 1999–2007 were able to snatch defeat from the jaws of victory.

Chapter 7 presents Senegal's unique regional experience with civil military relations. Senegal's long history as a consolidated and peaceful democracy stands in contrast to the experiences of many states of the region. And all the more so because Senegal has succeeded in consolidating its democracy while isolating its security sector from the same destabilizing effects of internal armed conflict that have brought low many of its neighbours. Cissé presents his own insider perspective on the foundations of democratic civilian control in Senegal as West Africa's oldest democracy marks its first democratic alternance in a new era of multi-party politics and even as one of the world's longest-running internal conflicts continues in the Casamance region.

Despite the wide range of national contexts covered across these chapters, a number of commonalities are nevertheless evident. Legacies of authoritarian governance have left behind specific security cultures with common features across all six contexts. This is evidenced by the fact that security is treated as a taboo area reserved for security professionals, or a little more broadly, elite politicians. These habits of interaction also contribute to cultures of adversarial relations between security forces and the political executive, between the political executive and other branches of government, and between government and the wider public represented by civil society. Moreover, there is limited tradition of discussing security issues beyond narrow elites. This reflects a focus on regime security, and the history of security institutions as defenders of state power. These characteristics have several direct consequences for SSR, which are brought out in the comparative analysis that concludes this collection in Chapter 8.

After a decade and a half of targeted support and sometimes heavy-handed interventions, the results of SSR processes have to date proven mixed at best and it is clear that things have not worked out as once was hoped. The challenges that SSR seeks to address can be summarized in the failure to tackle the dysfunctional patterns of security governance that maintain status-quo power relationships and undermine the legitimacy of the state as a provider of security. While the inherent complexity of security sector governance within a given national context is an important reason why SSR has not resulted in transformational change, the conclusion to this volume argues that the lack of an analytical perspective attuned to recognise iterative and gradual evolutions in governance has contributed to this failure. The narratives that follow seek to remedy this deficit by providing granular, insider descriptions of slow and unsteady change in West African experiences in security sector governance.

Notes

1 In its references to moments of change and the relevance of individual actors within sequential processes of institutional evolution, the analytical approach applied in this volume draws on historical and sociological theories of institutionalism. For key references in this literature please see further Hall and Taylor (1996); March and Olsen (1983); Peters (2011).

[2] While both Indonesia and South Africa constitute examples of strong national leadership, it should be noted that in both cases the record of reform in the post-transition era was subsequently challenged as a failure to adapt to the core normative concept of SSR by applying the principles of good governance to the security sector. For alternative views see further Baker (2015); Altbeker (2005).

CHAPTER 2

Resurrecting the Police Council in Ghana

Kwesi Aning

Director of the Faculty of Academic Affairs and Research, Kofi Annan International Peacekeeping Training Centre (KAIPTC), Ghana

Introduction

Since 1982 Ghana has enjoyed its longest period of sustained political stability since it gained independence in 1957.[1] While several periods of its democratic journey have been interrupted by military incursions (including attempted coups d'état, mutinies and the successful overthrow of democratically elected governments), post-1981 Ghana was transformed from being the 'sick state of West Africa', both economically and politically, to become a reference point for democratic practice and security sector governance processes. In a region beset by security challenges, several aspects of this 'success story' have yet to be documented. This paper addresses this lacuna concerning Ghana's security sector reform processes and how they have influenced security sector governance dynamics, examining some of the changes in the fundamental structures of power and governance behind Ghana's transformation. To this end, the paper analyses a particularly significant policy intervention: the re-establishment of the Police Council under the 1992 constitution and the contradictions in both how the institution has functioned over time and how it has contributed to the manner in which the Ghana Police Service (GPS) is governed. To appreciate the developments that have contributed to what this paper argues are first steps in a genuine case of deepening democratic control of the security sector, it is necessary to examine the history of the incremental changes that brought it about.

How to cite this book chapter:
Aning, K. 2015. Resurrecting the Police Council in Ghana. In: Bryden, A and Chappuis, F (eds.) *Learning from West African Experiences in Security Sector Governance*, Pp. 19–35. London: Ubiquity Press. DOI: http://dx.doi.org/10.5334/bau.b. License: CC-BY 4.0.

Ghana's political history and national security experiences have shaped the mechanisms and processes for managing its security sector. Understanding how the transformation of Ghana's security sector occurred relies on locating the processes of change within the developmental and historical trajectories of the country's turbulent post-independence politics and advances in security sector management and oversight. The statutory security sector institutions willingly and fully embraced the notion of democratic control. As a result, the governance voids and deficits that characterised periods of military rule have begun to close, though they have not been completely eliminated, as seen in relation to the Police Council.

From the early 2000s, Ghana gradually reversed the militarisation that previously characterised the country's political landscape, instead creating relatively stable security sector governance processes that have contributed to the development of a robust and responsive democracy. However, although several oversight institutions have been established to govern the sector democratically, they are not performing as effectively as hoped: the GPS and the Police Council are typical in this regard.[2]

The Ghana Police Service was established in the pre-colonial era. It has gone through several iterations, from a 'force' to a 'service', in an effort to improve its performance and deliverables. In this context, the Second Republican Constitution of 1969 recognised the need for a Police Council, which was first established in 1970. Yet a general perception still exists that the GPS has not been able to deliver and satisfy the expectations of those that it serves. Two key factors lie behind this dissatisfaction: the GPS's human resource capacity is weak and political will appears to be lacking in relation to enforcing democratic oversight through the Police Council.[3]

As a case study, the GPS and Police Council demonstrate how the very idea of the need for change arose, how this was pushed through the policy and bureaucratic jungles of successive military and democratic governments, and the limitations of the resulting structures. The paper begins by examining the political and historical conditions at stake in the policy shifts regarding Ghana's security sector. It then explores the processes that led to the 1992 resurrection of the Police Council, paying particular attention to the key actors involved and the sustainability of various shifts in policy. In sum, this chapter analyses the different facets of the legal and institutional frameworks underpinning the governance and functionality of an important actor within the security sector in Ghana with a view to identifying best practice that might inform wider SSR approaches in West Africa.

Context for Security Sector Governance in Ghana

In the immediate post-independence period, President Kwame Nkrumah's 1957–66 management of the security sector included creating a Presidential Guard and extending the control by his Convention People's Party over the whole security sector. There are different views on how the security sector either suffered or gained political support and currency during the subsequent regimes of Akwasi Amankwa Afrifa (1966–1969); Ignatius Kutu Acheampong (1972–78) and Jerry Rawlings (4 June–1 October 1979 and 1982–1992) when morale, as well as command and control structures, were severely undermined by political meddling. The end result was a situation where presidents were "able to subtly politicize the leadership of state security institutions resulting in partisanship" (Adu-Amanfo 2014: 99). Such political interference in the professional performance of duties and the delivery of public services culminated in a "demand for reciprocal loyalties, to the detriment of merit and professionalism" (Adu-Amanfo 2014: 100). Thus the "over-politicisation of the leadership of... security institutions has led to a virtual split of their loyalties and hence heightened partisanship among the rank and file" (Adu-Amanfo 2014: 100) contributing to "undue political interference with their routine administration and planning and execution of operations" (Adu-Amanfo 2014: 100–102). Indeed the political interference and meddling was not only limited to the military and police sectors, but also affected the intelligence community (Aning, Birikorang & Lartey 2013: 199–201). Hutchful (1999: 97) characterised the cumulative result as an "endemic process of militarization".

Yet, in spite of the negative impact on the professional cohesion and performance of these services, Ghana eventually succeeded in reversing this process. This shift was made possible by decisions initiated by the different military regimes that ruled Ghana from 1966 to 1992: the National Liberation Council (NLC), the National Redemption Council, the Supreme Military Councils I & II, and the Provisional National Defence Council. Although the Provisional National Defence Council was a dictatorship, a decade after it came to power it promulgated the 1992 constitution to restore democratic politics after sustained domestic and international pressure. This ushered in the Fourth Republic. The reversal of militarization was intensified during the Fourth Republic under the National Democratic Congress, which ruled between 1992 and 2000. Between 2000 and 2008, under the New Patriotic Party Government, these multiple processes contributed to improved oversight and the re-professionalisation of the security sector, leading to an increasing and genuine sense of democratic control of the security sector (Hutchful 1999: 109).[4]

The Creation of the Police Council

The Police Council was established after democratic rule was restored in 1970: thus, it was one of the first acts of the newly elected Progress Party (PP) Government, led by Kofi Abrefa Busia. But the initial drive to see the idea implemented was began under the dictatorial regime of the NLC following the first coup d'état (1966). A critical question is why a military-cum-police regime, whose democratic credentials were not entrenched, included such a provision in its 1969 Constitution?

The reason for the establishment of the Police Council lies in the country's history. During the immediate post-independence Kwame Nkrumah era from 1957 – 1966, the mistrust between Kwame Nkrumah's Convention People's Party (CPP) and the military caused a policy-shift to equip the Ghana Police Force (as it was then known) as a counter-balance to the Ghana Armed Forces: this was intended as a protective measure to forestall any of the security sector services from being able to overthrow the CPP. However, when Nkrumah's CPP became more dictatorial and progressively limited the democratic space, a combined force of police and army personnel collaborated to overthrow the CPP on 24 February 1966. The NLC was established in the aftermath of this coup d'état and was led by a combination of police and military officers.[5]

One of the NLC's first policy moves was to introduce a campaign to re-educate Ghanaians on their civic rights and responsibilities. Between 1966 and the introduction of the Second Republic in 1969, Busia led a number of civic campaigns around Ghana. Key among these was the Civic Education Forum, a civil society forum established by the NLC regime and led by Busia that aimed to inculcate the values of civil behaviour into Ghanaian society. Busia's leadership of the Civic Education Forum exposed him to the wide chasm between the availability and establishment of institutions and their functional ability to deliver. Busia subsequently became Prime Minister (1969 – 1972): his charisma and idealism was a key driver behind the move to introduce the Police Council. Busia was a scholar as well as a political figure: earlier in his career he wrote the seminal work on the role of chieftaincy in Ghanaian society (Busia 1951), stressing the importance of checks and balances in all institutional processes and procedures. Having experienced actual political power, he sought to fuse theory and praxis by arguing for the creation of an institution to provide oversight of the police's activities. The establishment of the Police Council was thus a novel initiative that sought to provide institutional oversight, simultaneously informing parliament about the performance of the police via an annual report on its activities and a parliamentary discussion of the report submitted by the Police Council.

Using his close affiliation with the NLC Government, when the process for the re-introduction of democratic politics began in 1968, Busia and his cohorts formed the PP, which subsequently won the election in 1969. Inducted into office as the Second Republic, one of their most abiding policy shifts was the introduction of the Police Service Act 1970 (Act 350) based on the 1969 Constitution. The Police Service Act 1970 (Act 350) remains the single most important piece of legislation governing the security sector, especially the GPS, with its intricate set of rules, regulations, checks and balances.[6] The enactment of Act 350 sought to improve the performance and oversight of the police service as a whole, with parliament performing a critical democratic oversight function. Act 350 is thus imbued with an intricate set of rules and regulations that establishes in detail facets of its administrative and oversight functions. When the original Police Council was formed in 1970, it was made up of ten members and operated as the constitutional body responsible for advising the president on matters of policy relating to internal security, including the role and operational capabilities of the GPS.[7] This represented a major and innovative policy shift that can partly be put down to the fact that the leadership of the Second Republic had worked closely with the combined police/military leadership of the NLC and, thus, had a clear vision of why oversight was so important and also how to make it palatable to the security sector and the wider public.

There are several key sections in Act 350. First, it requires the Inspector General of Police and, by extension, the GPS as a whole to submit annual reports to parliament through the Police Council:

> As soon as may be after the 30th day of June in each year, the Inspector-General of Police shall prepare a report giving details of the administration of the Police Service ... during the previous twelve months. The report shall be submitted to the Minister who shall cause it to be laid before the National Assembly.[8]

Under Act 350 the Police Council functions as an advisory body on appointments, welfare, discipline, selection, training, police-public relations and the adjudication of disciplinary appeals from serving officers.[9] Apart from the statutory demand to report to parliament, the Police Council is also mandated to:

- Review the constitutional and statutory oversight duties of the Police Service;
- Deliberate on the extent to which their mandates have been accomplished;
- Synthesize the rationales for their various successes and shortfalls;
- Identify targeted interventions in order to supply the operational deficit of the service; and
- Agree on a set on concrete re-orientations, programmes and activities for strengthening the oversight functions of the Council.

The Council may also, with the approval of the President, identify regulatory measures for the effective and efficient administration of the Police Service.[10]

Atrophy under Military Dictatorships

Although the PP government introduced the Police Council, the fundamental oversight responsibility of informing parliament through annual reports never took place. One can argue that, the Council under the PP government had insufficient chances to develop and institute its working modalities before a return to military rule. The military returned to power through a coup d'état in 1972 led by Ignatius Kutu Acheampong who then established the National Redemption Council which was followed 1978 – 1979 by the second Supreme Military Council of Frederick William Kwasi Akuffo. Though both Acheampong and Akuffo were military officers, there seems to have been a 'soft' spot for the police and this resulted in the police service being giving logistical support and other materiel much more than the armed forces. Several distinctive branches within the police were formed and the GPS was also renamed the Ghana Police Force. Changing the 'service' to 'force' was a clear indication by the new military rulers to give the police institution the necessary muscle to deal both with the public in times of agitation and to be able to serve as a countervailing force to the military.

Moreover, in 1974, the Police Force (Amendment) Decree 303 (NRCD 303) amended sections of Act 350. This change was critical because the GPS was institutionally removed from the administrative and bureaucratic control of the Public Services Commission. A further major distinctive change was that the Inspector General of Police (IGP) now chaired his own Police Council and was elevated to Cabinet Rank. Such an intrusive intervention meant that the guard became the guardian simultaneously, hindering effective oversight and concentrating too much unchecked power in the hands of the IGP.

Thus, between the coup d'état in 1972 and 1992 there was a democratic lacunae as Ghana's democratic institutions were hollowed out by one military dictator after another. The genesis of the Police Council was the exception, perhaps because it stemmed from the idealistic beliefs of an individual academic. Yet the intermittent interventions of the military into politics routinely suspended the working of the Police Council. Critical to appreciating these developments is the need to understanding how Ghana's security sector has always been controlled by a complex web of legal frameworks, some of which were suspended at times, while others were overlooked, abrogated or left in abeyance depending on the political dispensation at the time. When the legal framework governing the country was suspended following coups that established new coercive institutions, those already serving in the security sector felt unable to question their new leadership, not least because they were unsure from how high up the chain of command new orders were emanating. This proved especially problematic when new decision-making procedures created during military regimes sought to undermine the effectiveness of established institutions.[11]As such, during military regimes, when the current constitution was suspended, the armed forces and the GPS maintained their internal administrative and disciplinary regulations and procedures; however, these were kept in place for command and control purposes, as well as to create the impression of continuity in the case of the GPS. The Police Council – under whose remit these internal regulations were expected to be implemented in the interests of democratic oversight and accountability – was itself left in limbo and allowed to atrophy. It was only after the long hiatus between 1979 and 1992, when constitutional rule was reinstated, the Police Council saw a renaissance under the constitution of the Fourth Republic.

A key factor behind the Police Council's present form was the gradual opening of political space within which other non-traditional 'securocratic' institutions came to play critical roles in reshaping the sector (Aning 2008b). Gradually, Ghana's security sector has changed towards more inclusive and transparent governance processes. This provides:

> "an instructive study of security sector governance in West Africa, if only for the fact that an apparently endemic process of militarization appears to have been arrested and finally reversed in the late 1980s and 1990s, facilitating a transition to a fairly robust democracy. And while in some respects, Ghana's experience is representative of many transitions from military authoritarianism to electoral 'democracy' in West Africa, and shares many of the limitations and ambiguities of these transitions, it departs from most in that Ghana's initial exercise in regime rearrangement appears to be deepening into a genuine sense of democratic transition. Evolving stable security sector governance has been central to this experience." (Hutchful 2004: 1 – 2)

Hutchful's analysis demonstrates the extraordinary nature of Ghana's successful transition from largely autocratic military regimes following its independence in 1957 to the establishment of the democratic Fourth Republic in 1992. Despite the diverse nature of the regimes in power during this period, and the different changes and agendas that shaped the security sector, there has generally been a pragmatic approach to its management and administration. Even before the Second Republic in 1970, there were moves to reform, deepen and strengthen democratic governance mechanisms in Ghana with respect to the security sector, with institutional mechanisms for oversight gradually being accepted and their effectiveness enhanced.

The key to understanding Ghana's security sector dynamics is the combined power of the domestic demand for reform of the sector and the role of bilateral and multilateral institutions. Critically, most of these international institutions sought reform in the context of the "provision of a limited set of public services at the lowest possible cost": thus, there was a broad drive to make ministries, departments and statutory agencies more efficient and accountable as an essential part of improving overall efficiency in the public sector (Brzoska 2002: 1). In spite of demands from Ghana's international partners to reform the security sector as part of general public-sector reforms, the Rawlings administration of 1982 – 1992 resisted these pressures throughout the series of extensive reforms starting in the 1980s. These public-sector reforms, which benefitted from substantial external funding, resulted in the establishment of the National Institutional Renewal Programme but largely excluded security institutions.[12]

Only since 1996 has the idea gained ground that security sector institutions require extensive reform – and perhaps even to a greater extent than the rest of the public sector.

Resurrecting the Police Council

In 1992, after a sustained period of domestic agitation for the re-institution of democratic governance, a constitutional review process was undertaken. As a result, the political space opened up and a constituent assembly was tasked to design a new constitution. Following the introduction of democratic governance mechanisms with the inception of the Fourth Republic, the idea of a Police Council was reinserted into the constitution. Thus, the 1992 Fourth Republican constitution enjoined the reconstituted Police Council, under Article 203,[13] to advise the president on matters relating to internal security, including the conditions of service for personnel of the police service, budgeting, pensions, salaries, and finance for the effective and efficient administration of the GPS.

Thus, similar to the original version, by law the reconstituted Police Council is an advisory body to the president. Although the GPS is now institutionally located under the administrative purview of the Ministry of Interior (now a member of the Police Council), the Police Council itself is an independent body. At the headquarters level, the Police Council has two advisory bodies: the Police Appointments and Promotions Advisory Board and the Police Management Board.[14] While the former advises on appointments and promotions at all levels, the latter advises on major policy issues and decisions regarding the service's general administration and operations. Both are subject to the Police Council, so all GPS activities fall within its remit and responsibility. The issue remains whether these bodies have the effective authority to exercise their functions adequately. Despite these problems, there is general consensus among critical observers of Ghana's security sector landscapethat the continued existence of the Police Council is necessary and welcome.[15]

The new constitution made particularly significant changes to membership of the Police Council itself, making the vice president a member and, subsequently, the chair.[16] Under the new constitutional provisions, Police Council now comprises:

1. The Vice-President, who shall be chairman;
2. The Minister responsible for the Interior;
3. The Inspector-General of Police;
4. The Attorney-General or his representative;
5. A lawyer nominated by the Ghana Bar Association;
6. A representative of the Retired Senior Police Officers Association;

7. Two members of the Police Service, appointed by the President, acting in consultation with the Council of State, one of whom shall be of a junior rank; and
8. Two other members appointed by the President.

These changes reflected broader ones in the country as a whole and the GPS in particular. First, the addition of members of the retired Senior Police Officers Association recognised the immense expertise that was available in this body and its value to the work of the Police Council. Second, a police officer of junior rank was included to bring to the fore problems faced at this level of policing. However, it is unlikely that this move has had the intended effect as the hierarchical nature and institutional culture of the service makes it almost impossible for a single junior officer to bring the concerns of his or her colleagues to the fore without fear of being victimised.[17] This nominal inclusion of the junior ranks can be considered a legacy of the 1981 revolution during which junior ranks briefly took over the reins of government.

Regional police committees were also included in the new legislation to replicate some of the advisory functions of the Police Council on a smaller scale. However, these bodies have never been formally established. As such, all the developments regarding the Police Council since the advances accomplished under Busia can be considered technical adjustments and additions.

Despite the potential and intentions behind its establishment, the Police Council continues to suffer from a long history of close presidential control. The vice-president's position as chair was revoked, for example, in the aftermath of the potentially dangerous security crisis between President Jerry Rawlings and the late Vice-President Ekow Nkensen Arkaah.[18] Although progress was made insofar as the vice-president's position as chair of the Police Council has since been reinstated,[19] even in a democratic era membership of the Police Council remains biased towards the political executive and insufficiently independent. Out of the ten members, eight are appointed by the president, the exceptions being the member from the Bar Association and the retired police representative. Ideally, membership would reflect the three arms of government and also include civil society representation to make the Police Council more responsive to the public; instead, it is generally considered to fall largely under the control of the president. Moreover, most of the Police Council's since 1970 have worked and reached decisions by consensus with very little of their deliberations brought into the public domain.

The Police Council is generally perceived by observers – and, indeed, by members of the GPS – as primarily concerned with "promotions, demotions and dismissals".[20] Yet, although this is meant as a derogatory epithet, these are key mechanisms for enforcing accountability and ensuring professionalism. Thus, the Police Council's credibility has been called into question, including in relation to apparently unwarranted promotions that attracted resentment among the rank and file. However, in the last twenty years there have been instances where the Police Council has made capricious decisions. For instance, under the Kufuor Government in 2001 many senior police officers who had attained the compulsory retirement age, including the then IGP, were asked to retire. These officers still occupied positions as senior police officers as some had been given extended contracts by the government and others had remained for other reasons. While this decision was within the law and the GPS' regulations and procedures, many of those concerned were unhappy.[21] On the surface this decision was a show of strength by the Police Council; however, it later bowed to executive authority. Similarly, in a 2003 move attributed to the Police Council one senior police officer was promoted over the heads of many more senior personnel, creating agitation in the GPS. This was only one of a number of promotions and appointments that surprised many. The appointment of a retired officer as an IGP while serving officers were not considered was another example. The Appointments and Promotions Advisory Board claimed they were not consulted in all instances.[22] If so, the question remains as to who is advising the Council and how are these decisions made?

Immediately after the inauguration of the Police Council in November 2013, the chair, Vice President Kwesi Bekoe Amissah-Arthur, revealed that a new procedure for the appointment of IGPs would be instituted to avoid the ongoing instability that previously accompanied appointments: this primarily arose from associated political wrangling within the GPS causing tension across the ranks (Joy Online 2013a). However, just weeks after the vice president's public statement, the president renewed the appointment of the present IGP without consulting the Police Council, leading to serious consternation within the service (Joy Online 2013b).

The current barriers to improvement are two-fold and are both rooted in the Constitution. First, the mode of appointment of the IGP and the members of the Police Council make the GPS prone to the whims and caprices of the executive without adequate democratic control. The nature of the Police Council's work must not be seen to be in the control of the executive as this offers the possibility of illegitimate use for political advantage. The GPS should serve the people, so the populace must have a clear view of how the GPS is set up and controlled. Second, the office of the IGP is perceived to hold a great deal of influence. While the powerful nature of the office, including perceived tacit support from the executive, is primarily for operational reasons, a weak Police Council will be unable to provide checks and balances, especially where the GPS operates as a unified command institution. As a result, in practice the office of the IGP decides what to let the Police Council know and what to let it decide: provided the Police Council has the impression that the executive concurs, whatever is presented will be accepted, even if there is opposition. Thus, the performance of the Police Council ultimately depends on what the executive desires, not least because it is the executive that appoints the majority of its members. Every officer is aware of the current deficiencies and difficulties in the performance of the GPS but few raise their voices about these glaring inadequacies. In the past, more complaints were made when the situation was far better than it is now.

The sustainability of change

In Ghana's case, several key actors were involved in the most significant policy shifts regarding the Police Council. Busia, a long-term opposition leader, academic and human rights campaigner used his strong democratic credentials to institutionalise processes to bring about transparency. Although he established the Police Council, governmental difficulties and expectations prevented him from following through on ensuring that the Council functioned effectively.[23] Since the inception of the Fourth Republic, the usual constraints facing the Police Council – especially the lack of human resources, financial resources and executive control – have been offset by the opportunities, which have increased over time, to expand civil-society expertise and engagement within the security sector, though these opportunities are still too often adversarial. Nevertheless, the improvements in this arena have also been accompanied by opportunities to build capacity and deepen the interest of political parties and parliamentarians in security issues. In the immediate post-authoritarian period in 1992, the relationships between parliament/political parties and the security sector were full of distrust,[24] but since the inauguration of the Fourth Republic there have been attempts at widespread reform, including in relation to security sector institutions.

In analysing the effectiveness of the Police Council with regard to its mandate there is a close correlation between the effectiveness and accountability of the GPS as a whole and the performance of the Police Council. When the Council is perceived to be hands-on and engaging closely with the IGP and the headquarters management team, there is a positive effect on the general performance, effectiveness and service delivery of the GPS (Salia 2015).

Overall, there remains room for improvement in the activities and operations of both the GPS and Police Council. Moving forward, the GPS must clearly identify goals and set standards; there must be an agenda setting out major policy issues and also standard operating procedures for both administrative and operational matters. Some policies exist but enforcement is inconsistent, including with regard to eligibility requirements for recruitment. Publicly the police enforce these criteria, but there has been an emerging trend of 'protocolism' driven by persons of influence, especially the government, that has started to entrench incompetence across Ghanaian state institutions. Regulations and laws must be reinforced by the Police Council as provided for under Article 203(2) of the 1992 Constitution to ensure enforcement across the GPS. To improve the GPS, the Police Council must lend weight to the relevant regulations, laws and procedures or the improvements will be deprived of legitimacy. Similarly, if appointments to the Police Council are made more transparent without accompanying improvement in the GPS, this would be mere window dressing: the two are interlinked and intertwined in all respects.

Transparency on budgetary issues is key. The current administration seems to be concentrating its efforts on the creation of Formed Police Units: equipment has been procured and 170[25] officers will soon be sent on a mission to South Sudan. However even the Police Management Board seems to know nothing of the source of funding for this equipment. If the Police Management Board, which is supposed to advise the Police Council on policy decisions, lacks this knowledge, then who has it? This is especially important given that resource gaps are having a significant negative effect on the GPS' capabilities. Vehicles are not being serviced and some units and stations do not have the requisite staffing and equipment to carry out their duties. The popular strategy of ensuring police visibility has taken able officers away from stations to intersections, leaving other core duties unperformed or underperformed. In Accra alone, it is estimated that about 1000 officers perform these duties daily while stations lack investigators and officers to perform essential duties. This has a knock-on effect on policing across whole districts, divisions and regions.[26] The low level of investigated cases and commensurately high level of cases under investigation means that Ghana's prisons are full with remand prisoners. If the Police Council put more pressure on the IGP and the Criminal Investigative Department team, this problem could be reduced.[27]

Another area where the Council has so far failed concerns the appointment of the IGP and other critical headquarters staff. The existing job descriptions and specifications must be reviewed in is order that the persons appointed may be monitored and assessed according to clear criteria. This, in turn, would ensure adherence to the relevant laws, procedures and protocols, as well as conformity to performance requirements. Further on the subject of enforcing regulations, the fact that the rank and file of the Police Service do not understand the ethos of the GPS must be addressed. Since the GPS generally instructs commands, units and the rank and file through service orders, instructions, signals and circulars, the Police Management Boards could use the same avenues to clarify the GPS' mission statement and philosophy. This would make use of the extant system to ensure relevant information and documents are widely circulated to the command level and, in turn, cascaded downwards, creating conformity and a solid basis for measuring the efficiency and effectiveness of the GPS as a whole.

In sum, the reinstatement of the Police Council during the Fourth Republic represented a major and sustained policy shift in terms of re-establishing oversight of the GPS. The Police Council continues to be recognised as a necessary institution with good long-term prospects for strengthening the effectiveness and performance of the GPS even if much room for improvement remains.

Conclusion

Applying a historical perspective sheds new light on the under-analysed but critical issue of the Police Council's trajectory and the wider implications of this institution for security sector governance. In general, democratic oversight of the security sector in Ghana has improved since the 1990s. Nonetheless, in subtle ways the legacy of military control remains. In particular, parliamentary authority remains weak relative to the executive. To alter this balance, parliament will need to be endowed with better institutional capacity to exercise its mandated oversight functions; it must also have the resources necessary to enable and sustain such changes. Moreover, aspects of existing legislation, enacted to regulate the activities and performance of key security sector institutions, have come to limit rather than facilitate democratic oversight: these must be reviewed and amended. Frequent shifts in personnel and excessive politicisation of key oversight and accountability institutions have undermined an already weak human resource base. Even if all these issues were addressed, to be truly effective oversight institutions like the Police Council need to be complemented by more input from civil society actors. Ghana's civil society must become more active in networking, dialogue and advocacy if the country is to widen democratic space within the security sector and more generally.

It was not until 1992 that parliamentary processes began to impact on the security sector. The on-going failure of parliament to demand an annual report from the Police Council demonstrates that work remains to be done, though there have been important improvements in the legislation and constitutional provisions governing the security sector. Successive parliaments have been hampered by limited research on the security issue, party influence and the turnover of members of parliament as a result of elections. An efficient and functional Police Council, and appropriate oversight by parliament, must be guided by pragmatism and political realism rather than by party and individual interests. Despite the extremely limited literature about the Police Council and security service in Ghana, several general conclusions can be drawn. First, there is a need for a better fit between rhetoric and praxis. While the statute books recognise the important role that the Police Council can play, it has been rendered largely ineffective – wheeled out to make statements when Ghana's institutional credentials need to be shown to civil society and the rest of the world. Second, while the Council is given broad strategic functions and roles to play, it has generally limited itself to the more mundane tasks of listening to complaints from officers, and shying away from the more sensitive political issues of providing strategic guidance as stipulated by the constitution. Irrespective of its present weaknesses, there is consensus among Ghana's political and civil society that when properly resourced and led, the Police Council can and will contribute to the oversight and regulatory functions envisaged by the drafters of the 1969 Constitution and the Police Service Act in 1970. However, sustaining progress requires that the Police Council's statutory roles and powers be strengthened so that its decisions cannot be overturned by the executive or through the replacement of its members.

What implications does this have for governance-driven reforms in the West African region? In Ghana, the rhetoric of reform is not always backed by institutional independence, drive and effectiveness; thus, Ghana's ability to initiate and sustain governance-driven reforms are hampered. A more disturbing situation is to be seen across West Africa with the initial enthusiasm and optimism for such reform in the early 2000s replaced by lethargy and, in some countries, the reversal of advances in this arena.

Three issues remain outstanding. First, how can policy shifts to improve the effectiveness and efficacy of the Police Council be introduced? Second, how can such shifts be sustained over time? Third, what is the most effective and sustainable way to build a human resource base for maintaining intellectual and civil society engagement in these processes? Academia in particular must play a role not just in knowledge-creation but promoting access to other stakeholders and raising the profile of views different from those of the GPS. However, at present it is difficult to analyse and discuss the Police Council's work as, apart from short messages issued after formal meetings, there is no documentary evidence of its decision-making processes and the nature of its discussions. Improving civil society engagement with the Council requires innovative leadership to deliberately seek outside expertise to enrich and improve its knowledge base.

Ghana's institutional and legislative framework seeks to create an environment for democratic governance, including of the security sector. However, as law enforcement deteriorates in Ghana, with an antagonistic and potentially violent election expected in 2016, the future is not assured. There is the urgent need for a reinvigoration of the ethos behind the creation of the Police Council focused on creating a proactive and responsive police service that can resist an increasingly hostile political environment to ensure the continuation of democratic processes. As Ghana's democratic processes and mechanisms deepen, the Council's work will continue to be important: its strategic direction can and should play a crucial role as the GPS struggles to respond to public expectations.

The challenges ahead do not diminish Ghana's achievement in overcoming the political instability of the 1970s and 1980s to restore its democratic institutions, including the Police Council. Ghana has managed to provide at least a semblance of administrative oversight for the police and this is a major achievement that offers opportunities for improvement.

Notes

[1] I am grateful to several of my colleagues at the Faculty of Academic Affairs and Research of the Kofi Annan International Peacekeeping Training Centre

for helpful and critical comments on earlier drafts of this paper, especially Nana Bemma Nti and Paul Avuyi. I am also thankful for comments and editorial support from Dr Alan Bryden and his colleagues at DCAF. Finally, several high ranking police officers were helpful in providing comments and clarifying my thoughts. I am most grateful.

2 See, for example, the controversies surrounding the Ghana Police Service recruitment policy in which the GPS convinced the Police Council that it could investigate itself by establishing a Special Investigation Taskforce (Salia 2015: 32 – 33). See also Daily Graphic (2015a; 2015b; 2015c).

3 For a discussion of the historical developments of the Ghana Police Service, see Aning (2002).

4 See also Aning (2008a)

5 The National Liberation Council was a military-cum-police administration, headed by Lieutenant General Joseph Ankrah. The other members of the NLC were Commissioner of Police JWK Harley, Deputy Chairman Colonel EK Kotoka, General Officer Commanding the Ghana Armed Forces BA Yakubu, Deputy Commissioner of Police Colonel AK Ocran, Assistant Commissioner of Police JEO Nunoo, Major AA Afrifa and Deputy Commissioner of Police AK Deku (Barker 1979: 177 – 179).

6 Other legal frameworks that have regulated the Ghana Police Service, include, but are not limited to, the 1963 Security Service Act (Act 202), the 1965 Police Service Act (Act 284), Ch. XIII of the 1969 Constitution of the Republic of Ghana., the 1970 Police Service Act (Act 350), the 1974 Police Force (Amendment) Decree, Ch. XVII, s 172 – 175 of 1979 Constitution of the Republic of Ghana and the 1992 Fourth Republican Constitution.

7 See therefore the relevant provision in the Constitution of the Republic of Ghana (1992: Art. 203[10]).

8 Police Service Act (1970: Art. 36[1]).

9 See therefore Police Service Act (1970: s 10 – 16). Boyes (1971: 241 – 243) relates to this section in his 1971 Report.

10 See Art. 203 (2 – 3) of the 1992 Constitution. See also Act 350, Part III, sections 10 – 16. For how this relates to the Boyes Report of 1971, see Boyes (1971: 24 – 26). Article 201 of the 1992 constitution makes the vice president chair of the Police, Armed Forces and Prison Councils. However, the 1992 constitution was amended with Act 527 in 1996 to forestall a president and vice president from different parties in a coalition government not resolving relevant disagreements (Quantson 2000: 292 – 308).

11 In several interviews with senior police officers, mention was made of a politically-connected appointee from the revolutionary era (1981 – 1992) who contributed to undermining the sanctity of recruitment procedures by filling positions with party affiliates. Interview by the author in Accra, 7 March 2015.

[12] For a detailed discussion of these processes, see Aning and Lartey (2008). These reforms were variously described as 'public sector reform', 'national institutional renewal', 'public order' and 'rule of law' reforms. They were carried out in the 1980s within the context of the Economic Recovery Programme and the Structural Adjustment Programme. Under these programmes, a National Institutional Renewal Programme was set-up to see to the reform of several Ghanaian institutions. See also Atuguba (2007).

[13] These duties are familiar, with the notable exception of disciplinary oversight: they can be seen as a reinvigoration of the 1969 Police Council duties, with an extension to the original mandate.

[14] This structure is established by the Police Service Regulations (2012: reg 8, 10).

[15] Interview with senior police officer, Accra, 10 March 2015.

[16] See therefore the relevant section of the Constitution of the Republic of Ghana (1979: Ch.XVII, s 173[1a]).

[17] See, for example, Avuyi (1995); Assistant Staff Officer of Ghana Police (1990). See also Interview in Accra, 11 March 2015. According to the officer interviewed, the inclusion of a junior rank officer on the Council was "just for the numbers".

[18] In an interview with former Vice President, and later President, John Attah-Mills, he explained in detail the touchy nature of the problems raised by the split between President Rawlings and his vice president: the latter formally left the governmental coalition to head another party coalition, but retained his vice presidential position.

[19] See Ghana Web (2013). According to the report, "President John Dramani Mahama on Monday, November 11, 2013 inaugurated a new Police Council to be chaired by Vice President Paa Kwesi Bekoe Amissah-Arthur. The members of the Council are: Minister for the Interior, Kwesi Ahwoi, Inspector General of Police Mohammed Alhassan, Deputy Attorney General, Dr. Dominic Ayine, Commissioner of Police Ms. Rose Atinga Bio, Commissioner of Police Kwasi Nkansah (Rtd.), Inspector Charles Obiri Yeboah, Mrs. Nancy Amarteifio, Rev. Dr. Lartey Lawson and Alhaji Salifu Osman."

[20] Interviews with several stakeholders between January and September 2014 and January-March 2015.

[21] During the course of the research for this chapter, one of the most vexed political issues to emerge was the constant meddling of the executive in the functioning of the Police Council. As one officer retorted, 'check whether a new PC was composed by President John Kufuor (2000–2008) before the abrogation of the extended contracts. If no, then what did the PC do as its homework before approving the so-called extension of contract which it took the President to stop? There is also lack of consistency once again from the political leadership because Kuffour's government also extended the

appointments of some officers under the guise of contracts. As was expected, those contracts were cancelled or not extended when President John Mills (2009 – 2012) took over the presidency'. Telephone interview, Accra, 10 March 2015.

22 Interview, Accra, 8 March 2015.

23 For an alternative critical view, see Asamoah (2014).

24 Interview, Accra 13 December 2012.

25 Daily Guide News of Thursday, 23 October 2014.

26 A commissioned study is needed to assess the impact and effectiveness of this overt police strategy and to explore its implications. Has it reduced crime? Has it made the police more productive? Could the resources required for this level of visibility be entrusted to stations or the districts to police their own beat? What is the visibility team doing that the stations, if well equipped, would not do? According to an interviewee, "it is just depletion of resources if not misuse and or public sympathy winning activity". Interview, Accra, 15 March 2015.

27 Interview with senior police officer, Accra, 8 March 2015.

CHAPTER 3

Transitioning to Democratic Governance in Guinea

Dominique Bangoura
Professor at the Centre for Diplomatic and Strategic Studies, Paris.
Lecturer and researcher, University of Abidjan

Introduction

Security sector governance is an unfamiliar topic in Guinea. The subject remains taboo because it is generally left under the purview of the military, the police, men in uniform and the head of state. The reasons for this situation are historical as well as political and relate to the different, successive regimes in Guinea: the civilian dictatorship of Sékou Touré, who led the country from the time of independence until his death (1958 to 1984); the military (1984 to 1990) and authoritarian (1990 to 2008) regimes of General-President Lansana Conté and finally the military dictatorship of Captain Moussa Dadis Camara, who took power on 23 December 2008 and held it until 3 December 2009 when he was removed from power, following an attempt on his life.

Against such a backdrop, it has been difficult to establish the institutional and non-governmental conditions required to bring about change. It was only at the start of 2010, with the accession of General Sékouba Konaté, that a more favourable political environment was created and the first security sector governance and reform policy and stability measures were implemented. Also for the first time, civil society was able to influence the process and their demands were taken into account.

Nevertheless, it was only at the end of the transition, with the election of President Alpha Condé in November 2010 that security sector governance took on its full meaning, particularly as there was strong political will at the

How to cite this book chapter:
Bangoura, D. 2015. Transitioning to Democratic Governance in Guinea. In: Bryden, A and Chappuis, F (eds.) *Learning from West African Experiences in Security Sector Governance*, Pp. 37–59. London: Ubiquity Press. DOI: http://dx.doi.org/10.5334/bau.c. License: CC-BY 4.0.

highest level of state and that the various state and non-state actors were all very keen to pursue these efforts. The question now is whether these promises will be fulfilled during the term of office of the incumbent president.

Security sector governance in Guinea: background

The place and role of the armed and security forces have varied from one regime to another. Although Sékou Touré was a civilian leader, he established and developed a hard-line form of Marxist style authoritarianism, using and misusing the army, which he did not trust. He preferred to develop the Militia, the armed wing of the single party, which was totally devoted to him. Lansana Conté, who was first and foremost a military leader, used the army as one of the principal tools in seizing and maintaining power. Moussa Dadis Camara, who took power through a military coup d'état very quickly used the armed forces to entrench his regime and clamp down on both the political opposition and civilians.

Security sector governance under Sékou Touré (1958 – 1984).

Guinea was the first Francophone West African country to attain independence, on 2 October 1958, a few days after the historic "no" in the 28 September referendum proposed by General de Gaulle.[1]

A poorly endowed and politicised armed forces. The Guinean armed forces was created on 1 November 1958. It was made up of volunteers from the colonial army (Horoya 1993a; 1993b). However, not all Guinean soldiers were allowed to join the budding national armed forces and a number of them were denied access for political reasons (Bah 2009).[2] From the start, the Guinean army made a name for itself on the African continent through the contingent that joined the United Nations Blue Helmets in Congo, as well as their engagement alongside various national liberation movements (Angola, Mozambique, etc.) (Soumah 2004: 162). Nevertheless, under Sékou Touré, the Guinean military was deprived of resources, training, and equipment; some NCOs and officers were trained in eastern European countries and in Cuba. The army was provided with Soviet equipment but remained poorly endowed and badly organised.

There are two reasons that can explain the difficulties encountered by the army. First of all, Sékou Touré did not trust the military,[3] which had been responsible for organising coup d'états on the African continent and deposing several civilian heads of state. The first president of Guinea thus preferred to concentrate resources on the single party that he established, the Democratic Party of Guinea (*Parti démocratique de Guinée* – PDG). According to the Guinean journalist and politician, Siradiou Diallo, the party, which was designed to be the guiding institution, the driving force, and the instrument for controlling national life, was placed at the summit of the pyramid of government. All other institutions, including the armed forces and the militia, were subordinate to the party and only represented organs of implementation or instruments in the service of the party (Diallo 1986). The PDG was therfore named the party-state, which demonstrates its omnipresent (Bah 2009) and totalitarian nature (Camara 1998: 64).[4]

The regime thus exercised tight control over the military.[5] In addition, the army was subordinate to the PDG, the ruling party. This conception of the military was to have dire consequences. Strong politicisation of the armed forces led to indiscipline because an overzealous corporal with strong political affiliations, close to the seat of power, could easily question orders from a senior officer and even humiliate the latter. This lack of respect for the hierarchy led to malfunctions because subordinate officers had no respect for the military command structure. The politicisation of the military also led to other consequences at a later stage; it encouraged soldiers to take power (the 1984 and 2008 coup d'états) and to challenge the regime (repeated counter-coup attempts and mutinies under Lansana Conté, attempted assassination of Moussa Dadis Camara).

The Militia, a force to exert control beyond the armed forces. Under Sékou Touré, the People's Militia, a powerful paramilitary force, superseded the military. It was designed as a protective shield and to provide close security for the head of state. It was directly answerable to him and served as one of the main instruments of domination, in conjunction with the single party. Its mission was in theory to maintain law and order alongside the police, but in reality it was in charge of keeping watch over the armed forces and controlling the population. It was an armed, political police force that excelled in surveillance, denunciations and arbitrary arrests. Ranks in the militia were the same as in the military. Militia members frequently committed acts of violence against the police, gendarmes and soldiers. This parallel body garnered a lot of hostility from career military personnel, who sometimes spoke out or acted against it, but never succeeded in undermining it. Towards the end of his life, President Sékou Touré had a militia that matched the military in terms of numbers: 10,000 men on either side. The militia was however held in greater esteem.

Under such a regime, no social or political force could have even the slightest oversight or control, outside of the organs of the PDG. Sékou Touré died suddenly on 26 March 1984 from a cardio-vascular attack, leaving behind a country that was totally drained, with overcrowded prisons and countless victims who had died under torture or disappeared. In the absence of a proper count and an independent investigation, the precise number of victims of his regime has never been officially established. A few days later, on 3 April 1984, the military took over power under the leadership of Lansana Conté. After 26 years of civilian dictatorship, the country began an era of military dictatorship.

Security sector governance under Lansana Conté (1984 – 2008).

General Lansana Conté held power for 24 years. Between 1958 and 2008 therefore, Guinea had only two heads of state, one civilian and one military, but both shared a style of governing that used force and violence.

Three periods of governance under Lansana Conté. There are three distinct periods in the regime of Lansana Conté. The first, from 1984 to 1990 is the military period. The military regime dissolved the single party (PDG) and suspended the 1982 Constitution but did not undertake any reforms. This was an emergency regime. The second period, running from 1990 to 1995, represents the inception of the rule of law, with the adoption of the December 1990 Constitution by referendum. This was a time of liberalisation, marked by the adoption of a multiparty system and incipient public freedoms. Unfortunately, this period did not last very long. The ruling power organised and won presidential elections (1993) and parliamentary elections (1995), but both votes gave rise to strong protests, as a result of the massive electoral fraud. The third period is the period between 1996 and 2008. In February 1996, Lansana Conté faced the threat of being overthrown when a mutiny broke out in the armed forces, based on parochial demands. The head of state ended the mutiny by accepting all the demands, but he had many members of the forces arrested. This marked the restoration of an authoritarian regime. In November 2001, a referendum on the constitution led to the removal of the limitation on the number of presidential mandates and thus allowed Lansana Conté to stand for office indefinitely. In 1998, the president stood for re-election while the principal opposition candidate, Alpha Condé was arrested and imprisoned. The same occurred in 2003. In both of these elections, the head of state won the ballot, which the opposition condemned as fraudulent. A few months before, in 2002, the ruling majority had won the parliamentary elections under similar circumstances. With the exception of three parties, the opposition had chosen to boycott these elections.

Within such a context, there was little or no room for democratic forces to exercise oversight or control. The national assembly was considered a rubber stamp institution, in the service of the ruling government. In the socio-political arena, the ruling government did not hesitate to use deadly force on several occasions, in clamping down on trade unions and militant forces as they demanded social and political change (February, March and June 2006, January 2007).

A divided armed forces and the rivalry with security forces. The military was divided. It was often the theatre of generational conflict, ethnic tensions and personal rivalries, which resulted in the different groups of officers neutralising each other. Recruitment was based on political and ethnic criteria and training and exercises were inadequate; promotion did not depend on competence but rather on allegiance to the ruling power. There were huge disparities between the high-ranking officers, who were closest to the head of state and enjoyed great opulence, and the rank and file that lived in abject poverty. As a result, the indiscipline that had begun under Sékou Touré persisted in the barracks.

There was also an atmosphere of rivalry and mutual suspicion between the defence and security forces. This also applied between the military and the police because under Sékou Touré the military was subordinate to the Militia, the political police force. Being from the military, Lansana Conté directed more attention and resources to the gendarmerie than to the police, which is the security force that theoretically is responsible for protecting persons and goods. The police remained marginalised: their inferior role and status in the eyes of the army and gendarmerie led to violent clashes, most notably in June 2008 when police stations were destroyed. On 17 June 2008 for instance, soldiers clamped down violently on the police as they demanded increases in salaries and allowances.

Security sector governance under Moussa Dadis Camara (2008 – 2009).

President Conté officially died on the evening of 22 December 2008. His death was announced on national television at around one o'clock in the morning by Aboubacar Somparé, the Speaker of the national assembly and the information was relayed by Prime Minister Souaré and the army chief of staff, General Diarra Camara. For a few hours, therefore, there was the feeling that the process set out under Article 34 of the Constitution[6] to cover a vacancy of power had been initiated. The very next morning, however, at about 7.30am on 23 December, a group read out an initial statement over Guinean radio, announcing a putsch. Their spokesperson, Captain Moussa Dadis Camara announced the suspension of the constitution, government institutions and political and trade union activities, as well as the creation of a military committee known as the National Council for Development and Democracy (*Conseil national pour la démocratie et le développement* – *CNDD*). In the evening of 24 December he declared himself president of the republic.

Captain Camara himself announced the start of a political transition with clear objectives: to create the conditions that would enable Guinea to organise free and transparent elections and thus set up a democratic political regime through a democratic process of change (Bangoura, Bangoura & Diop 2006). He promised not to stand for election himself in this process.

In reality, however, the situation quickly raised some fears. The government that was established by decree on 14 January 2009[7] included a large majority of military officers. The 14 January 2009 programme statement appeared to be a vast undertaking, whereas the transition was only supposed to last a few months. Captain Camara would neither have the time nor the legitimacy to undertake all this, especially as the international donor community had condemned the putsch.

The style of governance of the head of the junta was characterised by volte-faces, contradictory signals, populism and angry outbursts during which he would summarily dismiss officials in public and once shouted at a western diplomat. No institutions were established to manage the transition. The knell sounded on the transition during the sixth session of the International Contact Group for Guinea (ICG-G) on 3 and 4 September 2009 in Conakry. On that date, Moussa Dadis Camara operated an about-face, breaking his word and dispelling any hopes of calming the situation. In an aside to the attending diplomats he said, "I shall stand for election because the people are demanding that I do so".

This first transitional period was a failure. It ended with the bloodbath in the stadium in Conakry on 28 September 2009 where government defence and security forces violently repressed political party activists who were demanding an open and democratic electoral process. Another serious event occurred on 3 December 2009 when Captain Camara himself became the victim of an assassination attempt by the head of his personal guard. This was after Toumba Diakité had refused to comply with the instruction from the president to answer questions before the UN international commission of inquiry on the 28 September 2009 massacres. Did Toumba Diakité act because he feared prosecution or because as a matter of principle he felt that the head of state was ultimately accountable for the acts perpetrated? The situation is a further demonstration of the extent of violence and indiscipline within the armed and security forces in Guinea.

In conclusion, it is clear that since independence, the armed forces, gendarmerie and police (including the militia under Sékou Touré) in Guinea, have distinguished themselves with acts of violence and repeated exactions against civilians and their fellow citizens. These forces have shown the signs of recurrent deep-rooted dysfunctions, excessive politicisation and lack of discipline. This situation can essentially be attributed to the type of political regimes that have held power in the country; between 1958 and 2010 Guinea never experienced a democratic regime. In-depth reforms of security sector governance are thus absolutely indispensable in this context. With this in view, it is important to identify the conditions that will enable such changes; the challenges to be met or the obstacles to be overcome; the efforts to be encouraged and the transformational approaches to be supported.

The conditions for change

What conditions are required to bring about change in the political, military and security environments? What are the hindrances and the enabling factors?

The state of the administrative, legislative and judicial systems

The issue is to determine what potential or real role can be played by the administrative system and the legislative and judicial branches of power in transforming or changing security sector governance. What possibilities can be developed in order to ensure effective separation of powers and a truly independent system of justice?

In Guinea, the administration is well known for being a tool of government and serves the ruling power. This has been demonstrated under every single government since the country attained independence. Far from being a neutral body, the administration serves the executive power. For example, under Lansana Conté, elections were organised by the government, in particular by the relevant ministries (local government and decentralisation, interior) in conjunction with the national electoral commission (1993), the high council in charge of electoral matters (1998) and the autonomous national electoral commission (2005), none of which were independent bodies. It was not until May 2007 that the national assembly adopted a draft bill establishing the Independent National Electoral Commission (*Commission électorale nationale indépendante* – CENI) (Bangoura 2007: 97). The CENI was a positive factor of change because it was, at least formally, the result of lengthy and difficult dialogue involving political parties (presidential majority and opposition) and government. In substance, the CENI was a novel institution that was supposed to be capable of organising and regulating the upcoming electoral process.

The establishment of the CENI by the national assembly can actually be considered quite an achievement because at the time the membership of the national assembly was not a true reflection of the entire political class. As a reminder, although parliamentary elections had taken place in 2002, most of the opposition parties had boycotted these elections, with the exception of the exception of three opposition parties.[8] At the same time as it created the CENI, during its first session in May 2007, the national assembly adopted the law amending the electoral code, the law on financing political parties and the law governing the status of opposition parties. It also passed a bill establishing an independent national commission of inquiry charged with investigating the June 2006 and January–February 2007 massacres.[9] Some of the factors that doubtless contributed to the passing of the bill include the weight of the prior democratic demands put forward by civil society and trade unions during the events in 2006 and 2007, which led to the 27 January 2007 tripartite agreement and the appointment of a consensus prime minister, Lasana Kouyaté, as head of government, in line with the terms of the agreement.[10]

Nevertheless, aside from these very important laws for the democratic process, the national assembly was unable in subsequent sessions in September 2007 and in 2008 to deal with defence and security issues that were still the preserve of the head of state General Lansana Conté. Although Article 59 of the constitution and its own by-laws allowed it to consider such matters, the national assembly was not yet familiar with the culture of democracy and did not enjoy sufficient independence to exert any control over government.

The justice system was no more independent than the rest. According to a Guinean lawyer, Mr. Thidiane Kaba, under Lansana Conté "the judiciary system was so subservient to the executive power that justice could not be properly administered" (Kaba 2007: 119) and the situation was compounded by the rampant corruption in the sector. The issue is not a lack of an institutional framework, because the December 1990 constitution does provide for the democratic rule of law, as well as the independence and smooth functioning of the justice system. The problem is the failure to apply the constitution, and in many cases the head of state was the first to infringe the fundamental law as, for example when he decided to personally travel to free his friend, the wealthy businessman Mamadou Sylla, from the prison where he had been incarcerated for embezzling public funds.

The same difficulties occurred under Moussa Dadis Camara who concentrated all powers in his own hands, with key ministries including justice being held by soldiers. Where the ministry of defence is concerned, the principle of civilian oversight over the military could not be applied since power was held by the junta. The national assembly, for its part, was dissolved at the time of the coup d'état. Captain Camara entrusted its role to the permanent secretariat of the CNDD, which was tasked with revising organic laws and the constitution, reforming the system of justice and supporting the reform of the defence and security forces. The secretariat was part of the junta and under the responsibility of a colonel who held the rank of minister.

It was only after the forum of militant forces of Guinea (civil society and political parties), meeting at the people's centre in Conakry on 12 March 2009, had put forward their demands and proposals that the principle of a transitional parliament known as the National Transitional Council (*Conseil national de la transition* – CNT) was reluctantly accepted, after lengthy negotiations. The practical establishment of this body was fraught with problems. A draft ordinance was submitted by the CNDD delegation during a visit to Brussels on 24 April 2009. This draft was rejected by the militant forces because it was not sufficiently independent of the junta. A new version was proposed by the minister and permanent secretary of the CNDD on 27 April. Based on this text, the militant forces negotiated with the CNDD early in May on the proposed CNT, outlining its mandate and the composition of its 163 members. The junta however subsequently amended the text unilaterally, increasing the number of members to 244, to be able to include individuals that were devoted to their cause. It was only under the new political dispensation (Ouagadougou agreement) and the authority of General Sékouba Konaté that the CNT was finally established as a transitional body and was able to play its role.

Oversight mechanisms established, but limited

Given the circumstances, it is clear that the system of governance under both Lansana Conté and Moussa Dadis Camara constituted an obstacle to change. Nevertheless a number of observation, oversight and control mechanisms were established under Lansana Conté, with the creation of the National Human Rights Observatory (*Observatoire national des droits de l'homme* – ONDH) in 2008 on the one hand, and the growing role played by civil society organisations on the other.

From the ONDH to the CNDH. In June 2008, a national human rights observatory was set up in Guinea, under the office of the prime minister. The institution was entrusted to the responsibility of Aliou Barry, a doctor of international public law and a professional in the area of defence and security matters, who was appointed by the prime minister on the basis of his competences. The ONDH was established a few months after the violent events of 2006 and 2007 during which the repression of demonstrations by trade unions and civil society resulted in a bloodbath. The ONDH, which was in charge of promoting human rights and ensuring their enjoyment, received the support of the United Nations. The establishment of the observatory was however not enough to prevent renewed human rights violations and the president of the institution was himself seriously injured[11] by members of the armed forces and the presidential guard in the course of discharging his duties (Conakryka 2010). The regime thus did not allow the ONDH to carry out its functions properly.

It was not until May 2010 and the adoption of a new Constitution of the Republic of Guinea by the CNT that an "independent national human rights institution" was enshrined under Title XVI of the fundamental law (Guinea 2010: arts. 146, 148).[12] Subsequently, President Alpha Condé created the National Human Rights Commission (*Commission nationale des droits de l'homme* – CNDH)[13] by decree dated 17 March 2011, soon after he was elected. Mamady Kaba, a civil society activist and former president of the Guinean chapter of the African Assembly for the Defence of Human Rights (*Rencontre africaine pour la défense des droits de l'homme*), was appointed president of the commission. The CNT then passed a bill establishing the organisation and functions for this independent national human rights institution on 14 July 2011. This institutional process aimed at improving the human rights situation was a major step forward, at least in formal terms.

The growing role of civil society organisations. It would not have been possible to create the CNDH without the sustained involvement of civil society and its lengthy advocacy. These activities were amply reported in the media. Civil society has gradually become more structured since 2002, culminating in a federation known as the National Council of Civil Society Organisations of Guinea (*Conseil National des Organisations de la Société Civile Guinéenne* – CNOSCG).

It distinguished itself by mobilising to demand social and political change in 2006 and 2007. Since then, it has been unrelenting in fighting against impunity and in favour of respect for human rights. It played a predominant role in providing support to victims of the 2006 – 2007 and September 2009 massacres. It was able to collect eyewitness accounts and proof of the violence and cooperated with international organisations (United Nations High Commission on Human Rights, UN International Commission of enquiry, International Court of Justice, etc.) and international NGOs (International Human Rights Federation, Human Rights Watch, Amnesty International, International Crisis Group, etc.) working in this area.

In conclusion, it has been possible to initiate a movement for change in favour of security sector governance, with the drafting and adoption of new laws, improved establishment of an oversight and human rights promotion commission, civil society involvement in monitoring the activities and behaviour of defence and security forces and the partnership between national and international civil society organisations.

It is clear that the efforts of the CNDH and other non-governmental/civil society organisations must be encouraged because they represent a form of checks and balances; they provide a different view and understanding of the issues of insecurity, injustice and human rights violations. Very often, it is through dialogue and discussion of ideas, consultations, adversarial debate and monitoring and observation that they are able to have their voices heard and put forward proposals. In spite of the paucity of their operational resources and sometimes their inadequate representativeness, these organisations are generally keen to enhance their capacities and professionalism, which augurs well for their sustainability and effectiveness. One example is the involvement of civil society in the implementation of a project financed by the Peacebuilding Fund.[14] The project, which aims to ensure civilian and democratic control of the defence and security forces, includes a component on capacity enhancement for civil society organisations.

This overall process is however not yet optimal, because of several obstacles related to the political violence that has held sway at the highest level of the state for more than 50 years, as well as the absence of a real political will to peacefully resolve the electoral dispute related to the preparation of parliamentary elections. These elections were postponed several times before they were finally held on 28 September 2013. Furthermore, to date, despite the progress made in civil-military relations, a strong feeling of mistrust still persists between the defence and security forces and the civilian population.

A favourable political framework for change under the transitional leadership of General Sékouba Konaté

Starting from January 2010, there were considerable improvements in security sector governance. This is understandable in the light of the situation at the time. The end of 2009 was a particularly trying time for Guineans. The massacres and gang rapes committed by forces of the Moussa Dadis Camara regime on the morning of 28 September 2009, followed by the assassination attempt on the head of state by the commander of the presidential guard on 3 December set off alarms throughout the country. In this instance, both the highest authority and those subject to authority had been affected. The violence had reached its paroxysm. The dysfunctions of the defence and security forces were at a peak.

While the vital forces of Guinea mourned their dead and cared for the injured, the UN International Commission of Inquiry sought to discern the truth regarding the 28 September 2009 massacres and to identify the perpetrators, in order that justice might be rendered. Militant forces called for protection from the international community in the form of a neutral force that could be interposed between the population and the DSF. They also called for an in-depth reform of the military and the police.

The Ouagadougou Joint Declaration (15 January 2010): a new framework for governance and security sector reform (SSR). In the absence of Moussa Dadis Camara, who was in hospital in Morocco, the second in line in the junta was in charge of expediting the affairs of State. This was General Sékouba Konaté,[15] the minister of defence. He decided to meet with Moussa Dadis Camara as soon as the latter arrived in Burkina Faso for his convalescence,[16] following the attempt on his life. The two men met on 13 and 14 January, in the company of the mediator, the Burkinabe president, Blaise Compaoré. At the end of their talks, they signed the Ouagadougou Joint Declaration on 15 January 2010. By this declaration, M. D. Camara officially conferred power to General Sékouba Konaté to govern during the transition. This declaration was obtained after strong pressure had been exerted by the militant forces of Guinea who approved the final draft, although they were not signatories.

This agreement comprised three points: it resolved the question of the succession; it set the principles and the roadmap for the transition (a six month transition to be used to organise presidential elections in which the present and former leaders would not participate) and set the reform of the defence and security forces as a priority. This was the first condition that marked the beginning of a transformation in security sector governance. From this point, other factors of change would apply.

General Sékouba Konaté holds the DSF accountable. One of the first measures taken by General Sékouba Konaté was to address the DSF and condemn the violent and barbaric acts perpetrated on the civilian population[17] and on their chief, Captain Moussa Dadis Camara who was at the time the commander in chief of the armed forces. He also paid tribute to the memory of all the victims. This speech on 23 December 2009 and his visits to various barracks were widely covered by the media, while the campaign to educate the troops and officers and call them to account was seen as a welcome overture from the General and served to appease tensions somewhat in the country.

Evaluation of the security sector by the ECOWAS-UN-AU Joint Mission.[18] The international community commended the president of the transition for his acts and offered its support in implementing the long-awaited reforms. The first of these was an evaluation of the various categories of actors in the security sector, as well as the sector as a whole. This exercise was carried out between 1 February and 30 April 2010 by a joint mission under the leadership of General Lamine Cissé, a well-renowned Senegalese officer both in his country and within the international community. The evaluation, which he carried out with a great deal of tact and professional experience, was the necessary starting point for any reform, as it provided a hitherto unknown picture of the security sector.

The evaluation report described the worrying state of deliquescence of the Guinean security sector where no standards had been applied for decades: totally disorganised defence and security forces, military interference in the political arena, absence of civilian control, a dysfunctional legal system and the involvement of non-state actors in security (militia, private companies). The report referred to the issue of the circulation of small arms and light weapons in the West African region, as well as other crosscutting issues such as gender. The report then made a series of recommendations under each of these points, at the end of a participatory process that took place in Conakry and other towns in the country.

The official report was submitted by the head of the joint mission to General Sékouba Konaté on 4 May 2010 during a ceremony at the *Palais du peuple* attended by the main socio-political actors in Guinea. These included representatives of government, the CNT, political parties, civil society, the security sector and external partners. Following the election of Alpha Condé, this report served as the reference document in preparing the SSR process in the country.

Early measures aimed at restructuring the DSF and the difference between restructuring and reform. From January 2010, after the signing of the Ouagadougou Agreement, General Sékouba Konaté initiated a vast restructuring exercise: imposing discipline and observance of the military hierarchy; a major project to construct new barracks; closure of the militia's Kaléah (Forécariah) training camp; a new military high command appointed by decree; recruitment of 8,000 trainee gendarmes to provide border security and ensure security during elections.

The restructuring exercise met an existing need and was warmly welcomed in the country. It however only represented a first step. The measures taken were technical and professional, aimed at bringing about functional improvements, but they did not tackle the root causes of the dysfunctions. They demonstrated the existence of a genuine political will to improve the living and working conditions of the defence and security forces, but fell short of overhauling the system. Furthermore, these measures were taken in isolation by the authorities, without taking account of the overall balance of numbers and without ensuring the participation of civil society.

Security sector reform is defined as both a policy and a holistic approach. Its aim is to establish highly performing defence and security institutions that are legally placed under the control of bodies enshrined in the constitution. It also aims to set up a strong and independent system of justice. In principle, reform must be carried out within a framework of national consultations. This is the type of reform that President Alpha Condé attempted to initiate when he acceded to power.

Establishment and role of the CNT. The ordinance establishing the CNT was signed by General Sékouba Konaté on 9 February 2010. Based on proposals by militant forces, the president of the transition appointed Hadja Rabiatou Serah Diallo, a trade union official, as head of this institution. On 17 February he sent a letter to the mission reminding them of the fact that the elections had to be organised within six months. The president of the CNT was invited to quickly set up the legislative body of the transition (101 members). The general indicated the quotas for each of these categories.[19] The list of members of the CNT, who were appointed by presidential decree, was published on 7 March.[20]

The CNT was finally inaugurated during an official ceremony where the president of the transition made a solemn statement (L'Observateur 2010: 2). The CNT immediately got to work. Barely a week after being set up, it decided to create nine commissions, each responsible for a specific area: constitutional review, revision of texts governing elections, finances, treaties and laws, assessment of government activities, monitoring and evaluation of the CENI, national reconciliation, defence and security and communication. One of the leading tasks of the CNT was thus to review the fundamental law and the electoral code, in order to draft the constitution and appropriate texts for the elections.

Security of the electoral process. Unlike his predecessor, General Sékouba Konaté, the president of the transition, succeeded in rapidly setting up the institutions to manage this transition: a prime minister (Jean-Marie Doré,[21] an opposition leader), a transitional national unity government, the national transitional council and the CENI (presided by Ben Sékou Sylla, a former president of the CNOSCG). General Sékouba Konaté officially took office in the middle of January 2010 and the first round of the presidential elections was held six months later, on 27 June. The president of the transition also ensured the security of electoral operations by passing a decree on 18 May 2010, establishing a combined force known as Special Force for a Safe Electoral Process (*Force spéciale de sécurisation du processus électoral* – FOSSEPEL), which was placed under the command of the army staff but under the authority of the CENI.

With the establishment of the CNT and the enhanced security of the presidential election, for the first time since independence the first round of democratic, open and transparent elections were successfully organised in Guinea. None of the leaders of the transitional institutions participated in these elections.

Unfortunately, the second round of the election did not take place until 7 November 2010. The delay was due to the moves to set up political alliances with the two remaining candidates, as well as other political manoeuvring.

During this period between two rounds of voting, the 'demons' of exclusion and ethnic-based hatred reared their ugly heads once again and led to various incidents, heightened tensions and violence. Faced with accusations of fraud by the Union of Republican Forces, (*Union des forces républicaines*), the president of the transition, General Sékouba Konaté even threatened to resign on 6 July 2010. The incident was fortunately resolved quickly. The elections were finally won by Alpha Condé.

The transition had achieved its principal objective of putting in place a system of political governance that would restore the constitutional order. To achieve this, General Sékouba Konaté had displayed firm political will and maintained a steady course. Nevertheless, the atmosphere of political conflict that characterised the period between the two rounds of voting had left deep scars that would affect the way in which the new head of state would govern.

The process of change since the election of Alpha Condé

Strong political will and broad-based consultation. In his inaugural address on 21 December 2010, President Alpha Condé identified security sector reform as one of the priorities of his government programme and requested the assistance of the United Nations. To this end, in January 2011, a UN mission led by General Lamine Cissé drafted the initial technical documents based on the recommendations of the 2010 evaluation. Other experts from the United Nations Development Programme (UNDP) Bureau for Crisis Prevention and Recovery, the Geneva Centre for Democratic Control of Armed Forces, the United Nations Office for West Africa and the United Nations Department of Peacekeeping Operations were also deployed to provide technical assistance to the committee in charge of organising the planned national SSR seminar.[22]

The new head of state, who was also commander in chief of the armed forces and minister of defence confirmed his political will by personally opening and closing the national seminar on security sector reform on 28 and 31 March 2011, respectively. Another important factor of success for this seminar was the calibre and high number of participants; the president of the republic, representatives of government and state institutions, diplomats, international organisations (in particular the UN, AU, ECOWAS), civil society organisations, invited countries, regional military commanders and commanders of the major units in Conakry. During this meeting, participants identified priority measures and the timetable for implementing SSR in the short (2011), medium (2012) and long (2013 – 2015) term, for each sector. The report of the proceedings was published.

At the same time, a general assembly *(états généraux)* on the justice system was being held in Conakry under the patronage of the president of the republic, from 28 to 30 March 2011. The summary report reviewed the justice system and set three objectives. The first was to ensure an independent system through a reform of the higher council of magistrates, with the creation of disciplinary bodies, a career management plan for magistrates, salary increases and a statute for clerks of court. Next was the construction and equipment of courts and tribunals and finally the redesign of judicial constituencies to improve access to courts, as well as a review of the prison system.

On 14 April 2011, the president of the republic signed a decree establishing the national SSR steering committee. The committee, which was under his authority, was in charge of supervising the reform process, defining its political and strategic orientations and monitoring implementation. It comprised a programme management unit, a strategic orientation commission, a technical monitoring commission and sector-specific technical committees. This was the first stage in implementing the reform process. The committee was supported by the government of Guinea and assisted by the United Nations system in the country.

Shared objectives in SSR. The reform process emphasised a new concept of the defence and security forces as part of a comprehensive, inclusive, consensus-based and participatory approach. This depended on buy-in from all stakeholders and national ownership at every level. Right from the start, this reform process was part of a democratic renewal and the inception of true rule of law; it aimed to establish an independent, impartial, competent and accessible system of justice.

The main purpose of SSR was to put in place the appropriate institutional framework; to provide professional and operational capacities to the legal apparatus and the defence and security forces (military, gendarmerie, police-intelligence, civil defence, customs and the environment); to bring these services closer to the population; to ensure civilian control and to guarantee the enjoyment of human rights. The reform process also sought to contribute, through various crosscutting areas, to controlling transnational crime and the circulation of light weapons in the region. To a large extent, the Guinean population agreed with these objectives.

Implementation of SSR and civil-military rapprochement. Indeed, the citizens warmly welcomed the initial measures under the reform process. These included ensuring the security of the civilian population by enhancing discipline within the armed forces, improving the behaviour of military personnel, dismantling roadblocks and demilitarising the capital. Measures were then taken to restructure the forces on the basis of defence requirements. New units were created and the members of the former presidential guard and the battalion of airborne troops (*Bataillon des troupes aéroportées* – BATA) or the 'red berets' were redeployed and dispersed. Finally, steps were taken to create a rapprochement between the DSF and the population; the civil-military committee was revitalised and a department of Civic Service for Development (*Service civique d'aide au développement*) was established. was established. The basic documents of the reform process, in particular those related to the legal framework (legislative texts such as the code of military justice, the general statute and the military statute), as well as those on the organisational structure of the forces were drafted or revised by the competent departments.

The second phase of the reform process consisted of drafting a national SSR action plan. Each ministry was required to work, sector by sector, in five technical committees (Defence, Security, Justice, Customs and Environment). By the middle of 2012, this work had been completed and each sector had drafted its action plan. The sector policies have since been validated by the various ministries. The overall plan now has to be harmonised and consolidated, but this has not yet been done.

SSR advanced further in 2012 with the implementation of three projects; a biometric register of military personnel, retirement of 4 000 military personnel and enhanced democratic and civilian control of the defence and security forces. UNDP recruited three experts to provide short-term technical assistance in these areas. The projects were financed by the United Nations Peacebuilding Commission Fund (PBC 2012).

Prospects of a national defence and security policy? On 23 August 2013, the deputy minister in charge of defence, Mr. Kabélé announced a new stage of SSR in Guinea, when he launched a national consultation throughout the regions, prefectures and communes of the country. The aim has been to involve all segments of the population in drafting the future national defence and security policy. This process is to be bottom up.

In the meantime, the United Nations system and technical and financial partners continue to support the SSR process. The European Union (EU) is providing assistance to three pilot projects on neighbourhood policing through the tenth European Development Fund. The aim is to bring the police closer to the population, to ensure more rapid access to security for individuals and to raise institutional awareness about police accountability. The EU is also providing support for civil defence (through the fire brigade in Conakry) and to the corps of forest rangers in high risk areas such as the Haute-Guinée park, the Ziama classified forest and the Mount Nimba protected area).[23]

All of the foregoing shows that SSR got off to a good start in 2011 – 2012, and progressed successfully because there was general consensus in the country on these matters. But can the pace be sustained?

Roles of the various actors

Various internal and external, institutional and more rarely, individual, actors constitute a driving force for SSR. It is however necessary to remain vigilant in certain cases because significant challenges persist.

Government and the challenge of policy dialogue and respect for human rights

Following the November 2010 presidential election, the executive demonstrated its willingness and openness with regard to the need for security sector reform. The policy foundation for sound security sector governance was laid. However, within the context of Guinea, SSR can only truly be successful under the framework of democratic rule of law, which has not yet been restored in the country. The rule of law has been seriously undermined by more than half a century of bad practices. Although the various institutions have been set up, they are not truly functional and political tensions persist due to the manipulation of ethnic sentiment and the disputed results of the 2010 presidential vote.

One of the main challenges facing this government is establishing political dialogue[24] with the opposition. Both camps are still highly suspicious of one another because of the incidents of past presidential and parliamentary elections. Indeed, the latter were greatly delayed and only took place on 28 September 2013. The ruling authorities and opposition leaders have absolutely no trust in each other. As a result, the current government is unable to prevent the use of force during demonstrations, as was the case on 25 November 2013, when a young student died during a march organised by the opposition in protest against the results of the parliamentary elections published by the Supreme Court.

From the CNT to the National Assembly: the end of the transition and the challenges of democracy

The election of the members of the national assembly marked a major step forward. The new, democratically elected assembly was to replace the CNT. The final results proclaimed by the Supreme Court on 25 November 2013 confirmed the provisional results published by the CENI on 18 October; of the 114 seats in the national assembly, Alpha Condé's party won 53, with 5 seats for his allies and 56 for the opposition. Although the ruling party had won, the opposition was well represented.

With the instauration of the new assembly the aim, in political terms, was to turn the page on the painful period of the transition, since the CNT was the only surviving institution of the transition, following the election of Alpha Condé. Guinea also needed to set up a true legislative body with the authority to ensure oversight of government activities. In the area of SSR, the new parliamentarians need to be educated and trained on civilian and democratic control of government.

A Reconciliation Commission but not Truth and Justice

The Provisional Commission for National Reconciliation (*Commission provisoire chargée de la réconciliation nationale*) was established by presidential decree on 15 August 2011 and two religious personalities[25] were appointed as co-presidents. It appears however that civil society was not adequately consulted on matters such as the mandate, powers and membership of the commission. The role of the commission appears to focus on reconciliation, but what about the 'truth' and 'justice' components that have characterised most truth and reconciliation commissions in Africa and in other parts of the world? Civil society would like the commission to deal with the question of impunity and make recommendations regarding the prosecution of individuals accused of perpetrating acts of violence.

The programme of action of the commission is divided into five phases: prayers, hearings, analyses based on the results of the work done at local, communal, district and national levels; defining orientations and finally setting up a body or institution in charge of national reconciliation.

After holding national and international consultations, the co-presidents of the Provisional Commission for National Reconciliation are expected to make proposals for the establishment of a real truth and reconciliation commission in Guinea. This is the fervent hope of civil society and some opposition leaders.

The Office of the Ombudsman: a vital institution embodied by a controversial figure

Title XI of the 2010 constitution, which was drafted and adopted by the CNT provides for the creation of an Office of the Ombudsman. Art. 127 describes the Ombudsman as "a body that intercedes, free of charge and independently, between the administration and the general public. According to the conditions established by law, it receives complaints from citizens relating to their interaction with government administrations, territorial constituencies, local authorities and public institutions, as well as any other bodies entrusted with a public service mission". The conditions for bringing a case before the Ombudsman, as well as the method of intervention and functioning of this body are set out by law.

While the creation of this institution is a welcome initiative, there have been concerns about the person selected to serve as ombudsman. In January 2011, President Alpha Condé appointed General Faciné Touré as the ombudsman. He was only able to take office in July, due to a controversy surrounding some comments that he had made which were considered inappropriate and likely to cause ethnic divisions. It is also important to note that this general was a former member of the Military Committee of National Recovery (*Comité milit-*

aire de redressement national), the military committee that took over power in the wake of the coup by Lansana Conté.

It would appear that someone who generates consensus, who is demonstrably neutral and objective, has never held any political office in the previous authoritarian regimes and is selected for their competence would be a more appropriate choice for this position. Many such individuals can be found within the civil society.

Role of external actors

External parties such as the International Contact Group for Guinea (ICG-G) played an important political and diplomatic role in supporting the transition in Guinea, while some individuals such as General Lamine Cissé and also the various technical and financial partners played a decisive role in providing guidance and assistance in SSR.

The ICG-G was remarkable for its ability to support all stakeholders in the transition and also to provide renewed focus on the road map for the transition. It was also able to impose sanctions when peace and security in the country were under threat and there was a risk of human rights being violated. The group was set up by the international community in January 2009 in Addis Ababa, of an African Union meeting.[26] The group met 17 times, at regular intervals, over a two year period between February 2009 and February 2011. The last meeting, which marked the end of its mandate and paved the way for the establishment of a group of the friends of Guinea, took place in Conakry on 10 February 2011, a few weeks after the newly elected president took office.

General Lamine Cissé is a retired Senegalese officer, who was instrumental in Guinea on several occasions starting from 2010, in providing advice, initiating, coordinating and monitoring the SSR process. He is well-renowned, in particular as a former minister of interior in his country, but also as the former Representative of the United Nations Secretary General and Head of the Office of the United Nations Organisation in the Central African Republic. His long years of experience, his interpersonal skills and his excellent knowledge of West Africa were valuable for this mission.

The technical and financial partners were the main bilateral and multilateral development partners of Guinea supporting SSR. These include France, the United States, the European Union and the *Organisation internationale de la Francophonie*. These external actors send civilian and/or military experts to the country to support the following areas respectively: department of Civic Service for Development (*Service civique d'aide au développement*); institutional capacity-building in security and SSR; justice system reform; and human rights training for military officers.

Conclusion

The question now is whether the changes will continue. It must be recalled that the need for SSR had become vital for Guinea as a result of the conflict-generating regimes and the violence that had prevailed since independence. SSR was however not possible under Lansana Conté because he prevented any attempts to implement reforms. The situation was the same under Moussa Dadis Camara. The first measures that foreshadowed a transformation in security sector governance and reform were introduced by General Sékouba Konaté. In a favourable political environment he demonstrated an unrelenting political will to begin restructuring the armed forces. He consented to the evaluation of the security sector and led the electoral process that resulted in a return to a constitutional order. The pre-requisite conditions for a veritable SSR process were put in place at that time.

The two first years of the Alpha Condé regime were very promising. The period from early 2011 to the end of 2012 was marked by a strong political will, openness and the search for a national consensus, followed by ownership and implementation, which were the first steps towards a real transformation of the security sector.

Throughout 2013, however, the process remained at a standstill. The main reason for this is the atmosphere of political conflict between the presidential majority and the opposition, as well as the violence that characterised the preparation and holding of parliamentary elections and the proclamation of the results. Furthermore, the fact that the process of drafting a national defence and security policy was initiated through consultation at the local and district levels could be interpreted as an attempt to postpone decisions and gain time. This inaction may be a government policy, until the reform can be resumed where it apparently stopped.

The initial enthusiasm has now subsided. The risk is that subsequently not enough attention will be focused on security sector reform. And yet the reform process, or rather the national SSR action plan has not yet been adopted, programmed, quantified or implemented. Quite an undertaking!

Notes

1. After breaking with France, President Sékou Touré turned to the Soviet bloc and initiated civilian and military cooperation with Moscow and other allies of the Eastern countries.
2. Sékou Touré wanted a docile military at the service of his regime and ready to execute his orders without asking questions. For him, the military, the party and everything that existed in Guinea was to serve to glorify his person (Bah 2009: 421).

3 Sékou Touré removed responsibility for the Deuxième Bureau (intelligence) from the military and entrusted the special service to his brother, Siaka Touré.

4 According to Camara Kaba 41 (1998: 64), the prison known as 'Camp Boiro' was constructed by the Czechs in 1961 – 62 under the authority of Keita Fodéba, who was at the time the minster of Interior and Security, as well as the minister in charge of the Guinean People's armed forces.

5 Despite being submissive to the regime, the military was not spared its tyranny: "obliged to blindly follow the orders of a single individual, the military largely assuaged the thirst for power… of the leader of the PDG throughout the twenty-six years of the revolution." Nevertheless, "some military leaders suffered the same fate as the victims that they tortured and killed before they themselves fell from grace" (Bah 2009: 153).

6 Art.34 of the constitution stipulates that, "should the function of president of the republic fall vacant following the death or resignation of the incumbent…, the speaker of the national assembly or failing him, one of the deputy speakers, shall perform the function of president. Such vacancy shall be duly noted by the supreme court, which shall be informed by the speaker of the national assembly…" (translation by the author).

7 Passed on 14 January 2009, this decree appoints the members of government (Guinea 2009).

8 The three opposition parties that took part in the elections were: *Union pour le Progrès et le Renouveau, Union pour le Progrès de la Guinée and the Parti du Peuple de Guinée.*

9 This law was not unanimously welcomed because human rights defenders and representatives of the victims wanted an independent and possibly international commission of inquiry.

10 Agreement signed on 27 January 2007 by unions, employers and governement, entitled Procès-verbal de négociations suite à la grève générale de l'Inter centrale syndicale CNTG-USTG élargie à l'ONSLG et à l'UDTG déclenchée le 10 janvier 2007.

11 After the first round of the presidential election in June 2010.

12 According to art. 146: "The independent national human rights institution is in charge of promoting and protecting human rights". Art. 148: "An organic law defining the membership, organisation and functioning of the institution".

13 These names are reminiscent of French institutions: in France, the 'national human rights advisory commission is the national human rights institution, established in 1947'. In Africa, independent national human rights institutions are statutory bodies established by government and they are in charge of promoting and protecting human rights in their respective countries. These institutions must be created and function in accordance with the United Nations human rights promotion and protection principles

(Paris Principles). Independent national human rights institutions are also required to assist the African Commission on Human and Peoples' Rights. Several African countries have established an independent national human rights institution. (Cameroon, Mali, Mauritius, Mauritania, Niger, Rwanda, Sierra Leone, South Africa, Togo, etc.) (CADHP 2015).

14 The Peacebuilding Fund is a fund for consolidating peace, which finances the projects of the United Nations Peacebuilding Commission (New York).

15 The December 2008 coup d'état was carried out by Captain Moussa Dadis Camara, who at the time worked at the army fuel depot, and Colonel Sékouba Konaté, Commander of the bataillon of the BATA, an elite unit. M. D. Camara had in the past served in the BATA. The two men knew each other well and were friends. M.D. Camara promoted Sékouba Konaté to the rank of general in January 2009.

16 Moussa Dadis Camara was initially evacuated to Morocco for treatment. Subsequently, in the evening of 12 January he arrived in Burkina Faso, the home of the mediator in the Guinean crisis, where he was to continue his convalescence.

17 General Sékouba Konaté could speak out against these acts because on 28 September 2009 he was away from the country on a mission. He was therefore not involved in the massacres.

18 Other participants in this joint mission included bilateral and international partners such as France and the United States, the European Union and the Organisation internationale de la Francophonie.

19 The Ouagadougou Joint Declaration provided for 101 members, distributed as follows in the Mission Letter: 30 (political parties), 15 (unions), 9 (civil society) 8 (external), 3 (professional orders), 4 (regional coordination units), 10 (defence and security forces), 2 (human rights), 4 (youth), 3 (employers), 3 (private media), 4 (women), 2 (farmers' organisations), 2 (craftsmen's organisations), 2 (religious bodies).

20 To their great surprise, the people of Guinea realised that the decree (Guinea 2010b) had increased the number of members from 101 to 155.

21 Jean-Marie Doré was appointed as prime minister by decree by General Sékouba Konaté on 19 January 2010 and he took up office on 26 January after a hand over ceremony with Kabiné Komara. In a brief address, the new prime minister indicated that his two main missions would be the elections and an overhaul of the military. This was a way of demonstrating that he had properly understood his duty as the head of the new transitional government.

22 The national SSR seminar was organised with funding from the UNDP and technical and logistical assistance from the United Nations system in Guinea.

23 See further, e.g., the press release of the European Union delegation to Guinea (Délégation de l'Union européenne en Guinée 2013).

[24] Various fora on political dialogue have been organised with the support of the international community (UN-ECOWAS-Organisation internationale de la Francophonie-EU-France-United States): Inclusive political dialogue, which was held in Conakry from 27 December 2011 to 22 February 2012, followed by Inter-Guinean Dialogue, also in Conakry from 5 to 9 June 2013 and on 2 and 3 July 2013, to try to arrive at an agreement on the preparation and holding of parliamentary elections.

[25] Mgr Vincent Koulibaly, Archbishop of Conakry and El Hadj Mamadou Saliou Camara, Imam of the Fayçal mosque in Conakry.

[26] Members of the ICG-G included: the United Nations, the African Union, the European Union, the Organisation internationale de la Francophonie, the Economic Community of West African States (ECOWAS), the Mano River Union, the Organisation of Islamic Conference, the Community of Sahel-Saharan States, the World Bank, Angola (as chair of the African Union Peace and Security Council) Nigeria (as president of ECOWAS), as well some African States (Burkina Faso, in charge of the mediation), the permanent members of the United Nations Security Council (the United Kingdom, France, Russia and the United States of America), Spain and finally Morocco (January 2010). Côte d'Ivoire, Ghana, Guinea-Bissau, Mali and Senegal also took part in the group.

CHAPTER 4

Developments in Legislative Oversight in Liberia

T. Debey Sayndee

Associate Professor and Director, Kofi Annan Institute for Conflict Transformation (KAICT), University of Liberia

Introduction

Liberia degenerated into what became a protracted civil war in late 1989. Not a single body of the security forces was at the service of the population. Although the fourteen-year armed struggle at last came to an end in 2003, true reconciliation and justice remain distant objectives. With the brutal civil conflict transforming the national army into an armed faction, establishing republican security forces oriented towards the public good is a crucial part of the country's process of post-conflict reconstruction and development. The country is facing a crisis of confidence in the state's security forces and needs a professional security sector that is regulated by a democratically elected government, and that is outside the immediate reach of the president. In other words, what is required is a transformation of the state security forces: shifting from their role as a prop of the regime in power to providing for the security of the population.

Liberia's history of conflict and authoritarian rule should put democratic security governance at the heart of any meaningful reform agenda. The challenge of becoming an open society in which everyone has at least the possibility of having his or her voice heard has not yet been achieved, but this transition, which started with the end of the war in 2003, is now well and truly under way.

This chapter takes stock of how far the objective of transforming governance dynamics in the security sector has been realised in Liberia in the

How to cite this book chapter:

Debey Sayndee, T. 2015. Developments in Legislative Oversight in Liberia. In: Bryden, A and Chappuis, F (eds.) *Learning from West African Experiences in Security Sector Governance*, Pp. 61–78. London: Ubiquity Press. DOI: http://dx.doi.org/10.5334/bau.d. License: CC-BY 4.0.

period 2003 – 13 through the lens of developments in the legislative framework for the security sector. Against the backdrop of the reform process as a whole, the chapter puts forward the argument that a narrow focus on training and equipping the Liberian security forces has not addressed the legacy of the years of conflict, nor the even longer history of regime-focused security dynamics. By contrast, it is argued that further support to reinforce national oversight and accountability of the security sector could help to overcome such deeply rooted pathologies. Specifically, this chapter examines the significance of parliamentary oversight in promoting democratic security governance and acts as a case study of the progress Liberia still needs to make in this area.

The following section discusses the scoping conditions underpinning security sector governance dynamics in Liberia. It focuses on the historical context for reforms, lending perspective to the changes already made to the architecture for security sector governance in Liberia, and the various actors involved in the process. The next section focuses on the governance gaps in the reform process and considers the first steps towards developing meaningful public and legislative control of the security sector based upon a new legislative framework. This chapter then assesses the extent to which these steps reflect sustainable progress towards a more robust culture of democratic governance. Finally, key lessons and potential next steps in security sector reform in Liberia are considered.

Scoping conditions

This section focuses on two sets of scoping conditions that need to be acknowledged in order to understand security sector reform (SSR) in Liberia. The first is the historical context of political governance in the country. The second is the approach to SSR taken by the international community and the priority given to different activities within that approach.

Liberia's historical trajectory of security sector governance

Liberia is currently making a transition from authoritarian rule to democracy. The coordinated efforts of the international community, led by the United States, resulted in the signing of a Comprehensive Peace Agreement (CPA) between the warring factions in August 2003.[1] This was a watershed moment in the history of Liberia because it brought to an end an authoritarian style of governance that had become entrenched since the country's founding in 1847.[2] The CPA was a hard-won victory, having been preceded by at least twelve failed attempts at achieving the disarmament of the warring factions before a roadmap for peace was agreed upon. Finally, the CPA marked the end of Charles Taylor's term as President of Liberia and sought to usher in a new era of genuine democracy. Following two years of a transitional administration between 2003 – 5, the country held its first ever free and fair elections, which brought to power Africa's first elected female president, and the country's 52nd Legislature. This new tradition of free and fair elections has been maintained as evidenced by the execution of a second set of post-war presidential and legislative elections in late 2011, when the 53rd Legislature took office.

This transition from authoritarianism to democracy also affected the security sector. In this respect it is important to understand the starting point for such a transition. In the past, the office of the President of the Republic controlled the security sector. The president had traditionally ruled in an authoritarian and sometimes arbitrary manner since the period of the original settler regime of the True Whig Party. For example, the 18th President of Liberia (1944–1971), William V. S. Tubman set the rules for the security sector, proclaiming that "[t]he military has three functions: to obey, to obey, and to obey" (Bright 2002; cited in Kieh 2008: 51).[3] His successor was William R. Tolbert, Jr., (1913 – 1980), who had been Tubman's Vice President for 19 years and became the 20th President of Liberia from 1971 until 1980, when he was assassinated in a *coup d'ètat*. An important event that contributed to the overthrow of his regime was the Rice Riot of early 1979, caused by a proposed price increase in the Liberian staple. Two thousand activists began what was planned as a peaceful protest march to the Executive Mansion. The march degenerated into a riot when the protesters were joined by large numbers of so-called back street boys – homeless, often drug-addicted youth living on the streets of downtown Monrovia. The widespread looting that resulted was ended by a contingent of troops called into Liberia by President Tolbert from neighbouring Guinea. This led to widespread disaffection within the Liberian security sector, which became the catalyst for the *coup d'ètat* that followed.

Under the regimes of Tubman, Tolbert and their predecessors stretching back to 1847, security policy was conceived and then implemented by a highly centralised authority based in the office of the president. It cannot be over-stated how the approach to national security under development in Liberia today, driven by democratic legislative initiatives and oversight, constitutes a radical departure from previous processes and policies. Yet challenges to democratic security sector governance remain, in particular those linked to Liberia's legacy of a patrimonial style of politics. This dictatorial style of governance was part of the source of later security sector problems in contemporary Liberia, such as corruption and physical threats to citizens.

The deeply entrenched networks of corruption and ethnic divisions were a central cause of the collapse of the security sector during the civil conflict and the resulting violence. Liberians have sought to move away from the past towards a clean, accountable form of governance that would place the rights of its citizens before the self-interest of its power-holders. However, dysfunctional political economic structures remain deeply embedded at all societal levels, including in the government.

Nevertheless, hesitant, albeit slow, progress is being made in the implementation of the reform process. For instance, the International Contact Group in Liberia and the Government of Liberia imposed the Governance and Economic Management Assistance Program in September 2005. Liberia was the first state to comply with the Extractive Industries Transparency Initiative rules, and the first West African country to pass a Freedom of Information Act to support more transparent governance (Glencourse 2013). Recently the government signed up to the Open Government Partnership and committed itself to a series of ambitious goals to become more accountable. Many of these initiatives have come about thanks to President Sirleaf, but former president and governance activist Professor Amos Sawyer has criticised the logic as faulty that "once a 'good' person is elected President the (institutional) problems will then be addressed" (Sawyer 2002). Professor Sawyer maintains that the high and continued risk of misuse of power derives from a failure to address the flawed political institutions, and specifically the problem of the centralization of power in the presidency.

Internationally driven security sector reform

The internationally driven attempt to radically reform the security sector after the war's end offered a chance to promote democratic security governance and prevent new destabilization. The UN family of organizations quickly identified security sector reform as a priority task. According to a report made to the United Nations Security Council, "in Liberia, one of the key reasons for the relapse into violence after the end of the first civil war and the 1997 presidential election was the lack of reform of the armed and security forces" (United Nations Security Council 2005a: par. 33; 2006: par. 6). Yet despite extensive efforts to reform the police and the military in Liberia, a comprehensive approach to SSR was the road not taken. This is one reason that SSR programmes in Liberia have been unprecedented in ambition, yet have enjoyed only mixed results (Malan 2008). Ten years after the signing of the CPA, and despite the support of many different actors from within the region and beyond, the vision of a legitimate, rights-based government is under serious threat with reform overly focused on the police and the armed forces, thus straying from the target of democratic governance for the sector as a whole.

SSR in Liberia began in 2004 with the first reform initiative of the Liberian National Police (LNP) to train 1800 new recruits in anticipation of the 2005 elections, which was introduced by the UN peacekeeping mission (United Nations Mission in Liberia – UNMIL) during the administration of the National Transitional Government of Liberia (United Nations Security Council 2005b: par. 30). Ten years of efforts to reform the LNP has resulted in an increasingly professional police force. However, the observed abusive behaviour, a culture of impunity and the endemic corruption, as disclosed by a Human Rights Watch report in August 2013, continue to erode public confidence in the LNP (HRW 2013). There are thus presently deep doubts about the competence and integrity of the police among Liberian citizens (IRIN 2013). Until these doubts are laid to rest or removed, in particular the suspicion of police involvement in crime, the LNP will not enjoy the cooperation it needs in order to be effective, and state authority may be undermined by citizens' attempts to provide for their own safety from crime and violence, e.g. through vigilante groups.

In line with the terms of the CPA, reform of Liberia's armed forces was heavily supported by the United States. The US-led approach to army reform in Liberia relied at first on a sub-contracting arrangement with the American security corporation, DynCorp International. This agreement was superseded in 2010 by a cooperation agreement with the US military to train and equip the new Armed Forces of Liberia (AFL). The Economic Community of West African States countries, Ghana and Nigeria, also supported the AFL's general staff. As a result of these efforts, Liberia acquired a pool of nearly two thousand rigorously vetted and well-trained military personnel (ICG 2009: 23), only 5 per cent of whom consisted of former AFL soldiers, with no ethnic group accounting for more than 15 per cent by 2008 (Malan 2008: 83). The vetting process, in particular, was a noted success; two experts involved described it as the best they had witnessed anywhere in the world (ICG 2009: 12). Despite having laid a sound foundation for further development, in 2009 the UN Secretary-General nevertheless reported a "significant capacity deficit" in the AFL (United Nations Security Council 2009). By 2013, however, the newly formed Liberian army qualified to participate in their first peacekeeping operation in Mali, sending a fifty-four person strong company. Since then, this operation has been renewed and expanded. The development of a capable management and leadership core within the military is an organic process that must be nurtured by both the Liberian government and its international partners. Despite some early missteps, army reforms therefore appear to be showing some successes.

Addressing Liberia's Governance Gaps

Despite these limited successes in creating new policing and defence capacities, a comprehensive approach to SSR has not been implemented in Liberia. The CPA and the external intervention that has followed constitute a transition from war to a negative peace characterised by the absence of violence; it is negative because whilst something undesirable has stopped happening, the desired result of wider social justice and positive social well being has not been achieved (Galtung 1964: 1 – 4). In order to move forward, Liberians needed to agree on the key challenges facing the country and establish their own priorities for reform. In response to this recognition a process for public consultation on national security was initiated, together with targeted support to the legislature in the area of security sector governance over the postwar period. This section describes the public hearings on national security and the legislative capacity building conducted for security sector oversight in 2005 – 6, which helped prepare the ground for revisiting Liberia's security sector legislation in the years that followed.

Public hearings on national security

In August 2005, and again in 2006, the Ministry of Justice of Liberia, in concert with UNMIL, conducted a national dialogue on the security sector (DCAF 2005). Such a broad-based and public consultation was unprecedented given Liberia's historical context of autocratic security sector governance. This novel step was based on the conviction that holding a dialogue on the needs and requirements of SSR would help broaden the constituency of actors working to develop a collective vision for security in Liberia. Stakeholders involved in the dialogue covered a broad range of national actors not historically involved in national security policy-making including the transitional legislature, the judiciary and civil society, as well as relevant ministries, organizations responsible for implementing reform and international actors, such as the United Nations. This hearing enabled a frank discussion among Liberians that identified challenges facing SSR in the country:[4]

- With respect to the security sector architecture at that time, the word used by some participants was "over-bloated", referring to the multiplicity of state security institutions, their large number of staff and their overlapping mandates. Moreover, the calibre of the personnel was questioned and it was suggested that many security personnel had been recruited on the basis of patronage, not experience;
- Another challenge that was much discussed in the dialogue was the need for a security sector in which the mandate of each security institution is clear and in which each security institution is comprised of and reflects all Liberia's ethnic and religious groups. At the same time, each security organization should be comprised of suitably qualified and well-trained personnel who are recruited through a transparent process;
- A key shortcoming of Liberia's security institutions was identified as the gross abuse of human rights of Liberians, often with impunity, by security personnel through torture, arbitrary arrests and the use of official powers for private gain. This state of affairs was able to flourish due to the lack of effective oversight. This, in turn, was due to several factors, including excessive presidential powers and a lack of capable parliamentary oversight. The lack of adequate remuneration made a difficult security situation even

worse by forcing security personnel to make ends meet through petty corruption and the abuse of power;

- It was also noted during the dialogue that Liberia's security system needs to have the capacity to secure its borders and natural resource endowments, and also to be responsive to sub-regional security imperatives;
- Last but not least, Liberia was seen as needing a security sector that it can afford, albeit with initial international support.

In light of these problems, the National Dialogue pointed to the need for institutions that were law abiding and respectful of human rights. Constructive civil society input was to be encouraged. Constitutional reform was also discussed. It was felt that there was a pressing need for revision in two areas: (1) constitutional clarification of the roles of all statutory institutions to deal with the overlapping of security sector institutions and (2) addressing the possible abuse of power by the president who has the constitutional authority to appoint virtually all of the leaders of the security apparatus. The dialogue concluded by underlining that while the international community may be available and ready to assist in SSR, Liberians have the primary responsibility for reform of their own security sector, and for the post-conflict reconstruction process as a whole. This was an insight from the public dialogue that would turn out to be prescient, as the degree of local ownership of SSR would later be challenged by Liberian civil society and the legislature, particularly with regard to US support for defence reform.

Support for the legislature

Following the 2005 elections, it quickly became clear that the 52nd Legislature consisted of some 75 per cent freshmen (first time legislators). A consortium, that included the author, was established to support the capacity building of this legislature, especially the Committees on Security and Defence of both the upper and lower chambers. The consortium worked together with the African Security Sector Network, the Conflict Security and Development Group, the Center for Democracy and Development, and the Geneva Centre for Democratic Control of the Armed Forces, among others. This process attempted to offer holistic, needs-based support in the form of working sessions, research and experience sharing (Jaye 2009: 7).

Through this process, members of the different committees were brought face-to-face with legislators in Ghana and the UK and were exposed to the learning experiences of past legislators from other countries. Through these sessions, Liberian legislators obtained insights into the process of civilian democratic oversight and how to make the security sector more accountable. Critical areas covered during the sessions included the development of a united, but differentiated, security architecture that is mutually supportive in contrast to the many overlapping functions of the existing structures. The appropriate separation of the roles and functions of the various agencies responsible for supporting the security sector was emphasised.

Exposing these freshman legislators to new ideas and giving them concrete guidance on how to fulfil their duties contributed to improving the legislative function, especially given the resource-poor environment where water, electricity and even paper were in short supply. There is a clear connection between these efforts to build the capacity of the freshmen legislators and subsequent changes to the security sector legislation. The 2008 National Defense Act, which these neophyte legislators produced, has proven to be a key pillar for security sector reform. This foundational piece of legislation also cleared the path for the 2011 National Security and Intelligence Act, which went further in establishing a rational basis for Liberia's various security institutions.

New National Defense Act

The main challenge to be addressed by the new National Defense Act of 2008 was to define the principle roles and responsibilities of the AFL. This also meant disentangling the overlapping mandates of Liberia's many security institutions. Defining the respective roles of the key sectors of the security system in Liberia was a difficult process. All of the major security institutions lacked a clear statement of their roles and responsibilities, including among others the AFL, LNP, the Liberian Seaport Police, the Police Quick Reaction Unit, the Special Security Service [now Executive Protection Service] and the Bureau of Immigration and Naturalization. This work had begun with the drafting of a national security strategy, which they only began to finalise in late November 2007 (United Nations Security Council 2007: par. 134).

The legislative process was completed and the new National Defense Act was passed in 2008. This Act superseded its predecessor from 1956 and envisaged a carefully vetted and well-trained professional force with the specific mandate of protecting Liberia's sovereignty. The 1956 legislation, in contrast, was based on out-dated US military legislation and mandated compulsory military service for all males and specialised training for officers. The number of soldiers was limited only by the ability of the government "to provide shelter, subsistence, uniform [sic], arms and ammunition and hospitalization". This model of military service contributed to building a huge force that was subsequently demobilised as part of the reform process, however, without appropriate care for the veterans, as explored further below.

In revising Liberia's approach to military training and personnel management, the new National Defense Act of 2008 also included provisions that Liberia should cooperate with the United States in the process of its security development but also draw on assistance from other international partners both in Africa and elsewhere. This has so far enabled Liberia to gain support from countries such as Ghana, Nigeria and China in training middle and senior managers of the security sector. This reorientation is affecting all sectors of the security structure. Personnel at top- and mid-management levels have been selected and trained in these countries, introducing best practices into operational protocols. Thanks to these collaborative efforts, Liberia has accrued at least some benefits of South-South cooperation and experience sharing. These efforts to broaden the training of Liberian security personnel in other countries marks a radical new departure from an exclusive focus on US-methods and training in the context of the post-2003 SSR period, in particular, but also generally since the founding of the Republic.

According to the National Defense Act of 2008, the primary mission of the AFL is to defend the national sovereignty and territorial integrity of Liberia. Along with national defence, the remit of the AFL includes international peacekeeping and humanitarian support of the civil authority in the event of disasters. Section 2.3 e of the National Defense Act states that the duties of the AFL include support to the national law enforcement agencies when such support is requested and approved by the President. However, it is further stipulated that during peacetime the AFL shall not engage in law enforcement and that the AFL will intervene only as a last resort, when the threat exceeds the capability of law enforcement agencies to respond. In Section 2.5 of the Act it is stated that the AFL should perform its duties in a non-partisan manner. All of these prescriptions are in response to the difficult experience of the AFL during the civil conflict, when it became entangled in the war.

The National Defense Act of 2008 did not deal, however, with some additional problems arising from the recent history of the AFL. For instance, the failure of the lawsuit filed by over 200 retired AFL soldiers and the widows of deceased AFL soldiers suggests that there are on-going problems in Liberia between civilians and the military. The claim that the court rejected in November 2013 was that the Government of Liberia disbanded the AFL unconstitutionally and failed to provide retirement benefits (Parley 2013; Gbelewala 2013). The ex-soldiers contended that instead of restructuring the AFL, as provided for by the CPA, the government had dissolved the army and done so without providing a retirement scheme for the former soldiers. Such controversies reflect some of the failings in Liberia's Disarmament, Demobilization and Reintegration process.

Despite its shortcomings, however, the National Defense Act of 2008 did succeed in providing a new legislative basis for the separation of law enforcement and national defence within a framework of democratic civilian control, rule of law and respect for human rights. Once a clear statement of the roles and responsibilities of the defence forces was established by law, producing the same degree of clarity for other security sector actors became a feasible goal. Achieving this clarity was the guiding purpose of the National Security Reform and Intelligence Act (NSRIA) that was passed in 2011.

The National Security Reform and Intelligence Act of 2011

The long awaited NSRIA was highly controversial because it entailed the closing down of a number of security sector institutions in order to organise domestic security provision across a smaller, more manageable number of service providers. The Act was submitted August 30, 2011 for approval by the president and was debated back and forth, resulting in two amendments. For example, the Ministry of National Security was abolished in the first version, but re-established by an amendment. Reducing the number of security institutions was seen by some as a way to reduce costs and complexity while dealing with the legacy of autocratic governance, whereby the interests of security institutions were played off one another to the benefit of the president. For others though, reducing the number of security institutions meant putting too much power in the hands of only a few key institutions, while overburdening new, weak institutions with a broad remit of duties, leaving the nation potentially unprepared to confront future threats. Many interests were put forward in the attempts to dissolve institutions deemed to have served the ends of divided political elites. Some concerns centred on varying understandings of these institutions. Several executive and legislative joint-working sessions took place to bridge the impasse. The NSRIA was finalised only in May 2013, although the Act refers to itself as "work in progress" seemingly owing to the many challenges and unresolved issues that still surround these questions (Liberia 2011).

The NSRIA of 2011 did indeed prove to be a work in progress. In 2013 several important amendments were made in order to revise the security architecture it had initially set up.[5] Two new chapters were added to the original Act, re-establishing the Ministry of National Security (MNS) and reactivating the National Bureau of Investigations (NBI). Security institutions recognised under the most updated version of the National Security Reform and Intelligence Act as a part of the national security architecture include:

- The Liberia National Police;
- Bureau of Corrections and Rehabilitation (Ministry of Justice);
- Ministry of National Security;
- Bureau of Immigration and Naturalization;
- Drugs Enforcement Agency;
- Bureau of Customs and Excise;
- National Bureau of Investigation;
- National Fire Service;
- National Security Agency;
- Executive Protection Service
  (formerly called the Special Security Service).

The MNS and the NBI regained some of their former duties and responsibilities that had earlier been reassigned to the LNP and the National Security Agency by the 2011 NSRIA. The MNS assumed the task of organizing and validating data provided to the Government of Liberia by different branches of the security sector and coordinating and sharing this information with relevant agencies, such as the National Security Agency. Cyber-crime and other high tech criminal activity are also part of the remit of the MNS along with the duty to advise the president on the activities of the other security agencies. The NBI investigates major crimes such as murder, arson, illegal entry into Liberia and the theft of government property. It is the NBI that maintains and updates records on known criminals and passes this information on to the LNP and other relevant agencies.

These amendments to the original 2011 National Security Reform and Intelligence Act bear testimony to the challenges faced in security and intelligence today. While the obligations of those entrusted with state secrets are stressed, other than the general oversight of the legislature, the president and the executive, there is no clear protection mechanism to prevent the MNS, the NBI or the National Security Agency from over-stepping their authority. This is because the role of the judiciary is not mentioned in the original NSRIA or its amendments. There is no independent avenue of appeal available, nor is there recourse for someone who feels himself wrongly suspected of crimes.

Thus, although civilian oversight is a cornerstone of the NSRIA, this call for oversight has not been fully translated into mechanisms that are adequate to this task (PBC 2012: par. 35). In a similar way, the actors governed by this Act do not possess the basic equipment needed to carry out their tasks and more advanced training is required. Without greater attention to civilian oversight, effective community outreach, reduction in the rates of corruption and adequate working tools, the current plans described in the NSRIA could be thwarted (PBC 2012: par. 35).

Progress and challenges in the Liberian legislature

The above discussion illustrates that the Liberian Legislature is a crucial actor in SSR that has come to play an unprecedented role in actively shaping Liberia's security sector governance during the transition to democracy. According to Thomas Jaye, effective security sector reform in Liberia requires strengthening legislative oversight in three areas: authority, ability and attitude (Jaye 2009, 9). From this perspective, the legislature still faces many issues that include: executive domination, lack of integrity among individual legislators and corruption.

A sound legal framework exists as a basis for legislative oversight even if the presidency is imbued with a great degree of constitutional power: Article 34 of the Liberian Constitution gives ample power to parliament to deal with all security sector issues (Ebo 2005: 23). Furthermore, the way that the legislature operates provides space for the establishment of committees on security and defence, which could supervise the security sector through their power to hold hearings and summon witnesses. The process of selecting committee members has been broadened beyond appointments by the Speaker, thereby, making for more robust work and more openness in the legislature.

Efforts aimed at transparency, such as the Open Budget Initiative, have further extended legislative authority over security sector governance by making budget provisions for the military and other security institutions publically known. The opening of security budgets by the legislature to public scrutiny has the potential to improve public confidence, and more robust legislative oversight should further enhance these positive effects. One reported limitation of this system is the constant budget shortfall, which permits the executive to make many re-allocations without legislative approval. This is even more pronounced in situations dealing with emergencies and security threats.

However, authority is not the only variable for effective legislative oversight. Legislators must also enjoy the ability to make use of the powers at their disposal. The complexity and especially the secrecy of the security sector represent serious problems to oversight. Security officials can and do hide behind so-called national security interests in order to limit the role of legislators. Another challenge is turnover. By the time legislators develop some knowledge and expertise on defence, security and intelligence matters they find themselves moved to another committee or their tenure in the legislature will have ended. Finally, there is the problem of the generally low educational level of legislators.

Ability, secrecy and turnover are interrelated issues. Ability relates not only to educational attainment but also to personal integrity. Secrecy is a cultural variable in Liberia that can be negotiated and is open to compromise. Finally, in due course, turnover is likely to lessen as the electors gain confidence in their chosen representatives and return them to office in subsequent elections by voting on the basis of this gained confidence rather than following a 'vetted assessment' of all candidates. A key challenge for future elections will, therefore, be to improve the role and participation of the population in the process.

The final condition for effective oversight of the security sector is attitude. Historically, Liberia's legislature has usually yielded to the will of the executive. This is no longer the case. The relevant committees have been active in insisting that they provide input on security issues and do not hesitate to summon ministers to explain issues to them. Thus, the emerging role of the legislature should help to provide legitimacy for the state security apparatus, on the one hand, and empower the legislature vis-à-vis the executive, on the other hand.

Yet the problem of attitude is not only in the control of the legislature. The executive must also respect the role of legislators in ensuring democratic governance of the security sector, which has not always been the case in Liberia. Since independence, the will and commitment of the legislature to fulfil their oversight role has been hampered by single party rule and the imperial style of the presidency. Due to these two factors, the legislature has historically yielded to the will of the executive and party loyalty has undermined the independence of the Senate and House of Representatives. This is changing. Even though the president is vested by the constitution with considerable power, the legislature has begun to use its legal authority to address issues that were previously rubber stamped by its predecessors.

Security sector reform in Liberia: the sustainability of change

Making public consultation more inclusive, establishing a new legislative basis for national security and strengthening legislative capacity constitute unprecedented changes in security sector governance in Liberia. They are, however, only the initial steps towards closing the gaps in the democratic governance of Liberia's security sector. These efforts to improve democratic governance took place within a wider context of internationally led efforts that dealt with the technical dimensions of reform but did not sufficiently address governance concerns. Increasing Liberian-owned efforts, such as reform of the legislature, may potentially offer transformative potential. This section considers the extent to which SSR in Liberia has the potential to be transformational in nature and how likely it is to be sustainable based on the SSR process to date.

Local ownership versus international intervention

There are a number of critical actors in the Liberian SSR process. Given that Liberia had become a failed state, the involvement of the international community was, and is, seen as necessary to improve the capacity of security institutions. As a result, Liberia has been obliged to undertake SSR with extensive external involvement. While a great deal of assistance was forthcoming, these support relationships have exclusively engaged the executive. Thus, with respect to local ownership and democratic participation, all local actors with the exception of the executive were marginalised in the SSR process, especially early in the process (Onoma 2014; Ebo 2008; Loden 2007).

The most egregious example of this marginalization was a relationship the US built with a private contractor to implement defence reforms on behalf of the US State Department. The company in question, DynCorp, refused to report to the Liberian parliament on the rebuilding of the AFL, citing contractual obligations to the US State Department. The contracting out of reform made it extremely difficult for the legislative body and civil society actors to exercise any kind of monitoring function, let alone provide genuine input into the process. The definition of the nature, content and character of Liberia's new armed forces was, thus, decided without consultation with parliament or civil society, highlighting a serious lack of inclusion in the SSR process. Both government officials and civil society groups have voiced their concern about a lack of local ownership, and have called for a "Liberianisation" of the process (Anderson 2006: 4 – 5; Onoma 2014: 1).

Civil society should be a crucial actor in the new Liberian security sector, as emphasised in the national dialogue and the legislative development process that followed. Strengthening the role of civil society in public security oversight would also contribute to improving local ownership. In the past, civil society was confined to information sharing rather than consultation. This role needs to be expanded beyond the limited initiatives described above. Civil society was mentioned explicitly in Article VII (3) of the CPA section regarding the strengthening of civilian oversight and local participation in Liberia's SSR. Broader governance processes gave them a limited platform for engagement. A number of civil society groups active in security related issues organised themselves into a coordinated Working Group on SSR. The SSR Working Group became much more active in reform by 2008. Community policing forums were designed to increase civil society and public input into policing, although this process went through a number of missteps before finally being re-launched in 2011 as a programme for Community Watch Teams.

Although the extent of civil society participation is much greater than at any time in Liberia's past, these initiatives remain limited in their impact. This is because civil society was not incorporated into the Government of Liberia's reform framework from the outset. The exclusion of civil society in Liberia's SSR illustrates the common tendency to posit a tension between the principle of efficiency and the principles of legality, transparency and accountability (Bendix and Stanley 2008: 27). This lack of local inclusion seems to have contributed to the US decision to sever its relationship with DynCorp and take on direct responsibility for mentoring the AFL through Operation Onward Liberty, a five-year mission to assist in training the AFL. This cooperation arrangement specifically provided for a process of "Liberianisation" of leadership characterised by fast-track promotions and ultimately a Liberian Chief of Staff appointed in 2014, replacing a Nigerian general who had served the post in a caretaker role.

New oversight opportunities

Another important initiative after the enactment of the National Defense Act of 2008 was the Governance Reform Commission (GRC) made permanent in 2009 as simply the Governance Commission. The GRC was originally established under the CPA as a transitional body mandated to advise on issues of good governance. From this position, it played an important role in shaping early reforms, including leading part of the national dialogue on SSR since

2006, and was eventually mandated by the president to draft reform proposals.[6] The President of Liberia has already tasked the Governance Reform Commission to provide advice and leadership on matters of national interest, including security, making this role permanent in 2009 (Liberia 2006). The GRC assessed the country's security sector and reviewed existing legislation. It concluded that the SSR process in Liberia was "taking place within very volatile, uncertain and fragile internal and external environments" (Jaye 2006). The centralization of power in the presidency, the lack of an independent judiciary and the past one-party rule represented significant challenges according to the GRC. The NSRIA of 2011 was an important step in helping to establish the kind of SSR called for by the GRC (Jaye 2009).

Other independent bodies created to support the effective functioning of SSR include: (1) the Liberia Anti-Corruption Commission established in August 2008 by an Act of the National Legislature with a broad mandate to implement appropriate measures and undertake programmes geared toward investigating, prosecuting and preventing acts of corruption, including educating the public about the ills of corruption and the benefits of its eradication (United Nations Security Council 2009: par. 2) and (2) the Independent National Commission on Human Rights, required by article XII of the CPA and established by the Truth and Reconciliation Commission to implement its recommendations (ICTJ 2015). Both these developments are promising and positive. However their long-term importance depends on how they are implemented, and to date they have enjoyed only mixed results.

Over the past decade, Liberia's security architecture has evolved from a many-headed monster full of duplications to a stream-lined sector with clearly defined boundaries of function and responsibility; this is in part thanks to some of the legislative capacity building efforts previously mentioned and the legal framework it subsequently has helped to develop. The legal framework for the security sector is almost complete with the passage in 2011 of the NSRIA and its amendments in 2013.

Future SSR work that awaits attention includes several pieces of legislation: a police act, reform of the drug enforcement agency, the National Defense Strategy and the Firearms Control Act. In addition, several legal topics also need attention: a clarification of the relationship between the security services and the political process in order to avoid the politicization of security and the process of appointments of top officials, whether political or non-political.

Police reform

In light of the damage to public confidence due to continuing police dysfunction, enacting a new police law is perhaps the most pressing of Liberia's immediate security priorities. Indeed, "Just because the guns have been silent for 10 years doesn't mean everything's OK here," said Thomas Nah of the

Center for Transparency and Accountability in Liberia (Stroehlein 2013). According to Nah, "Liberia is going nowhere as long as the police remain like this" (Stroehlein 2013). Although corruption is widespread in Liberian institutions, the abuses found within the LNP are especially egregious because, in the words of Cecil Griffiths, president of the Liberia Law Enforcement Association, it is "the face of the state".[7] Given the LNP's capabilities and complexity, the question of oversight is critical (Gompert, Davis and Stearns Lawson 2009; Gompert et al. 2007).

An important recent initiative has been the establishment of the Professional Standards Division, the LNP's internal monitoring unit. Since it began its work, LNP officers have been more inclined to report the abusive behaviour of other officers. However, Human Rights Watch and local bodies alike have urged the Government of Liberia and the LNP to go further to establish an independent civilian oversight board to field complains about acts of misconduct.

There is a clear need for full implementation of a new police law. There are a variety of modalities through which this need can be met. Although it would be challenging to enact, such a law could be part of an omnibus security bill. Another possibility would be to update the Act to amend the Executive Law with respect to the National Police Force of 1975 (Jaye 2008: 169). Among the provisions such an act would need to address itself are arrest and detention practices. Without an efficient, fair and transparent system of arrest, trial and incarceration, those accused of crimes might simply find themselves in jail without due process or, alternatively, might find their way right back onto the street without prosecution (Gompert et al: 57). This, unfortunately, is the reality in today's Liberia. The LNP in this legislation should come under the authority and management oversight of the Ministry of Justice, and the ancillary police services should be consolidated into the LNP (Gompert et al: 77).

A comprehensive police law would complement the National Defense Act of 2008 with respect to the AFL, and give the LNP a sound legal footing on which to rebuild its reputation and fulfil its mission. A new police law is an essential piece of Liberia's new national security architecture that remains missing and evidence of the crucial responsibilities Liberia's legislature must still assume in regards to SSR.

Conclusion

The years of slow descent into crisis and the fourteen years of intermittent civil war that followed were devastating for Liberia and its people. The challenge of resurrecting a viable state security sector amidst the chaos that followed was daunting. Yet, within the ten short years since the CPA was signed, Liberia has rebuilt its military and established a new civilian police force built upon a stronger technical foundation, with an improved capacity to secure the nation's population and its borders and even participate in international peace missions.

This internationally led effort to improve the effectiveness of Liberia's security sector, however, failed to ensure a more locally owned approach to reform. Liberia has been unable to reap the full benefit of improvements in the security sector because of the failure to match these gains with improvements in democratic accountability. As this chapter has shown, inconsistencies and the missing pieces in Liberia's legal framework for national security remain to be filled. Problems of executive dominance cut to the core of Liberia's national security architecture, preventing more effective security sector oversight by the legislature and other government actors. These dynamics facilitate old patterns of patronage-based elite politics, undermine good governance and contribute to corruption. Structural failings in security sector governance translate into ineffective service delivery, harming the population through petty corruption and abuse of power. Even though national-security policy-making has become more inclusive, civil society voices remain on the margins and Liberia's legislature and judiciary remain beholden to the executive. Failing a radical revision of Liberia's constitution, the executive will continue to enjoy more control over the security sector than the other two branches of government, and Liberia's democracy will suffer as a result.

Yet this long list of work still waiting to be done should be understood as a measure of how much progress has been made in Liberia's security sector, as well as a measure of what is yet to be achieved. The extent of progress in SSR needs to be understood against the scale of the task that presented itself. Ten years is too short a timeframe to transform security sector governance dynamics completely, yet in the past ten years much progress has been made. In particular, the new National Defence Act of 2008, together with the NSRIA of 2011, constitute a far-reaching revision of the legal basis for security provision, management and control in Liberia.

In terms of the transformative potential of governance-driven SSR, the *process* that led to these changes is perhaps the most significant aspect. More than the soundness of Liberia's new legislative framework, it is the fact that this new legal framework was enacted on the basis of a public policy dialogue that was unprecedented in Liberia for its inclusiveness and openness. It is equally important that these ideas were translated into legislation by newly elected legislators able to apply themselves to the task successfully despite such imposing capacity constraints. Moreover, it is also significant that this progress was made in spite of a general neglect towards improving democratic governance within externally led SSR programmes and in the face of many barriers to local ownership of the reform process. Liberia's experience thus symbolises the potential offered by targeted support to legislative processes, such as the parliamentary capacity-building for security sector legislators, as this process contributed to empowering legislators to contribute to the process of improving security sector governance. It also shows the usefulness of an inclusive policy-making process, including opportunities for civil society participation and broader public dialogue. These examples suggest that a more open process can generate ideas for more responsive reform proposals, fostering political support and building consensus around potentially contentious issues, as well as improving public confidence in new legislative processes and the provision of public security.

Although the future is never assured, there are many reasons to be optimistic that Liberia is now heading in a new direction with its security sector, one that has begun to establish legislative supervision and civilian control. If so, this marks a remarkable departure from a long historical precedent of presidential dominance over security affairs. Liberia's experience so far suggests that the new assertiveness among Liberia's legislators should be supported and maintained, together with increased public dialogue and more inclusive policy-making.

Notes

1 Comprehensive Peace Agreement Between the Government of Liberia and the Liberians United for Reconcilation and Democracy (LURD) and the Movement for Democracy in Liberia (MODEL) and Political Parties Accra, August 18, 2003.

2 On the historical roots of Liberia's crisis in democratic governance see (Jaye 2009).

3 As William Barnes (2013) argues, Tubman's three rules applied to public servants in general.

4 The following discussion draws on the Summary Report of the Liberia National Dialogue on Security Sector Reform (Geneva Centre for Democratic Control of Armed Forces 2005).

5 An Act to Repeal and Amend Sections 1, 2, and Section 6(IV) of the National Security and Intelligence Act of 2011 was passed on 23 May 2013 by the Honourable House of Representatives of the Republic of Liberia (Liberia 2013).

6 On the role of the GRC, see (Jaye 2009).

7 Private communication with author, Monrovia, 2014

CHAPTER 5

Missed Opportunities for Comprehensive Security Sector Reform in Mali

Zeïni Moulaye

Foreign Affairs Advisor and former Minister of Transports and Tourism for Mali

Introduction

Following the democratic revolution in March 1991, Mali became an example and even a model of democratic governance in West Africa, including in the area of transformational management of the security sector. The events of 2012 however called all this into question. That year was marked by the resurgence in the Tuareg rebellion in January, followed by a coup d'état in March against a regime that the organisers of the putsch described as "incompetent" (Konaté 2013: 252). Then, in April, Islamist jihadist movements also made their appearance. A temporary alliance of the rebellion, the jihadists and other transnational criminal operators (Moulaye 2014) including drug traffickers was created, which enabled them to occupy the northern regions of the country, constituting two thirds of the national territory. For almost a year, these criminals pillaged, plundered, raped, destroyed and carried out grave human rights violations marked by an unprecedented degree of violence. These events revealed the overall lack of governance in Mali, in the political, economic, social and cultural and security spheres.

The serious shortcomings in the security sector had not been addressed by the timid process of security sector reform initiated by the government of General Amadou Toumani Touré in 2005. Why? Most certainly due to a

How to cite this book chapter:

Moulaye, Z. 2015. Missed Opportunities for Comprehensive Security Sector Reform in Mali. In: Bryden, A and Chappuis, F (eds.) *Learning from West African Experiences in Security Sector Governance*, Pp. 79–95. London: Ubiquity Press. DOI: http://dx.doi.org/10.5334/bau.e. License: CC-BY 4.0.

lack of leadership, political backing and acceptance. It appears that these grave shortcomings were the result of a rear-guard conservatism on the part of certain senior officers who wanted to cling to their often undeserved privileges in terms of recruitment, rank, positions and allowances. They risked losing such privileges if the reform process led to sound security sector governance, democratic control, transparent management, efficiency and accountability. The situation can be attributed first and foremost to the lack of political will at the highest level since the head of state, according to the constitution, is commander in chief of the armed forces and in this case, was also a former senior officer.

The modern history of Mali has provided various remarkable opportunities to redesign and reform the security sector. The first of these was at the time of independence on 22 September 1960. At the time, the new Malian authorities called on all citizens serving in the ranks of the French armed forces and within the colonial security services to come back to their newly independent homeland to set up the Malian armed forces and Malian security services. The concept and practice of security was not however redesigned to take into account the new political, economic and social and cultural realities of the nascent state of Mali. The defence and security forces (DSF) were established immediately after independence, but their members were not 're-programmed'. During the colonial period, these personnel had been 'trained' to serve the French administration against the same colonised peoples who had now declared their independence. As a result, unwittingly, the mind set (domination) and behaviour (repressive) of the troops at the disposal of the new regime were the same as within the colonial forces. In their defence, it is most likely that this was exactly what the new leaders wanted, as they sought to entrench their authority and power. This would later lead to the establishment of a dictatorial regime.

The start of a democratic era on 26 March 1991 provided a second opportunity to redesign and reform the security sector. Already in 1990, the rebellion in the north of Mali had revealed the scope of proliferation of small arms and light weapons, as well as their devastating effects on human security. At the time of the democratic revolution in 1991, the security forces were reviled and accused of being 'repressive forces', at the service of a 'dictator'. The forces were such a subject of public opprobrium that during the days of unrest in March and even some weeks later, policemen could not move around in uniform without attracting condemnation from the population. The change of regime provided an opportunity to operate a qualitative shift in security sector governance by making this an integral part of the overall democratic governance of the country. What happened instead was that the security forces, in particular the police, were violently condemned and marginalised because they were accused of having served as the repressive arm of the dictatorial regime. Even worse, defence and security institutions were overlooked, relegated to the background and provided with negligible resources.

Twenty years later, Mali was to pay a high price for this negligence. Faced with the upsurge in transborder and transnational crime, starting from 2000, individuals, communities and local and national elected officials had started to raise many questions and call the attention of the authorities to security matters. However, due to the failure to implement sufficiently in-depth reforms, ten years later in 2012, hordes of narco-terrorists allied with a group of irredentists razed the institutional and democratic structure to the ground in just a few days. Due to lack of adequate training and equipment, and above all lack of motivation, the defence and security forces were incapable of containing the enemies of the republic.

In the first part of this study, we shall review the state of security sector governance prior to the launch of the 2005 reform process. The second part will describe the stages in the process of policy change conducted up to the events of January 2012. The third part will touch on the roles of various actors and the challenges of reform. Finally, in the fourth part we shall review some of the outcomes and suggest proposals for creating the best possible conditions to enable the reform process, which is even more vital for Mali today, to be continued and enhanced. In the conclusion, we shall examine the prospects for security sector reform in Mali.

The state of security sector governance prior to the reform

The system of security sector governance in Mali dates back to colonial times and is characterised by a half century of accumulated flaws from this period. Indeed, for many years, the security sector was plagued by a lack of leadership, vision, strategy, communication and good governance. Up to 2009, the authorities had never adopted a single official, public security policy document, nor had they initiated any analysis on possible fundamental changes in the paradigms of security governance. For fifty years, security matters were kept out of public debate and excluded from democratic control. As a result, people generally felt that security was the exclusive domain of the security services. This led to total disinterest in the governance of this sector on the part of the population. Over time, this situation has become extremely detrimental to the efficiency of security services, in particular when they required the collaboration of the general public in fighting against insecurity and organised crime. Finally, although a number of mechanisms for the control of the security services do exist formally, they have never functioned effectively, probably due to the exclusive, sensitive and sovereign nature of the security sector.

The institutional framework in Mali makes a clear distinction between defence and security. Since 1992, they have been under two different ministries; the ministry of defence and former combatants and the ministry of internal security and civil defence. Defence is solely responsible for the armed forces.

Security includes the police and civil defence, which have civilian status, as well as the gendarmerie and the national guard, which are military forces. The gendarmerie and the national guard are managed by law by the ministry of defence, but they are placed at the disposal of the ministry in charge of security. This blend of forces is actually meant to make up for the deficit in human, material and financial resources.

Security institutions function in accordance with international law. The security services were established in accordance with existing legislation and regulations in Mali (laws, decrees, ministerial orders, administrative decisions, etc.). They are under the orders of the democratically established civilian authority. The budget allocated for security is included in the planning of the national budget, which is submitted to the council of ministers and the national assembly for approval. Expenditure by the security services is not subject to state secrecy. The information is available to all and the resources are managed by specialised public administration departments in the ministry of security.

Security in Mali falls within the public domain. The missions and prerogatives of the security services are defined by the constitution of 1992.[1] Institutional mechanisms are responsible for their functioning and management. In practice, security sector governance in Mali has to take account of some deeply entrenched endogenous security management mechanisms, in particular in the hinterland. In rural areas in particular, communities more often call on custom and traditional authorities (chiefs, qadis, imams, griots, etc.) when dealing with local security governance. This is one of the emergent issues of democratic security sector governance in Mali.

The national assembly is responsible for direct control of the security services through its oversight of government activities and may put questions to the authorities in charge of security at any time. The 'parliamentary committee on defence, security and civil defence' is in charge of considering security matters, analysing them and taking such decisions as are required by law: If necessary, it may question the minister or other security officials.

Furthermore, various provisions of the constitution confer political control over the armed and security forces on the president of the republic, who is commander in chief of the armed forces.[2] The president of the republic presides over the higher council for national defence and the national defence committee, which are responsible for defence policy in military management and crisis management respectively.

The judiciary also has constitutional and legal prerogatives to control the security sector. Under the terms of the code of criminal procedure, the judicial police, made up of police officers, is mainly in charge of recording crimes and offenses, of gathering evidence of such infringements and of identifying the perpetrators. Judicial police officers are agents of the justice system who work under the authority and the responsibility of the office of the prosecutor. The judicial power also includes mechanisms for control of the security services, in the form of certain provisions of martial law, as well as military tribunals and courts.

The existence of all these institutional control mechanisms was nevertheless not enough to prevent the dysfunctions, excesses, shortcomings and failures that came to light in 2012. Why? Because in reality, parliamentary control in Mali is often limited to adopting the security budget and considering draft bills and, very rarely, to putting questions to the minister in charge of security. Parliamentarians have never initiated any draft bills in this area. This phenomenon is due first of all to the lack of adequate knowledge about security sector issues and also to the fact that, like all ordinary citizens, parliamentarians believe that security is a 'reserved domain'. In addition, government has always communicated very little about security matters and there is a clear lack of political will to subject the security sector to democratic control.

Since the beginning of the 21st century, the country has experienced increasing insecurity. In addition to the existing risks and vulnerabilities, the most worrying threats have come from organised crime: trafficking in drugs, weapons and human beings, cybercrime and terrorism. These criminal activities have had immeasurable effects on human security, social cohesion, enjoyment of human rights, political stability and the efforts to build a democracy and ensure development. The weaknesses in security service oversight and delivery have heightened the country's vulnerability.

Security sector governance faces two types of challenges. There are firstly the numerous, physical security challenges that take various forms and, secondly, the abundant and varied issues of governance in the security sector.

The issues related to governance include the lack of leadership or a vision and strategy, as well as the lack of communication or a system for managing resources; inadequate personnel, training and equipment; the absence of a framework for coordinating the actions of the security forces and for consultation with other actors in the security sector. Finally, strategies have not been adapted to take account of new forms of criminal activity, in particular cybercrime and transborder and transnational crime. All of these make it clear that there is a need for a new form of security sector governance that will transform security into a factor of social cohesion, national unity and development. To achieve this some of the fundamental paradigms of security will have to be modified, but this also implies that people are ready in their minds to accept the idea of change.

How then can the requirements of democratic participation be reconciled with the exclusivity of security services? How can parliamentarians, communities, civil society organisations and sometimes individuals be enabled to contribute to establishing a secure environment at a time when the security forces themselves are unable to tackle the multiple internal and external security challenges head on? The answer lies in making security an integral part of the overall democratic governance of the country and promoting a new form of governance that enables direct and indirect control of the security services by parliament, as well as the community and individuals, respectively. This will improve the overall framework for security sector governance.

The process of change: towards security sector reform

A nascent atmosphere of change in security policy

Following the traumatic events of 1991, the security services, in particular the police, began to think about their future and the nature of their mandate. However, it was not until 2001 that structured debate actually took place during the 'Journées de reflexion de la police nationale'. This time of reflection was organised on the initiative of the general directorate of the national police service and took place in Bamako from 21 to 23 February 2001. It was an opportunity to review some of the difficulties facing the security forces in areas such as human and material resources, logistics, finances and infrastructure. Participants in the three days of reflection also spoke about the possible new face of the police service describing it as one:

> "whose presence will enhance the feeling of general security by the public; one that observes the law and individuals' rights in carrying out its missions; that remains discreet in order to gather information, communicate with citizens, prevent crimes and offences and improve the efficacy of its services to the general public; that is tolerant of the surrounding traditional and socio-cultural concepts, in order to preserve the social harmony of families and the community; that is disciplined in organising and executing its traditional and specific public security missions, and one that is strong enough to protect persons and goods and fight banditry and crime, in line with existing legal regulatory and administrative provisions." (DGPN 2001: 4)

In 2003, the permanent secretary of the ministry of security and inspector-general of police, Anatole Sangaré, presented the overall approach of his ministry to a visiting delegation from the Nigerian Centre for Strategic Studies that had travelled to Bamako to learn about the experience of Mali in the area of security sector governance. This approach focused mainly on developing a policy of prevention, consolidating the basis for community policing (politique de proxmité) and clarifying and harmonising different security roles. It also sought to adapt means to immediate ends, consolidate and enhance public outreach and pursue a meaningful communication strategy. Based on these elements, the ministry intended to adopt a national security policy that was described as "pragmatic and consistent, in an environment characterised by apparently contradictory demands; on the one hand, the need to preserve public order and state stability and on the other, the need to ensure the rule of law and respect of individual fundamental rights, as well as our tradition of tolerance and hospitality" (MSIPC 2003a: 7).

For the implementation of these guidelines, the ministry drafted an operational plan covering seven priority intervention areas: enhancing the security of persons and goods; enhanced operational capacity of the security forces; improved design of the security coverage structure; adapting the legal framework; design of a real communication policy; improving the methods of governance and promoting a policy of bilateral and multilateral cooperation (MSIPC 2003b: 4).

The reflection exercise named 'Journées de reflexion de la police nationale' did not result in a security sector reform project. This may be due either to some form of self-censorship on the part of the security forces, or the fact that the required approval from the hierarchy was not forthcoming. The police service is a vertical structure where even general analysis has to be driven by the superstructure. It took four years for another opportunity to arise in 2005. Prior to that, in 2003, there were signs that the hierarchy was more aware of the values and criteria of sound security sector governance, but these values had not yet been shared with the grassroots and even less with other security sector agencies. The very concept of security sector reform was far from the minds of those involved. Nevertheless, some key players had begun to realise that there was a need to move towards the change for which the general public had long been calling. All it needed was something to trigger off the whole process. In reality, various warning signals had been going off and others were to sound even more alarmingly and sometimes rather suddenly. The events of March 2005 therefore became a catalyst for another attempt at reform.

Triggers of the reform process

On 27 March 2005, an event that could have been quite banal set off a shockwave. An African Cup of Nations eliminatory round football match between Togo and Mali ended with a win by the visiting team. Throughout the night, a horde of hooligans, joined by thousands of young people, occupied and ransacked Bamako, the capital city. Law enforcement forces failed to protect the population and indeed were completely absent during these events. This violent reaction was a way for idle youth to express their dissatisfaction at the difficulties facing them daily, which included endemic unemployment, poverty and deprivation, marginalisation and exclusion. It was a way for them to challenge the authority of government, whom they blamed for all their woes, and to express their disgust with its system of management. The spontaneity and the degree of violence of events caught everyone unawares, including the president of the republic.[3] On 7 April 2005, the prime minister met with civil society representatives who expressed their exasperation and demanded the establishment of a strong state that could guarantee the safety of persons and their property and that nevertheless would not be a dictatorship. This situation highlighted at least three systemic shortcomings in security sector management:

- Malfunctions related to the breakdown of government authority and poor communication, which meant that there was a need for an in-depth analysis of the security sector;
- A government system of management where rewards were distributed more readily than responsibilities;
- A considerable absence of accountability and efficiency on the part of public security forces, with regard to the resources allocated to them.

Following these events, the responsible authorities were removed from their positions, but this was not enough to appease the general public, who called for deeper change. And yet those involved in the security sector did not all have the same degree of awareness or the same vision of change. Within the security services, many felt that all that was needed to allay this dissatisfaction was an amendment of existing texts and some improvements in the living and working conditions of security agents. A small number of them, as well as a good part of civil society actors however realised that the security situation was in need of a new form of security sector governance in order to meet the requirements of democracy and deal with major security threats such as drugs, weapons and human trafficking, natural disasters, the presence of Algerian Salafists on the national territory, etc. It is against this backdrop that the minister of internal security and civil defence launched the General Assembly on Peace and Security in Mali (*Etats généraux de la sécurité et de la paix au Mali*) in 2005.

Major implementation milestones and developments in the reform process

The idea of holding the General Assembly on Peace and Security in Mali was put forward by the ministry in charge of security. This meeting became the entry point for the security sector reform process and marked a historic moment in the annals of the sector in Mali. For the first time since independence in 1960, the security services were making overtures to other actors in the sector. No subject was taboo and all the issues were raised and debated. It was a gathering of flag officers and farmers, soldiers and hunters, police and herders, senior civil servants and labourers, women, men, young people and the elderly. The participants worked together to identify the security challenges, assess the security needs of the population and propose solutions, as well as the most desirable form of national security sector governance.

The General Assembly on Peace and Security in Mali took place from 21 to 23 November 2005 under the auspices of the ministry of internal security and civil defence and was attended by the president of the republic, President Amadou Toumani Touré. The event had been prepared in three successive phases. During the first phase, the ministry sent out missions, travelling sometimes all the way to communes and villages to raise awareness among various stakeholders about the need for national debate on security matters and to gather their reactions. During the second phase, the ministry organised regional consultations spearheaded by the regional governors, on major themes such as urban and peri-urban banditry, the proliferation of light weapons, community conflict management, rising religious intolerance, transborder crime, etc. The third phase was the actual event in Bamako where 245 participants from various walks of life attended the General Assembly. There were representatives of government, the general administration and the administrative regions, commanders of military regions, defence and security forces, civil society, the private sector, political parties, local authorities, communities and technical and financial partners.

The General Assembly on Peace and Security in Mali was assigned four objectives:

- To encourage all categories of the population to participate actively in a discussion of security issues and the design of a coherent and harmonised security programme;
- To identify the components of a 'national security policy' by examining the problems in the security sector from different points of view;
- To put together the makings of a draft security orientation and planning bill;
- To establish a framework for consultation, coordination and participatory management of security issues, involving all security sector actors.

To meet these objectives, participants alternated between plenary sessions and workshops over the three-day period, with accounts from senior officials and also ordinary citizens who recounted their experience of security in Mali. The inaugural presentation focused on security issues in West Africa and was followed by 21 other presentations on topical subjects. The workshop discussions were centred on five major themes: 21st century societies and the emergence of new risks; the precautionary principle and the culture of prevention; security and decentralisation; security and intercommunity conflicts and security agents and accountability. Each workshop was run by a moderator and the discussions were collated by a rapporteur, working closely with the general rapporteur of the event.

With regard to the vision of security, two conceptions emerged from the General Assembly. Most of the security forces called for enhanced government authority and the reinstatement of a strong state in order to provide security. The other stakeholders, in particular those from civil society, political parties and local authorities (communities), who represented the vast majority, called for a new vision based on more democratic security sector governance where the individual would be the central focus of security concerns. In various communications and presentations, appeals were made for this new vision to be based on human security (MSIPC 2005). The supporters of this predominant approach were convinced that a security system that was based on democratic governance and focused on the individual would give renewed impetus to development. This vision is based on the fact that the end of the cold war also marked the end of inter-state conflicts. The centre of gravity of threats has now suddenly swung from external factors to internal factors, thus revealing a multitude of vulnerabilities, risks and real threats to peace and national security. The proponents of this approach pointed to the fact that violence was spreading at all levels of society and emphasised the need to review the conventional state-centric approach to security. Ultimately they stated that while state security must be assured, from now on human security must be the first priority.

On 23 November 2005, after three days of intense, frank and open debate, 127 recommendations were published. The following are among the key recommendations:

- Drafting of a national security policy based on a new vision (human security) and a new comprehensive strategy (prevention);
- Implementation of a programme for shared governance of peace and security;
- Design and implementation of a communication strategy to promote shared governance of security and peace;
- Drafting of a long term action plan for implementing the strategic pillars of the national security policy, with the aim of moving towards a security planning act.

These recommendations outlined a road map for improving the democratic quality of security sector governance in Mali and identified the first step as the drafting of a new national security policy.

National security and civil defence policy

In the wake of the General Assembly on Peace and Security in Mali the ministry of security set up a commission in charge of drafting a national internal security policy and establishing a programme for shared governance of the security sector. These were practical steps in the implementation of security sector reform. The aim of the programme was to make a qualitative contribution towards creating an enabling atmosphere of social peace and political stability for economic and social development by integrating security in the overall democratic and developmental governance of the country. The objective was to meet democratic demands, as well as the criteria for good governance and to improve the ability of the security forces to deal with both internal and external factors of insecurity and meet the security expectations of the population.

The national internal security policy took the form of a simple policy outline that emphasised the polysemous, crosscutting and multidimensional nature of security and described the nine strategic pillars that should serve as the backbone of the national security and civil defence policy:

- Prevention of situations that could undermine security;
- Strengthening the capacities of the security forces;
- Enhancing national disaster prevention and management capacities;
- Control of insecurity on roads and rivers;
- Creation of a neighbourhood police service;
- Implementing shared governance in the security sector;
- Anti-terrorism;
- Enhanced bilateral and multilateral cooperation;
- Implementation of a communication strategy to promote a change in attitudes and behaviour.

Through focusing on these areas, the government intended to implement measures that would enhance the national capacity to deal with the broad range and complexity of security problems and ensure an atmosphere of social peace and political stability throughout the country, thus promoting development.

This outline of a national security policy also included a five-year action plan that was to serve as the security sector planning law. The council of ministers postponed the adoption of this action plan for both budgetary and political reasons. The council of ministers felt that the required budget was not available. In addition, the head of state in particular was of the view that a security sector planning law needed to go hand-in-hand with a military sector planning law, which was still pending. Nevertheless, the idea of a programme to support the implementation of a national security policy was approved and gave rise to the establishment of the Programme for Shared Governance of Peace and Security (*Programme de gouvernance partagée de la sécurité et de la paix* – PGPSP).

The Programme for Shared Governance of Peace and Security

The implementation of a concept of shared governance of peace and security as an instrument for executing national security policy was a significant starting point for the security sector reform process (Moulaye & Niakaté 2011). The overall objective of the programme was to contribute to establishing an atmosphere of security, peace and stability, which would promote sustainable human development and contribute to poverty reduction in Mali. The programme was assigned three specific objectives as follows: (i) to assist in drafting and adopting a new national security policy, following the General Assembly on Peace and Security in Mali (ii) to support the implementation of the shared governance of security and peace programme at national and decentralised levels and (iii) to support the construction of lasting peace and security in the north of Mali. The programme included the following major activities:

- Drafting and implementation of a national security and civil defence policy framework document, as recommended by the General Assembly on Peace and Security in Mali;
- Capacity enhancement for security and civil defence departments, civil society organisations, the private sector, local authorities and local communities, in the area of security governance;
- Prevention and resolution of community conflicts, in close collaboration with civil society organisations, local government and government representatives;
- Enhancing disaster prevention and management capacities;
- Design and establishment of a pilot municipal police service;
- Drafting and implementation of a communication strategy on shared and decentralised security;
- Promoting a culture of peace;
- Control of light weapons, etc.

The programme also provided assistance to various national institutions (national assembly, economic and social council and the ministries of local government, defence, women's promotion, justice, etc.). The programme provided technical and financial assistance to numerous communities, local authorities and civil society organisations involved in conflict prevention, management and resolution. The opportunities for dialogue and consultation that it provided generated valuable debate on security issues in the country. These discussions often inspired the artisans of peace and those involved in the security sector and helped them to identify appropriate solutions which contributed to consolidating peace and security in the hinterland of Mali. Finally, the programme was able to build a network of partners, which contributed significantly to its funding. These results are even more important as they relate to the most valuable assets of a nation, namely its citizens. They enabled some actors to realise the importance of investing in security, an area which until then had been totally foreign to them. With conviction and perseverance, the programme was able to involve other stakeholders and thus attain a critical mass that made the reform process irreversible.

By the end of the three years of implementation (October 2008 – December 2011), the programme had achieved some remarkable results that included the drafting of a national internal security and civil defence policy framework document. Furthermore, a number of studies were carried out and served to consolidate the basis of the reform. These include a feasibility study on a communal police service, a study on the establishment of a database on criminal activity and a study on the communication strategy, with a communication plan for the ministry of internal security and civil defence.

The positive results of the PGPSP include about a hundred capacity building events organised for security sector stakeholders, in particular lecture-debates on security challenges in Mali, Africa and the rest of the world, as well as on institutional responses and the issue of security sector reform. The PGPSP also focused on a number of training activities including training 170 security agents in public accounting in order to improve financial management of the security sector. 50 agents were also trained on airport safety. The programme also included a component focusing on involving communities, whereby 15 intercommunity or intercommunal meetings were organised, as well as a local governance capacity building support project for the Kidal region, which was facing specific difficulties in the area of security and grassroots development.

Beyond these results, the programme kick started the process of civil society involvement in security sector governance, which continued independently of the upheavals in the country. Communities in particular became more aware of the need for concentrated efforts to build peace and security as the prerequisites of local development. The resources allocated to the programme also helped to mitigate the usual atmosphere of suspicion between civilians and the military, appease some social tensions and reduce the level of violence in the country. However, all of this was not enough to meet the immense security needs and turned out to be ineffective against emergent threats such as organised crime.

All of the militant forces of the nation were represented at the General Assembly in November 2005. They helped to start the security sector reform process, but not all of them demonstrated the same level of determination. Civil society organisations and grassroots communities were the most enthusiastic. For some of these non-state actors, it was the first time that their status and usefulness were being given full recognition and they were convinced that reforms would respond to some of their concerns. They therefore engaged fully in the debate.

One year after the holding of the General Assembly, it was clear that the most positive reaction to this initiative had come from civil society. In fact, several civil society organisations working on peace, security and human rights came together to form the National Coalition of Civil Society for Peace and the Fight against the Proliferation of Small Arms (*Coalition National de la Société Civile pour la Paix et la Lutte contre la Prolifération des Armes Légères* – CONASCIPAL). They spontaneously decided to support government efforts to promote democratic security sector governance. In January 2007, CONASCIPAL organised the first national civil society forum on democratic security sector governance in Mali. The report of this forum was published (Moulaye 2008). From that date, people throughout the country began to demonstrate a real acceptance of the ideals of the reform and various information, awareness-raising and training activities were organised, as well as intercommunity and intercommunal meetings.

During the General Assembly on Peace and Security in Mali, the defence and security forces remained in the background, although they did make their voices heard. They however frequently referred to their duty to maintain a certain reserve and the fact that they were unused to speaking out in public. In reality, many members of the armed forces were not optimistic about the success of the reform process, which may be quite normal because learning to live in a democracy also implies a culture of questioning things. However, such questions must lead to analysis, followed by bold commitment. A few officers nevertheless realised what was at stake, right from the start. They understood the need for reform and the positive effects that it would have for the country in the future. They got fully involved in the process, but there were only a handful, none of whom held decision-making positions. Although the military hierarchy constantly spoke out in support of the initiative, with the benefit of hindsight, it appears that this support was only superficial. Some other individual stakeholders were also very active, generally researchers who made decisive contributions to the analysis of the security situation, as well as to the understanding of certain concepts and approaches.

The ministry received support from UNDP in organising the General Assembly because the Malian government had made certain statements that appeared to show that human security would be the pivotal concept orientating the overhaul of the security sector. Since the UNDP was promoting this concept at the time, they were initially the only partner involved in the reform process. Subsequently, Norway, Luxemburg and Switzerland also provided strong support to the initiative. The support from UNDP to the reform process was initially cautious and consisted mainly of organising consultations in the hinterland, in addition to the General Assembly on Peace and Security in Mali. Later on, the UNDP granted a budget extension for the design and implementation of the PGPSP.[4]

Conclusion: Lasting change and prospects for consolidating reform

A few weeks after the General Assembly, the ministry of security drafted a five-year action plan (2008 – 2012) aimed at implementing all the 'hard' and 'soft' aspects of security sector reform, with a budget of FCFA 88.4 billion. The action plan was to be submitted to government for approval, in the form of a security planning act. The expected sources of funding were the government budget and external contributions to be gathered through a sector roundtable meeting. The project was however not approved by government, under the pretext that a military planning act had first to be adopted. This clearly demonstrates the absence of the required political will at the highest level of state and highlights the competing parochial interests between defence and security. In reality, government had not assigned any substantial resources to security sector reform and was rather counting on the support from the sector roundtable meeting of UNDP and other external donors, which is a reflection of the degree of political will or lack thereof.

At various times in the reform process this lack of political will was made manifest. For example, it took a very long time for the national, internal security and civil defence policy framework document to be finalised. It was initiated in January 2006, but was not adopted by the council of ministers until October 2010. Such a length of time either shows a lack of strong determination or internal tensions regarding its content. Similarly, the shared governance of security and peace in Mali programme was designed in 2006, but was not implemented until 2008. There again, the two-year delay appears to indicate a lack of strong political will.

Since the president of the republic and commander in chief of the armed forces was also a former senior officer, one wonders whether he was really in favour of security sector reform. Why did he want to tie the military planning Act to the security planning Act? Was he afraid of the differences that the reform could create between the armed and security forces? Was he aware of the reluctance of certain military officers with regard to any form of reform in the defence sector? Did he realise that by delaying the planning act he was undermining the whole process of security sector reform? These are some questions that legitimately come to mind after the fact.

In practice, the reform efforts were mainly limited to implementation of the activities under the PGPSP. Poor government enthusiasm for the reform led UNDP to withdraw from the programme as soon as its financial contribution was exhausted. Meanwhile, certain actors such as civil society organisations, local authorities and the communities, continued to call for the technical and financial support of this UN agency, which shows that they were interested in pursuing the reform process.

In reviewing the events, it appears that internally, there should have been more in-depth communication from the start, as many stakeholders within the security forces and even more outside (civil society, political circles, private sector, local authorities and communities) had no idea of what was involved in reforming the sector. A good part of the security hierarchy was not convinced of the usefulness of the exercise or feared its effects on their personal privileges.

Externally, funds had to be mobilised to carry out reform activities, but most external partners felt that security was an area of national sovereignty where they could only intervene on the basis of an express request from the

Malian government. Furthermore, the security services themselves had little experience of development programmes funded directly through international cooperation. The security forces were thus not used to the methods for mobilising external resources and tended to keep to themselves because of their duty to maintain a certain reserve. The solution found was to promote democratic security sector governance so that security would be considered by partners as an area that was open to official development aid, in the same way as health or education.

Obviously, things could have gone differently if there had been greater political will at the highest level of state and stronger commitment on the part of all the institutions of the republic. It would have helped if senior security officials had not been so reluctant and if right from the start, the defence and security forces had understood that security sector reform was a broad-based undertaking. They should all have worked together to ensure its success. Ideally, Mali should have had a single, overarching reform programme based on a 'single vision, a comprehensive strategy, synergy of action and appropriate communication'. Instead, several programmes working in the fields of peace and security coexisted without any organisational link and failed to collaborate in their activities. Merging them all would have gone against certain personal interests and ambitions.

In the end, the only component that was implemented relatively satisfactorily was the awareness-raising on security challenges and the need for security sector reform that involved a wide range of stakeholders. Only civil society organisations, local authorities and grassroots communities demonstrated genuine interest in the reform process. There are therefore whole areas of the reform process that still need to be designed and implemented, in particular those related to legislation and regulations that would induce a true transformation. The concept of shared governance of security has made some headway. It needs to be broadened in order to open the way for effective security that will underpin sustainable development.

In the light of the unfortunate events of 2012, attitudes have evolved considerably in Mali. The humiliation of the defence and security forces and the psychological shock to the Malian people were such that today no one is against security sector reform. What is required now is to find the most appropriate, intelligent, reliable, effective and efficient way to go about it.

On 30 December 2013, the ministry of security relaunched the reform process with the establishment of a 'multidisciplinary analysis group on security sector reform'. The ministry of defence, which had been rather reluctant in the past, also set up a defence review commission. It would be better if both ministries could work together to transform the security sector and thus design a shared vision, a national domestic security policy and a national defence strategy that would lead to a more peaceful environment, a factor that is more conducive to productive investment and sustainable development. Such an undertaking should be lodged within the office of the president in order to facilitate decisions, coordination and synergy in action. This would make up for the past lack of leadership and political backing and ensure greater buy-in from institutional actors, something that had been missing in the initial phase of the reform process.

Notes

1 The Constitution of the Republic of Mali was passed on 25 February 1992.
2 See, for example, Title III, Art. 44 of the 1992 Constitution.
3 Meeting between the president of the republic and the press (8 June 2005) on the occasion of the 3rd anniversary of his accession to power.
4 For a report on this programme, see Moulaye and Niakaté (2011).

CHAPTER 6

Democratic Security Sector Governance and Military Reform in Nigeria

E. Remi Aiyede
Senior Lecturer, Department of Political Science,
University of Ibadan, Nigeria

Introduction

Nigeria began to reform its security sector as part of the transition from military to civilian rule at the start of the new millennium. The reforms began with an effort to convince the armed forces to return to their barracks and keep to their constitutional role as guardians of the state. Elections were conducted and a civilian administration took control of the government and military in a short transition programme organised by General Abdulsalami Abubakar's regime. The Obasanjo Government (1999 – 2007) implemented a series of reforms to strengthen political institutions after years of tyranny and economic recession. The National Economic Empowerment and Development Strategy focused on four main areas: improving the macroeconomic environment, pursuing structural reforms, strengthening the management of public expenditure, and implementing legal and statutory reforms. The Vision 20:2020 document became the blue print for the drive to make Nigeria the 20th largest and most competitive economy in the world (NNPC 2009).

Although there were no explicit references to the reform of the security sector in these documents, the Obasanjo Government sought international assistance to support its military reform process. External agencies involved in the reform of the military included a private corporation, Military Professional Resources Incorporated (known commercially as MPRI), the American government's International Military Education and Training programme

How to cite this book chapter:
Aiyede, E R. 2015. Democratic Security Sector Governance and Military Reform in Nigeria. In: Bryden, A and Chappuis, F (eds.) *Learning from West African Experiences in Security Sector Governance*, Pp. 97–116. London: Ubiquity Press. DOI: http://dx.doi.org/10.5334/bau.f. License: CC-BY 4.0.

and the British Defence Advisory Team. As Nigeria continues to face severe security situations, reforming the security sector has remained on the political agenda through successive governments, not least because the legacy of the country's extended military rule post-independence has inflicted great damage on the psyche of both civilians and the military itself (Siollun 2013).

Key reform issues include the prevention of coups, the demilitarisation of society, the subordination of the military to civilian control, the use of the military for policing functions, the need to decentralise the police, the need to build the capacity of the military to combat insurgency, and prison and criminal justice system reform. These elements of security sector reform have become a major on-going feature of public discourse in the media. The recent engagement of the military with the fight against terrorism, especially the Boko Haram insurgency, has brought these issues to the fore across Nigerian society, not least because the controversies that have surrounded the faltering and protracted engagement of the military with Boko Haram has raised issues about the military's readiness and capability.

In 2014 Governor Kashim Shettima claimed that Nigeria's soldiers were poorly armed and ill motivated, making the debates all the more urgent (Onuoh 2014). He also spoke of cases of desertion, soldiers' wives publically demonstrating against their husbands' deployment without proper equipment, recurring cases of corruption within the military and reports of soldiers shooting commanding officers for orders leading to fatalities. In a context where a military transformation programme is supposed to be in place and there are increasing demands on the military to aid civil authority (accompanied by a concurrent increase in the budget for the defence sector), the call for engagement on the issue became more urgent across the country and even around the world (BBC 2015).

What has happened to the effort to reform the military in Nigeria? What trajectory has it taken? Has the reform of the military stalled or was it wrong headed from the start? Which actors have been involved and what roles have they played? How can the reform be revived and redirected to address contemporary security challenges? This study explores the answers to these questions and demonstrates that Nigeria lost several opportunities to transform its military into an effective and efficient force capable of deterring external aggression and maintaining internal security within the framework of democratic civilian control.

Critically, General Obasanjo's move to alter the constitution to provide for a third term for the president and state governors slowed down his government's commitment to military reform. This provided space for the military to take control of the defence sector reform from civilian authorities; thus, the reform became coloured by the preferences of the emergent military leaders, their failures to address structural defects in the management of the military due to self-interest and frequent changes in the military's leadership: this, in turn, derailed the implementation of a systematic transformation of the military. Other structural factors that have affected the reform process include the ill-health and eventual death of President Yar' Adua, who succeeded President Olusegun Obasanjo, and the emergence of Boko Haram as a major security threat. Under President Goodluck Jonathan, the military's counter-terrorism engagement with Boko Haram not only affected the trajectory of military reform, but also revealed the limitations and failures of reform efforts to date and underlined inter-agency rivalry, especially with the police. Reform efforts had failed so drastically that the 2014 Minister of Defence, Senator Musiliu Obanikoro, talked about a fresh move to reform the military (Eghaghe 2014: 1).

This paper argues that Nigeria lost several opportunities to transform its military into an effective and efficient force capable of deterring external aggression and maintaining internal security within the framework of democratic civilian control. It argues further that the trajectory of democratic politics as shown in the move by General Obasanjo to alter the constitution in order to provide for a third term for presidents and state governors slowed down the commitment to military reform by the Obasanjo government. This provided the space for the military to take control of the reform of the defence sector from the civilian authorities, derailing the implementation of a systematic transformation of the military. The argument begins with an overview of the development of the military since the colonial era; it also explores the series of post-independence efforts to develop the military into a reliable institution for the defence and security of the country. It outlines the broad context of military reform under Obasanjo from 1999 to 2007, when the country returned to civilian rule after over two decades of military dictatorships. The paper then examines in detail the counter-programme of transformation instituted by the military, its level of implementation and the key factors behind the current state of military reform. Finally, the paper proposes a way forwards based on the requirements for systematic transformation that have remained unaddressed.

Context for Security Sector Governance in Nigeria

Nigeria became independent of British colonial rule on 1 October 1960. Thereafter Nigeria operated a parliamentary system of government as a federation of three regions (Northern, Eastern and Western). In 1963, it became a republic. The same year, a fourth region was created: the Midwestern region.

The Federal Defence Council was established in 1957: it comprised representatives of federal and regional governments and the governor general chaired it. The Federal Defence Council made the first set of formal defence-policy decisions and determined the structure of the Nigerian army, including its recruitment criteria and the nature of the parliamentary procedures to determine and approve its annual budget. The Federal Defence Council became fully responsible for the Nigerian army in the immediate post-independence era, completing the Nigerianisation of the army in 1960, even though a large proportion of British officers continued to serve in the highest ranks. At this time, civil society and the media were heavily involved in security policy, as seen in the demonstrations that greeted the proposed Anglo-Nigerian Defence Pact and Nigeria's continued participation in the international peace-support operation in the Congo after the execution of Patrice Lumumba. Meanwhile, parliament played a role in the introduction of a quota in officer recruitment policy to reflect the diversity of the country (Alaga & Akum 2013).

However, progress in defence reform was halted when the First Republic came to an abrupt end on 15 January 1966 in a coup d'état. This coup was the ultimate result of the governance crisis that characterised the First Republic's brief rule: key issues included the muted confrontation between the president and the prime minister arising from the 1964 federal elections and the rigged Western regional elections of 1965 that resulted in the breakdown of law and order in the region. The coup was largely viewed as a sectarian Igbo coup because almost all of the First Republic politicians and military leaders killed, with the exception of one Igbo officer, were from the north or south west.

The country descended into civil war following a counter-coup on 29 July 1966, which was viewed as a revenge coup because apart from General Ironsi and Fajuyi, only one of the ten officers killed was not of Igbo extraction (Dudley 1973; Post & Vickers 1973). With the counter-coup, the cohesion of the army under a single command was lost; the army command was disrupted when Lieutenant Colonel Ojukwu objected to the ascension of Lieutenant Colonel Gowon as head of state because he was not the next in command after General Ironsi. Although efforts were made to reconcile the parties, killings of Igbos in the Northern Region, and the subsequent declaration of the sovereign state of Biafra, heralded the beginning of a civil war that would last from 1967 until 1970. Thus on 27 May 1967 the Eastern Regional Consultative Assembly mandated Ojukwu to declare the independent Republic of Biafra: this was followed by the declaration of a state of emergency and the creation of a 12-state federal structure for governing Nigeria by General Yakubu Gowon (Osaghae 1998; Panter-Brick 1970). As a result of these political dynamics, the Igbo were marginalised in the military in the post-war period.

Another consequence of the civil war for the military was the increase in the size of the army: from about 7,000 personnel organised into only two infantry Brigades in 1967, the Army grew to over 250,000 officers and men in 1970 (Bali 1989: 164). Thus in the post war era, the effort to reduce the army into a more nimble force became a central element of the military reform and the transition from military rule to democracy. Although General Gowon promised a demobilisation of the army, little effort was invested in the exercise. Gowon was overthrown in 1975 for failing to keep faith with the transition programme intended to terminate military rule in 1976. General Murtala Mohammed, who became head of state after Gowon, planned to transition to a civil programme in 1979. He set up a constitution-drafting committee and restructured the country into 19 states. However, he was assassinated in an unsuccessful coup on 13 February 1976.

Following his assassination, General Murtala Mohammed was succeeded by General Olusegun Obasanjo, who carried on with the programme of transition to civil rule that ended in 1979 when the country returned to democracy with President Shehu Shagari as elected head of state. It is significant that only about 50,000 members of the armed forces had been demobilized at this point (Osaghae 1998: 82). Thus, in the post-civil war era the effort to reduce the armed forces became a central element of debates on military reform and the transition from military rule to democracy.

The 1979 Constitution outlawed coups and banned the military from partisan politics. It mandated the chief of defence staff to report directly to the president rather than the minister of defence, as was the case during the First Republic. Under the new system, legislative oversight was strengthened with committees for police, defence and intelligence affairs in both the House of Representatives and the Senate. However, having the chief of defence staff report directly to the president undermined the oversight functions of the legislature. Moreover, the military disregarded the new administrative tendering processes for contracts and also the legislative approval required for its expenditure. This was partly because the military commanders felt powerful enough to defy presidential orders. For example, Major General Dumuje ignored the orders of President Shagari over military action in aid of civil authorities during a religious insurgency in Kano. The military also tried to influence political appointments, including through sending "a list of their preferred candidates" for ministerial positions to the president in 1983, shortly before the coup of 31 December 1983 (Alaga & Akum 2013: 221 – 222).

Despite these difficulties, the civil war and the immediate post-civil war years coincided with a double oil boom that enabled Nigeria to expand its Import Substitution Industries, invest in infrastructure, and finance massive imports of intermediate and capital goods, as well as raw materials and other consumer goods. Between 1975 and 1979 the economy grew by 8.3 per cent per year and Nigeria recorded a trade surplus of N2 billion in 1980, in spite of a sudden fall in oil prices in 1978 (Olukoshi 1993). The military expanded and acquired more modern equipment and artillery and also built barracks across the country. However, the development of urban roads and highways, and the introduction of social programmes, was accompanied by corruption involving military decision-makers and their bureaucratic aides. Although the Murtala Mohammed and Olusegun Obasanjo governments made efforts between 1975 and 1979 to establish budgetary mechanisms, many statutory institutions such as the military only used these processes when it suited them. Thus, as Omitoogun and Oduntan note, budgetary processes and expenditure were generally driven by the personality of the current head of state rather than by institutional mechanisms (Omitoogun & Oduntan 2006: 158).

It was in this context that Nigeria's trade surplus turned into a deficit of ₦300 million by 1983, with external debt at ₦21.38 billion: a bewildering 989.2 per cent increase since 1980 (Adesina 1995: 18). Internal public debt rose from ₦4.6 billion in 1979 to ₦22.2 billion in 1983, while national output fell by 8 per cent in 1982 and a further 5.5 per cent in 1984. Inflation, at 23 per cent in 1979, rose to 40 per cent in 1983. To address the resultant sudden and severe payment crisis, Nigeria had to run large budget deficits and embarked on massive borrowing from private and official international sources to deliver on its financial programmes. In the process the country amassed huge debts. In an attempt to stem the crisis, the Shagari administration promulgated an Economic Stabilization (Temporary Provisions) Act in April 1982, in addition to attempting various austerity measures to reduce government expenditure and curtail imports. These measures were reinforced by the Buhari government, which had overthrown the Shagari government in a military coup d'état in 1983.

When Ibrahim Babangida took over from Buhari in 1985, he instituted an economic-reform programme alongside a transition back to democracy programme. However, under his rule power was concentrated in the presidency. To garner support for his government, he used promotions, redeployment, the appointment of military officers to political positions, and preferential treatment regarding the award of contracts for retired officers, in addition to buying cars for officers in certain ranks. At other times, he tried to incite members of the armed forces against civil society during public protests against his government, describing these protests as attempts to "destroy the credibility of the military" or "humiliate the military out of office", declaring that "it is only the military that can lead the armed forces back to the barracks" (Adekanye 1997: 45, 47).

Despite these problems, under Babangida's administration the lot of the Igbos in the military gradually began to improve for the first time since the civil war when Ebitu Ukiwe, an Igbo, was briefly appointed chief of general staff. However, the question of regional balance has remained a major challenge in Nigeria, in spite of subjecting the enlistment of candidates into the military and other statutory services to the federal character principle – a provision in the 1979 Constitution requiring public appointments fairly reflect the linguistic, ethnic, religious, and geographic diversity of the country.

Babangida's annulment of the 12 June 1993 presidential elections, which was supposed to conclude the protracted transition programme to civilian rule, catalysed a major political crisis, provoking civil discontent, deepening divisions among the various ethno-linguistic groups and generating calls for the reconstruction or reform of the military. As a result, Babangida stepped aside, leaving an interim government to conclude the transition to civil rule. However, the interim government was declared illegal by a court of law: General Sani Abacha removed it from power later in 1993 in a bloodless coup. Abacha demolished all existing democratic structures and began a fresh attempt to transition to democratic rule with a programme designed to transform him into a civilian president. However, he died suddenly on 8 June 1998. His death provided a window for democratic and military reform. Abacha's successor, General Abdulsalami Abubakar, began a campaign to encourage the military to return to their barracks by 29 May 1999.

General Abdulsalami Abubakar's government commenced their attempt to reform the military with a 10-month transition-to-civil-rule programme. The major plank of this reform was Abubakar's plan to persuade the military to return to barracks. He also took steps to improve their welfare, increasing salaries for both enlisted ranks and officers by the end of 1998. He set up a committee that organised a series of workshops for the armed forces and the police on welfare, re-professionalisation and the need to return to democracy. He also eased the political atmosphere by releasing political opposition figures and civil society activists who had challenged the regime of General Sani Abacha. This was followed by a repeal of several decrees that legalised arbitrary arrest without trials and other restrictions on civil liberties. He also promised to look into cases of human rights abuses. He then began the process of producing a constitution for democratic rule.

The new constitution put the command chain and operational use of the military under the control of the president as civilian commander-in-chief, but with mandated oversight by the National Assembly. To a large extent this separated the military from direct involvement in the politics of the transition process, although the military continued to exert indirect influence over the choice of presidential candidates. However, beyond these basic measures no specific programme of long-term reform was introduced. Comprehensive reform of the security sector was therefore left to the incoming civilian administration.

Democratisation of the Security Sector: 1999 – 2007

In May 1999, Olusegun Obasanjo became president of a civilian administration known as the Fourth Republic. Five key issues ensured that military reform topped the new administration's agenda. The first factor concerned the need to address the Southern Region's claims about the dominance of the Northern Region, including the ethnic dominance of the Northern Region in the military. The second concerned the fear that military rule for 15 of the first 25 years of independence had led to the development of a culture of using coups to solve disagreements and that this would jeopardise future democratic rule. The third factor revolved around the need to reorganise the military to make it more compact and efficient, including by addressing corruption within the military to restore prudent and proper use of resources to increase the battle-readiness of its forces. The fourth issue concerned the need to develop an appropriate civil-military relationship that subordinated the military to civilian leadership and demilitarised Nigerian society by addressing its culture of violence, aversion to debate and the use of extreme measures in internal conflicts (Adejumobi 1999). The fifth factor comprised a number of related issues but centred on the need to depoliticise the military by removing soldiers from political office so that military service no longer conferred political power or extensive financial privilege; this was especially important in light of the tradition of cadets enlisting as a shortcut to political office. However, there was concern that soldiers exposed to the privileges, rapid promotions and stupendous wealth that political office could confer in Nigeria might no longer be content with the drab and unprestigious life of the barracks (Adekson 1979); thus, reform was needed to re-orientate the military to its primary function and encourage its officers to abstain from political power. A related issue was the need to re-professionalise the military in order to address the adverse effects of its politicisation on *esprit de corps*, respect for the military hierarchy and general discipline. The economic and political failures, and reoccurring coups and counter-coups under military rule have undermined claims by the military that they were on a corrective course; moreover, the rampant corruption that characterised military rule soiled the image of the military as a custodian of the unity and integrity of the Nigerian state.

Shortly after he assumed office in 1999, President Obasanjo retired over 100 generals and other officers in the middle ranks who had held political office. This strategic move purged the military of politicians in uniform and created space for a comprehensive reform process to commence. Thus the reform effort under the Obasanjo regime was informed by the desire to pre-empt any attempt by the Northern Region to use the military to re-establish political hegemony. Given the disproportionate number of officers from the Northern Region who had held political appointments under military rule, the move to re-professionalise the military through retiring these officers helped to improve the balance in regional representation across the higher military ranks. Following a review of the appointment of chiefs of defence staff and other services, new high-ranking officers from more diverse backgrounds were appointed to take the place of those who had been retired. The 2010 appointment of an Igbo, General Azubuike Ihejirika, as chief of army staff was celebrated in the media because he was the first Igbo officer to have occupied the post since the end of the civil war in 1970.

In his speech at the National War College (now the National Defence College) in 1999, he outlined the key elements of the proposed reform programme:

1. An elected civilian president as commander-in-chief of the armed forces, and the supremacy of elected state officials over appointed officers at all levels;
2. Civilian leadership of the ministry of defence and other strategic establishments;

3. Decisions regarding the goals and conduct of military operations must serve the political and strategic goals established by the civil authority;
4. Application of civil principles to all military investigations and trials;
5. Right of Civil (Supreme Court) authority to review any actions or decision taken by the military judicial officers;
6. Other instruments for achieving supremacy of civil authority include constitutional clauses and legislative oversight functions (Manea & Rüland 2013: 65).

Although Obasanjo later elaborated a series of reform programmes across a broad spectrum of governance, these often failed to include military reform. Indeed, both the National Economic Empowerment and Development Strategy and the Vision 20:2020 documents (NNPC 2004; 2009) articulated under Obasanjo administration ignored security sector governance and reform. Reviewing the content of, and effort behind, the reform of the security sector during this period, Manea and Rüland (2013: 64) observed both the absence of a comprehensive concept of reform and insufficient political will to ensure its implementation. The measures implemented by the Obasanjo administration to reform the military included the following:

1. The exercise of the power to appoint and remove service chiefs;
2. Making the Ministry of Defence a primarily civil body;
3. The institution of a Human Rights Violations Investigation Commission known as the "Oputa Panel" and a Human Rights Commission;
4. Reform of the military justice system by making all military court decisions subject to review of the Supreme Court;
5. Reform of civil-military relations (with MPRI);
6. Legislative oversight of the defence budget by requiring the National Assembly to scrutinise and pass the defence budget with oversight powers throughout the process;
7. The formulation of a National Defence Policy in 2006 (Nigeria 2006).

However, towards the end of the Obasanjo regime the pursuit of reform lost impetus due to the constant troubles between the president and the legislature, including controversy over President Obasanjo's effort to change the constitution to provide for a third presidential term. The president's pre-occupation with these political challenges distracted him from the reform effort, weakening the prospects for the National Assembly to enact both new legislation concerning the military and constitutional amendments to support military reform.

As Aiyede (2013: 177 – 179) and Manea and Rüland (2013: 64 – 69) note, the prospect of military reform was further undermined by the absence of widespread media and social support for democratic control of the military. Several opportunities for the reform of the military were wasted, including the possibilities offered by the recommendations arising from the Political Reform Conference of 2005. The Conference recommended a constitutional provision against coups amending section 1(2) of the 1999 Constitution, in addition to establishing the National Security Intelligence Council and the National Security Service Commission. Other recommendations included the political re-orientation of the military; retraining of the armed forces to encourage greater professionalism; the reorganisation of the defence industries corporation of Nigeria; investment in research and development focused on military applications, supported by committing at least five per cent of the defence budget to this work; the establishment of a Faculty of Technology at the National Defence Academy to support graduate/postgraduate studies in maritime/aeronautical engineering, armament technology and computer science; the establishment of a joint warfare school; improving welfare services for military personnel; and making the most of the military's engagement in peace-keeping operations. However, of the 116 constitutional amendments proposed, none was devoted to military issues. In the end this mattered little as the National Assembly's opposition to the proposal for a third presidential term resulted in them denying all the constitutional amendment proposals at that time.

The reform process also suffered from the resistance of the military to the use of foreign assistance, especially under Victor Malu, Chief of Staff from 1999 until 2001. However, President Obasanjo invited MPRI and the British Defence Advisory Team to support the reform programme. In response, some senior military officers argued that MPRI's knowledge about civilian-military relations, which was the focus of their intervention in Nigeria, was already taught at Nigerian military institutions. They further argued that the support offered regarding the re-professionaliation of the military was not based on any needs assessment or determined in consultation with the leaders of the military and, indeed, that it ran contrary to their expectations regarding external assistance.[1]

Under the Yar' Adua government that succeeded President Obasanjo in 2005, efforts by the civilian executive to pursue military reform were further stymied, despite security being one of the seven agenda items of the administration. This was largely because of the ill health and eventual death of the president, who was incapacitated for the better part of his 2007 – 2010 time in office. The presidency was run by his kitchen cabinet, a cabal that included his wife. When the president went to Saudi Arabia, he did not formally hand over power to the vice president, Goodluck Jonathan, for the duration of his trip, as stipulated by the constitution: instead, the Kitchen Cabinet kept the state of his health a secret. There was palpable fear that the military would take over in March 2010 when the president surreptitiously arrived back at Abuja Airport at night without informing the vice president, who eventually succeeded him later that year (Adeniyi 2011: 237).

President Goodluck Jonathan went on to win the 2011 elections. However, the transformation agenda of his government did not include any significant move on the issue of military reform, despite the fact that the threat from Boko Haram intensified under his rule. There was high turnover in the leadership of the military, demonstrating civilian control over the appointment and retirement of the military leadership, but there was also a remarkable increase in the budget for defence. These decisions have been subject to parliamentary oversight. In the case of the appointment of service chiefs of the tri-services of the military, the President began to seek the confirmation of the Senate in 2013 after Justice Adamu Bello ruled on 1 July 2013 that the appointment of service chiefs was subject to confirmation by the Senate as noted earlier. Before them the president had removed and appointed the service chiefs without regard to parliament. The current practice is for the president to name the service chiefs and then refer the list to the Senate for confirmation. So far, none of those sent to parliament has been rejected.

The Sustainability of Change

In spite of the apparent slow-down in military reform, and the military's opposition to external involvement in this process, the military leadership has developed and implemented its own reform programme. However, the reform measures have depended on the priorities of each succeeding chief of army staff. For instance, in May 2004 the current chief, General Martin Luther Agwai, constituted a Change Management Committee with the responsibility to determine the structure, equipment and training needs of the Nigerian army to meet the threats and challenges for the next decade and beyond. *A Framework for the Transformation of the Nigerian Army in the Next Decade (Volumes 1& 2)* was subsequently developed. The Office of Nigerian Army Transformation was established in 2006 to monitor and evaluate the transformation process, and to conceptualise, develop and ensure implementation of short, medium and long-term plans regarding the army's future.

In 2006, when Agwai became Chief of Defence Staff (CDS) he tried to extend these ideas to the other armed services. He set up the Armed Forces Transformation Committee within the Ministry of Defence to provide a guide for transforming the military as a whole. In 2008 the Committee produced a national military strategy document, two volumes of joint doctrine for the armed forces and a proposed structure for the higher management of defence (MOD 2008a; 2008b). These documents show that the Committee envisaged that military strategy would be revised every five years and the joint doctrine reviewed every two years. However, no revisions have occurred to date, nor was the planned management structure achieved.

The Committee also published documents about its plans:

1. to restructure the Ministry of Defence for enhanced management of national defence;
2. to develop a National Military Strategy and Joint Operational Doctrine;
3. to provide ways and means of achieving highly professional and motivated human resources;
4. to establish joint acquisition and maintenance processes for both minor and major military hardware;
5. to set up a military Research and Development and Defence Industrial Base; and
6. to establish a credible military structure with the capabilities required to meet current and future challenges.

Of all these documents, the 2006 National Defence Policy was significant, not because it was produced with little or no input from parliament and civil society (Aiyede 2013: 176). Critically, the Policy adopted the joint-operation concept to enhance the operational efficiency of the military; however, the lack of centralised control made the practical application of the concept difficult. The structural issues that underlie this lack of centralisation are the result of ambiguities in the provisions of the Nigerian Armed Forces Act 2004, which assigned operational directives to the CDS, and section 217 of the 1999 Constitution, which was silent on the powers of the CDS as it related to the service chiefs, who take directives directly from the minister of defence or the commander-in-chief. This system effectively reduces the role of the CDS to that of an adviser to the commander-in-chief, who has operational command of the armed forces despite the CDS being theoretically responsible for the coordination and integration of the activities of the three armed services. A further complication is that the CDS is usually appointed from amongst the service chiefs and continues to serve in both capacities. This system recognises that effective and combat-efficient armed forces require that the CDS exercise operational control with powers to supervise, coordinate and determine the activities of the services. However, such powers would limit the president's influence over the leadership of the military: a system placing the president or the minister of defence in a position of power over the CDS and the three service chiefs provides a more robust opportunity for cultivating loyalty, dispensing rewards and exercising significant influence over the armed forces. Thus, these contradictions arose from the fact that the Nigerian Armed Forces Act 2004 was designed to preserve presidential control of the military's chain of command. The fact that service chiefs compete for audiences with the president and minister of defence has been perceived as a bulwark against coups or the possibility of the military speaking with a single strong voice to place demands on the political leadership. However, dispersing powers away from the CDS, especially regarding budgetary and operational issues, and instead giving them to individual services enables service chiefs to enjoy significant autonomy and budgetary powers: powers they are unwilling to relinquish. The practical result, as Menea and Ruland argue, is that "Purchase of military hardware are largely controlled by the service chiefs and to a lesser extent by the Chief of Defence Staff and the Defence Ministry" (Menea & Rüland 2013: 73). There is also a tradition of the president financing military equipment through executive orders that allow access to extra-budgetary resources. Thus, both the presidency and the service chiefs are interested in maintaining the status quo.

The fact that the procurement process is often fraught with corruption made possible by these contradictions has seen them entrenched rather than addressed.[2] However, as Oyegbile (2014) notes, a corruption-ridden procurement process accounts, at least in part, for the poor equipment holdings of the military and their weak morale. He quotes a retired senior military officer in demonstrating how unpopular this situation is amongst all but the highest-ranking officers:

> "The war against terrorism or even a conventional war in this country cannot be won with the way things are going presently. Our system of military funding is fraught with corruption and open to clear abuse. Military budgets should never be given to military commanders or Chief of Army Staff as it is obtained presently." (Oyegbile 2014)

The joint doctrine contained in the 2006 National Defence Policy sought to emphasise the primacy of political leaders, elected officials and their appointed subordinates in establishing broad national policies and procedures in the defence sector, while ensuring that military officials rendered advice and recommendations on professional matters, including military capabilities, limitations and projections. The same policy also required military leaders to be responsive to public opinion by providing timely and accurate information to citizens in the course of their assigned missions and especially while employing force (MOD 2008b). While the military is best placed to offer timely, complete and accurate information on military matters so that the National Assembly can fulfil its constitutional responsibilities for military affairs effectively, civilian leaders chose not to fully implement the joint doctrine as envisaged. For instance, since 1996 civilian presidents have appointed and retired the top leadership of the armed services in line with the provisions of the constitution, but they have exercised these powers without due regard to the legislature, as required by law. Thus, Festus Keyamo, a human rights activist and lawyer, obtained a Federal High Court judgment in 2013 that challenged the practice of appointing service chiefs without the approval of the National Assembly. The court declared previous appointments null and void. This caused President Jonathan to formally seek confirmation from the Senate regarding appointments he made on 16

January 2014: the Senate confirmed the new service chiefs on 29 January 2014 (Ojiabor 2014: 6). As a result of this case, the vigilance of civil society was able to use the court system to challenge abuse of processes by the executive, yet this remained an isolated victory.

Ultimately, in the post-Obasanjo period, the efforts invested in promoting the transformation programme within the military establishment foundered because of a lack of commitment. As a result, limited reform measures have been designed and implemented by the leaders of each service to serve their own interests. For instance, under Air Chief Marshal Paul Dike as CDS, several programmes, seminars, tours, conferences and workshops were held to explain and move the change process forward. The Transformation Office at the Defence Headquarters drew on the resources of independent think-tanks and private organisations to educate the military in an effort to improve its relations with the media and civil society (Onwudiwe & Osaghae 2010). The three services also developed effective public relations directorates, while the army created a Wide Area Network Infrastructure to facilitate access to information to improve productivity, proficiency and operational effectiveness (Bojie 2011: 3).

Within the Nigerian army, sensitisation lectures, seminars, workshops and a revision of books and manuals were carried out to enhance the knowledge of personnel about the transformation process. These seminars and workshops were organised in Abuja and all divisional headquarters; they concerned issues such as civil-military cooperation, the Continental General Staff System and also attitude change. A new uniform was introduced to present a more friendly public face to society. Similarly, in 2011 General Onyeabor Azubuike Ihejirika, then chief of army staff, established the Department of Civil-Military Affairs to improve the image of the military, win public support and deal with matters relating to human rights, rule of law, and negotiations, liaison, and conflict management with the civilian populace (Alaga & Akum 2013: 229).

Just as military reform finally seemed to be underway, Nigeria's security challenges began to deepen. Cases of kidnapping and robbery, as well as the rise in terrorism largely perpetrated by Boko Haram, led to a series of changes in the work of the security agencies. Virtually all security agencies are now involved in efforts to curb these problems. For instance, the military, the police and other security agencies have all established counter-terrorism units. Moreover, the military has been progressively engaged in key policing activities across 28 states of the country, meaning that it is often spread thin. The military's intervention in communal conflict zones, crime control and counter-terrorism have catalysed but also provoked controversies (Falana 2014). Crisis Group identifies three ways the Nigerian government has responded to the security challenges (ICG 2014); namely, budgetary increases, strengthening anti-terrorism legislation and boosting military capacity.

In the past few years, counter-terrorism efforts have been extended to cover the non-governmental security sector, including civil defence, private security companies, citizen-security agency collaborations and the justice system. The Terrorism (Prevention) Act was signed into law in 2011. This was followed by a 2012 amendment that designated the Office of the National Security Adviser as National Coordinator for Anti-Terrorism Efforts: a move intended to prevent in-fighting among security agencies over which should assume the lead in joint operations. The government also sought to improve training, personnel management, equipment (especially for close-quarters combat) and coordination. For example, over 7,000 security personnel from the military, police and Nigerian Security and Civil Defence Corps have been variously trained in urban warfare, counter-terrorism and counter-insurgency, intelligence and amphibious operations, demolition and explosive breaching, and tactical communication. The specialist military training institution, the Counter-Terrorism and Counter-Insurgency Centre in Jaji, Kaduna State, trained graduates from across the armed forces and the police.

However, Leren Blachard of the African Affairs Congressional Research Service observed that successive Nigerian governments have been slow in allowing the security services to participate in US training programmes; describing Nigeria as an "extremely challenging" partner to work with, she noted that Nigerian troops are "slow to adapt with new strategies, new doctrines and new tactics" (Akinloye 2014: 1). Nonetheless, in the wake of the Chibok kidnappings President Jonathan called for external support: China, America, Israel, France and the United Kingdom committed to providing assistance, and the California National guard is currently helping to establish the 143 Infantry Battalion – a force trained in special tactics for the express purpose of engaging Boko Haram in their rural strongholds (Iroegbu &Adinoyi 2014: 1).

In response to persistent conflict in the Niger Delta and the wave of criminal activities (especially kidnappings) in South-East Nigeria, the president re-established the Ahiara Barracks, which had been shut down in 1992 as part of the restructuring of the army. The facilities accommodate the newly created 14 Brigade with its garrison, a battalion and other supporting elements. A 145 Battalion has been proposed for Ikot Umoh Essien, Akwa-Ibom State; a 144 Battalion at Umuna, Rivers State; and an artillery regiment in Ebonyi State (Onuorah 2011: 4).

The government has increased the defence budget from ₦100 billion (US$625 million) in 2010 to ₦927 billion (US$6 billion) in 2011, and to ₦1 trillion ($6.25 billion) in 2012, 2013 and 2014. Although the defence sector took a third of the federal government's budget for 2014, in August 2014 President Jonathan presented a proposal for a loan of $1 billion to the National Assembly to enable him to re-equip the military to fight insurgency and deal with other security challenges. Over 30 armored tanks and two helicopter gunships with in-built night vision technology were recently purchased and deployed to fight insurgency in the northeast, while the air force has taken delivery of six jets (McGregor 2015).

Emergency rule was first declared in the three northeastern states on 13 May 2013 as a result of the intensity of Boko Haram's activities. Three extensions were routinely approved by parliament in its oversight capacity. On 17 November 2014, the National Defence Council decided that emergency rule in Adamawa, Yobe and Borno States be extended a fourth time; however, the House of Representatives turned down the request when it was presented for parliamentary approval. The Senate, which was divided on the matter, did not take any action until the emergency rule expired. The dominant view in parliament was that emergency rule had not made any difference to the counter-insurgency operations and that the president should resort to the provisions under the constitution and section 8 of the Armed Forces Act 2004 to empower himself to deploy the military to troubled parts of the country (Adejuwon 2014). Emergency rule was previously approved because the military had explained to parliament that it was necessary given the unpredictable situation and the threat to peace in the relevant part of the country, it would aid intelligence gathering and the operation against Boko Haram terrorists and provide legal backing for foreign military collaborators to enter Nigerian territory in aid of the counter terrorism operation.

Thus, the counter-terrorism effort has come to define current activities in the security sector, especially since the kidnapping of over 200 girls in Chibok in April 2014 and the subsequent escalation in the activities of Boko Haram. These events show the limitations and reversals that have occurred in the security sector reform programme. The counter terrorism effort has also attracted foreign interest and support, though partially through exposing the weaknesses of the military to the media and the public. Statements by interested foreign governments offering to work with the military have been damning regarding its capacity and preparedness. For instance Alice Friend, the Pentagon's Principal Director for African Affairs, stated that the "Nigerian military has the same challenges with corruption that every other institution in Nigeria does. Much of the funding that goes to the military is skimmed off the top" (Schmitt & Knowlton 2014). Media reports on engagements with the insurgents generally agree that recent efforts at reform have proven at best ineffective and incomplete, while many positive developments have been reversed.

Corruption has been a particular concern of late. For instance, in 2014 Nossiter (2014) of the *New York Times* reported that foreign diplomats believe the Nigerian military has inadvertently hampered the hunt for the abducted girls of Chibok through their ineffectiveness and lack of capacity:

> "the military is so poorly trained and armed, and so riddled with corruption, that not only is it incapable of finding the girls, it is also losing the broader fight against Boko Haram. The group has effective control of much of the northeast of the country, as troops withdraw from vulnerable targets to avoid a fight and stay out of the group's way, even as the militants slaughter civilians." (Nossiter 2014)

The Nigerian media has made similar claims. Meanwhile, in February 2014, Kashim Shettima, Governor of Borno State, declared that Boko Haram fighters were better-armed and better motivated than government troops. In May 2014, soldiers of the main army units tackling Boko Haram, angry about deaths among their ranks following an ambush, opened fire on the car carrying their commanding officer, Major General Ahmadu Mohammed. Thus, controversy came to characterise military-media relations over the military's engagement with Boko Haram; there is a high level of distrust at least partially attributable to the military's poor public-information management.

The persistence and intensity of criticism regarding the military's failures in the war against Boko Haram led military spokesman Major General Chris Olukolade to appeal to the media to stop damping the morale of officers and men at the front (Agbambu 2014: 8). However, poor information management has led to wild speculation in the media about the possible complicity of some of its high-ranking officers in supporting Boko Haram with equipment and funds. For instance, Stephen Davies, the Australian who was appointed by the Nigerian government to help negotiate the release of the kidnapped schoolgirls, named a former chief of army staff as one of the sponsors of Boko Haram. There have also been claims that information provided by army officers has helped insurgents in ambushing military convoys (e.g. in the ambush that led to the May 2014 mutiny against Major General Ahmadu Mohammed) and in attacks on army barracks and outposts in Boko Haram's northeastern strongholds. In June 2014 several reports were published in the local media of senior officers under court martial for providing arms and information to Boko Haram extremists; in response the military confiscated newspapers from vendors to prevent them from circulating in nearby cities.

However, in August 2014 the media exploded with concerns about the strength and capability of the military when Boko Haram took over Gwoza, a small town in southern Borno: the insurgents hoisted a flag and declared a caliphate state. The inability of the military to root the insurgents out of the territory quickly, and the subsequent battle over Bama and Maiduguri, fueled further concern about the military's capabilities. The situation worsened when about 480 Nigerian soldiers made their way into Cameroon after a gruelling encounter with Boko Haram militants. The media reported this incident as desertion, while the military described the movement as a tactical manoeuvre (Onuorah 2014: 4; Akinlotan 2014: 80). Alongside these problems, the military has also come under severe criticism over its human rights record. For instance, Amnesty international have accused the Nigerian military of torture and extra-judicial killings in several recent reports (Amnesty International 2012; 2014).

It is in this context that media editorials have moved from advising the government to review its military strategy to calling for an overhaul. At the 58th Nigerian Navy Week in May 2014, the defence minister, Senator Musiliu

Obanikoro, approached President Jonathan with a proposal for a presidential retreat where stakeholders, the parliament, the private sector and other interested parties could meet to "develop a transformational roadmap for the Nigerian military" (Eghaghe 2014: 1).

Conclusion

President Olusegun Obasanjo's regime was the key actor in post-independence security sector reform, especially with regard to the military. Although Obasanjo's government set out a broad outline for reform, the process was largely centred on the executive without engaging significantly with the legislature and civil society; moreover, his drive to amend the constitution in order to provide for a third presidential term undid much of the good work and momentum that had been achieved, stalling efforts to amend legislation that would have encouraged further progress. After Obasanjo, the subsequent presidents, Yar' Adua and Jonathan, placed little emphasis on reforming the security sector, despite having to deal with severe security challenges. While they continued to exercise presidential powers over the appointment and retirement of the military's leadership, both largely left the armed forces to carry on with the process of reform in their own way. Thus, further reforms have reflected the preferences of the prevailing military leadership for more technical and effectiveness focused enhancements over substance democratic governance.

The reform agenda enjoyed significant momentum under Lieutenant General Martin Luther Agwai, who introduced the military transformation concept to the army during his time as chief of army staff, though he employed the term across all the forces when he became CDS. However, his successor, Lieutenant General Azazi, did not agree with this approach: indeed, as chief national adviser to the president he later stated that:

> "the concept from the beginning has been that we should go beyond secrecy in security and accept public participation because at the end of the day, a security strategy should look at national objectives and how the nation could make progress without any hindrance." (Oloja & Onuorah 2011: 1)

Military reform was revived when Air Chief Paul Dike became CDS, in a reform programme focused on improving civil-military relations through a community relations programme to expand, complement and strengthen existing public relations strategies. Reform has since stalled. Today, there are many unresolved issues, including new issues thrown up by the military's counter-insurgency efforts in the northeast. There are also disagreements among senior military officers not only about the best methods for achieving military reform, but the very content of military reform and transformation. Indeed, some officers take the view that reform efforts have been concluded and what is needed now is routine re-equipment and training to respond to new challenges.[3] The fact that the military has been suspicious, cautious or even hostile to seeking external assistance regarding reform has further limited the degree of change achieved and sustained.

As Aiyede (2013: 176) and Manea and Rüland (2013: 67–69) note, since 1999 parliament has not been able to live up to the expectations generated by its extensive formal powers of law-making, including the creation of oversight powers regarding defence and security issues. This is partly because parliament lacks the required competence, political will and confidence to intervene in security issues. Thus, its role has been limited to defence oversight, including confirmation of new appointments to the position of CDS and approval of several requests by President Jonathan to extend emergency rule in the three north-eastern states where the military is engage in counter-insurgency operations.

The media has started to cover security issues in greater detail, as the failures of the counter-insurgency activities against Boko Haram have demanded increasing public attention. However, there a sustained and detailed media and public debate about the security sector is yet to emerge in Nigeria. Civil society involvement in the military reform process is also relatively weak in Nigeria. Although a small number of organizations have been involved with police reform, there is an absence of specialist civil society expertise to promote democratic control of the military in the media, and civil society. This has translated into the weak contribution of the legislature, media and civil society and leaving the defence establishment to lead discussion. These absences have further contributed to the stagnation of the reform process.

Nevertheless, the military reform and transformation process has made modest achievements in the form of establishing civilian control of the armed forces and purging the military of those who held political office. However limited it remains, the parliamentary oversight exercised over defence affairs has increased. A systematic agenda for reform was worked out, notably under the auspices of the Office of Nigerian Army Transformation and later the Armed Forces Transformation Committee, involving how best to restructure the management of the military, revive discipline and *esprit de corps*, rejuvenate research and development, re-equip and train men and officers with appropriate skills. However, this agenda was not effectively or consistency pursued. This was due largely to a lack of will on the part of parliament as well as political and military leaders. It was further hampered by corruption and severe security challenges, including internal conflicts and terrorism.

In recent years, the Boko Haram terrorist challenge has become the key factor in determining the direction of change in the military's organisational structure. The Boko Haram counter-insurgency effort revealed the limitations of security sector reform in Nigeria and exposed the military's weakness to the public, especially with regard to the kidnapping of over 200 schoolgirls in Chibok at a time when that State was under emergency rule. Cases of mutiny, soldiers' disregard for orders, protest by soldiers' wives over the deployment of their husbands without adequate equipment and weapons support, the treachery of officers and claims of corruption have become a matter of major public concern, bringing the issue of security sector reform to the fore if not yet giving birth to a substantive public debate on the road ahead.

The main lesson to be learnt in and from Nigeria is that security sector reform must take into account the larger context of governance, especially the commitment of the political leadership, the interface between the military and civilian components of the Ministry of Defence, the interest and capacity of parliament and civil society to address security issues, and the general values that drive politics. The political enthusiasm for security reform that accompanied the democratisation process was lost early, while the initial promise of independence regarding ownership and continuity for the military could not be sustained. The changes in military operations and organisation provoked by its engagement with internal conflicts and counter-terrorism have translated into unsystematic changes in the military's operation and organisation. The 2008 reform documents must be reworked to take these changes into account if they are to be used to rejuvenate the military, re-structure the defence leadership in order to reap the benefit of the joint doctrine and inter-agency cooperation, and provide a framework for effective use of foreign assistance.

Nigeria's challenges include the need to develop sufficient capability, including adequate manpower, to deal with contemporary threats to security. It must also include reorganising the procurement process to ensure value for money, reduce corruption and improve the conditions of both lower ranking officers and men. The current engagement with Boko Haram and other terrorist groups means that it must also develop its intelligence network and capabilities to preempt and apprehend terrorists before they strike. Above all, reform must deal with broader issues concerning the renegotiation of power needed to build an inclusive system of governance with a strong parliament and civilian institutions, as well as media engagement to encourage debate through keeping the population informed so that they can make their views known. This, in turn, would strengthen the degree to which democratic principles are embedded in all aspects of Nigerian society – a critical pre-condition for security sector reform.

Notes

[1] Interview conducted by author 2014.

[2] Author's interview with military officers in February 2014.

[3] Discussion with military officers conducted by author in February 2014.

CHAPTER 7

Security Sector Reform in Democratic Senegal

Lamine Cissé

Former Chief of Staff of the Armed Forces of Senegal, Minister of the Interior of Senegal, former United Nations Special Representative of the Secretary General for West Africa

Introduction

Generally speaking, Senegalese political institutions observe the legal principle that all segments of the state are subject to the law. The construction of the Senegalese nation can no doubt be considered to be a success since ethnicity is absolutely irrelevant in the political arena and does not affect the distribution of positions of national responsibility. Within such an environment, it might therefore be considered inappropriate or even inopportune and irrelevant to speak about security sector reform (SSR) in Senegal. This is however not the case. This study aims to carry out an analysis that will contribute to consolidating Senegalese institutions and further disseminating the best practices that have, to a large extent, contributed to the stability of the country and its excellent civil-military relations.

There are also other reasons for undertaking this study. First of all because Senegal like other countries, but to a lesser degree, experienced a single party political system followed by a limited multiparty system with one dominant party. It is common knowledge that such a regime is often based on an authoritarian definition and conduct of public policy. Secondly, where security is concerned, since 1981 the southern region of Senegal has been the theatre of a conflict whose origins lie in the demands for independence of the Movement of Democratic Forces of Casamance *(Mouvement des Forces démocratiques*

How to cite this book chapter:

Cissé, L. 2015. Security Sector Reform in Democratic Senegal. In: Bryden, A and Chappuis, F (eds.) *Learning from West African Experiences in Security Sector Governance*, Pp. 117–137. London: Ubiquity Press. DOI: http://dx.doi.org/10.5334/bau.g. License: CC-BY 4.0.

de Casamance, - MFDC). Although the Senegalese political authorities have always considered this to be a question of internal security, the conflict has led to the engagement of the armed forces, whose traditional mission is geared towards defending the country's territorial integrity. The armed forces are thus involved in continuing security operations that often include conducting missions that can reasonably be said to exceed the simple framework of keeping order due to their degree of intensity, the tactical and strategic objectives, the resources committed and above all the modes of action adopted. Because of the conditions under which they are conducted, these security operations can have numerous consequences for the security forces. As part of their mission, they are required to interact with the population, as well as administrative and traditional authorities, the justice system, the media, civil society and even their counterparts from neighbouring countries, along the national borders. This situation also raises a number of questions, in particular regarding observance of international humanitarian law; the relations among the various security forces engaged in the conflict affected areas; the legal implications of having the armed forces engage in internal security duties that are not normally their responsibility; mainstreaming the gender dimension in situations of operational engagement and the requirements of secrecy and confidentiality surrounding these operations. It may therefore be necessary to evaluate these effects and assess the need or relevance of initiating reforms aimed at refocusing the activities of the DSF on standards that are more in line with the requirements of the rule of law.

Another dimension is the new paradigm of human security, which is now an obligation for all stakeholders. In conjunction with advancing democracy and its attendant effects, this paradigm implies that populations are now seen not only as beneficiaries of security, but above all as stakeholders who are fully involved in implementing security. This means that the right frameworks must be put in place to ensure the participation of the various segments of the population. Additionally, certain observers have noted that following the inception of a new political dispensation with the change of regime after the 2000 presidential election, a series of constitutional reforms, as well as a number of administrative and political practices gradually placed the president of the republic in the forefront of government and relegated other institutions of the republic to the background. Some analysts feel that this led to a diminution of political freedoms and shifted the balance of powers among the legislative, judicial and executive branches in favour of the latter. It is also worth taking time to examine the effects that these factors have had on the security sector.

After describing the context of security sector reform in Senegal, this study will touch on the crisis in Casamance, which is the main security problem facing Senegal, and describe the importance of this issue from the point of view of SSR. The study will then examine the components of transformational change in the security sector to date, as well as the sustainability of such changes. The study will conclude with a number of recommendations.

Security sector governance in Senegal: background

After roughly three centuries of French colonial domination, Senegal acceded to international sovereignty on 20 June 1960, first within the framework of the Mali Federation, then when this was dissolved, as a separate nation on 20 August 1960. The political evolution of the country was characterised by a certain de facto political stability, with the single party system. Since 1976, the country has had a fully-fledged multiparty system and a presidential regime that includes an executive branch headed by the president of the republic, who has authority over the prime minister and head of government, the national assembly, which serves as the parliament and the economic, social and environmental council. After two democratic changes of head of state in 2000 and 2012, Senegalese democracy can be considered to have come of age.

The judiciary, which is made up of courts and tribunals in all the administrative regions of the country, administers justice. It is generally felt that the system of justice is credible and accessible to all citizens, although some observers point to some functional shortcomings. Finally, the DSF are unanimously appreciated for their service to the republic and their professionalism. Indeed, the DSF do not play any political role and in professional terms, they seek to satisfy the expectations of the authorities and the population in carrying out the missions entrusted to them both within and without the national territory. Senegal also stands out as one of the few countries in West Africa that has never experienced a military coup d'état.

Political institutions

Political institutions, which were redefined by the 22 January 2001 constitution, are based on the sacrosanct principle of the separation of executive, legislative and judicial powers. Following a tradition established by the 7 March 1963 constitution, which succeeded the 26 August 1960 constitution establishing a parliamentary regime with a bicephalous executive power, the 22 January 2001 constitution placed executive power exclusively in the hands of the president of the republic. The constitution nevertheless provided a number of checks and balances, with oversight functions in the hands of the national assembly and the judiciary power in the courts and tribunals (Fall 2012).

The workings of the political party system however gradually upset the balance of these institutions, to the advantage of the president's party. The national assembly, which the political opposition describes as being "subservient", is also seen by many observers as a rubber stamp parliament. It must however be acknowledged that all the socialist governments that preceded the change in 2000 enjoyed an absolute or qualified majority in the national assembly. Similarly, the majority of opposition political forces are of the view that the constitutional council, whose members are appointed by the president of the republic, has demonstrated its lack of independence by regularly handing down decisions that appeared to serve the partisan interests of the head of state instead of being based on the letter and the spirit of the electoral code.

This situation has led to repeated reforms of the fundamental law, with a view to resolving incidental political issues. It also contributed to imposing the will of President Abdoulaye Wade who sought to implement a process that some of his opponents described as "monarchical devolution" of political authority. The inception of the youth *'Y'en a marre'* (Enough is enough) movement, as well as M 23 in 2011 represented a major turning point. The latter was an alliance of various youth and civil society organisations and some political parties. After a standoff between opposition parties allied with civil society, and under pressure from international organisations and several western diplomatic missions, the government had to give up its plans. Consequently, the Senegalese people peacefully and transparently operated another change of regime in 2012 and voted Macky Sall, the candidate of the *Alliance pour la République*, a member of the 'Benno Book Yaakar[1]' coalition of opposition parties, to the highest office in the nation.

In reality, the institutional framework established by the 22 January 2001 constitution had shown its weakness and as a result, the authorities that came into power after the 2012 presidential elections were compelled to initiate a reform process that was entrusted to a committee chaired by a renowned civil society representative. The terms of reference of the mandate of the committee indicate that its task is to:

> "restore the prestige and authority of parliament, to replace the present constitutional council with a true constitutional court, to protect the constitution against any amendments that would undermine democratic progress and, in particular, to consolidate the Senegalese electoral framework by enhancing the independence of election management bodies and setting up mechanisms for continued policy dialogue." (Fall 2012: xxi)

The justice system

According to the provisions of art. 88 of the 22 January 2001 constitution, the judiciary is independent of the legislative and executive branches of power. This power is exercised by the constitutional council, the supreme court, the court of accounts and other courts and tribunals. The legal system is based on two principles; the unity of the legal order, made up of the courts and tribunals, and the hierarchy of courts, with first and second degree courts, as well as other higher jurisdictions. In the eyes of the general public, the Senegalese system of justice is plagued by three main shortcomings; inadequate independence, lack of transparency and inefficiency (Sy 2012).

The system of justice in Senegal has to deal with several difficulties: insufficient numbers of staff (magistrates and officers of court); difficult access for citizens to this public service which is an important part of the enjoyment of their rights, and inadequate judicial coverage, namely the distribution of first and second level courts throughout the national territory. Above all, the fact that the constitution grants the president of the republic the power to appoint magistrates to the higher courts is likely to considerably hamper the independence of the justice system. For example, the five members of the constitutional council are appointed by the president of the republic for a non-renewable six year term. Similarly members of the supreme court are appointed by decree of the president of the republic. The president also chairs the Higher Council of Magistrates (*Conseil supérieure de la Magistrature*), with the minister of justice as vice-chair. Since the Higher Council of Magistrates plays a decisive role in the career development of senior magistrates, one can easily understand the issues inherent in controlling this body.

President Abdoulaye Wade did make considerable and unprecedented efforts to improve the remuneration of magistrates. He also initiated a project to reform the judicial coverage and thus facilitate access to justice for citizens, while freeing up the courts to deal with cases more promptly. Nevertheless, magistrates, law theoreticians and civil society organisations all feel that the justice system will only be truly independent when the presidents of higher courts are elected by their peers and the president of the republic has less influence over the Higher Council of Magistrates. The issue is still debated in judiciary and political circles where there are fears about the establishment of a 'magistrate-state'.

On this issue and based on the recommendations of the national assizes, President Macky Sall, who took over power after the second democratic regime change, has called for proposals for institutional reforms. The National Commission for Institutional Reform (*Commission nationale de réforme des institutions*) was established for this purpose and submitted its conclusions in December 2013. Some of its proposals, which sparked off various reactions, related to the legal system: a less influential prosecution service, the chairmanship of the higher council of magistrates and a fully-fledged constitutional court to replace the constitutional council. They also touched on the combined roles of president of the republic and president of a political party, etc. Some people protested that the National Commission for Institutional Reform had exceeded its mandate in suggesting a new constitution. Within political parties and civil society, and depending on their affiliation with one group or the other, some spoke about reforms that would consolidate or deconsolidate the constitution.

In any case, it is clear today that in spite of some political reticence or apprehensions that may initially have appeared justified, the national assizes marked an undisputable step forward for democracy in Senegal.

Defence and security forces

The defence and security forces are made up of the armed forces, the gendarmerie, the police, the prisons service, the customs service and the department of water, forestry, hunting and soil conservation. However, since these services do not all have the same degree of involvement in ensuring security in the military sense of the term, this study will only focus on the first three corps mentioned above, namely, the armed forces, the gendarmerie and the police. In describing the lessons learned from the security operations in Casamance, the focus will be on the armed forces, as they bear the greatest responsibilities in this engagement.

The armed forces. With a total of about 15,000 soldiers, the principal mission of the armed forces is to provide external security. This mission is executed by defending the integrity of the national territory on land, sea and in the air. While the terrestrial forces are made up of professional and disciplined troops led by competent officers with excellent authority over them and cover the national territory extensively, albeit insufficiently, their operational capacities are limited because their equipment is largely outdated. The navy and the air force are unable to carry out all their maritime and air defence missions, for similar reasons.

Since 1982, the armed forces have been engaged in continued securitisation operations in the Kolda, Sédhiou and Ziguinchor regions, which have been the theatre of a rebellion by the MFDC independence movement. They are also a key player in dealing with natural disasters and emergency situations.

Finally, they have long been involved in peace missions under the auspices of the United Nations (Contingent of the Mali Federation to the Belgian Congo in 1960), as well as African international organisations such as the African Union and ECOWAS. It is in this capacity that contingents of troops were sent to Darfur, Côte d'Ivoire and Mali. Senegalese staff officers have also served in South Sudan, the Democratic Republic of Congo and more recently in the Central African Republic.

National gendarmerie. With about 6,000 soldiers, the gendarmerie is a military force that has attributions related to military policing, public security and criminal investigation. Under the authority of a senior officer known as the senior commander of the national gendarmerie and director of military justice, the national gendarmerie is divided into territorial and mobile units, as well as units specialised in crime investigation, anti-terrorism, port surveillance and environmental defence. The gendarmerie also participates in international peace missions.

Like the armed forces, the gendarmerie is renowned for its professionalism, competence and observance of republican values. In its activities, it respects human rights. Although there have been sporadic reports of torture being used in certain cases, this practice is frowned upon by the high command. Generally speaking, such violations of the law are dealt with through legal process and the perpetrators are punished.

The principal challenge facing the gendarmerie is its inability to cover the full extent of the national territory. Also, in the hinterland, the gendarmerie is not adequately represented in the areas of the national territory that are affected by the MFDC rebellion. This security vacuum has led to the absence of any government authority and makes it particularly difficult to ensure effective administrative activities for the population.

The armed forces were kept out of national political life for a long time because they did not have the right to vote. This right was granted to them by law n° 2006 – 20 of 30 June 2006. The same applied to the paramilitary forces, as well as all government agents who were deprived of this right because of their specific status. The military command however never demanded to be allowed to enjoy this right, which is considered by many observers to be a major component of citizenship (Esambo Kangashe 2013: 159). Indeed, the hierarchy was rather apprehensive about the issue, due to the risk of politicisation of a corps whose strength till then had lain in its ability to maintain the same distance from all political trends.

National police force. The police force is under the responsibility of the minister of interior and public security. It is a paramilitary body entrusted with a public service mission, intelligence, criminal investigation and the control of organised crime and terrorism. It is made up of territorial units in charge of public security in urban areas and mobile units that are responsible for law enforcement. It also includes specialised criminal police units such as the criminal investigations division and the departments in charge of combatting major crime and terrorist acts.

The reputation of the police force has been tarnished by its poor image with a part of the population that accuses it of corruption and inadequate professionalism. Also the recent frequent changes in management following a series of dismissals have led to some instability. Steps have however been taken to improve this image. For example, two non-hierarchical ranks have been instituted; the position of controller general of police (where no appointment has been made since it was created in 2009) and that of inspector general of police. Like the gendarmerie, the police is unable to cover the national territory adequately due to a lack of personnel and infrastructure. The police force nevertheless participates in peace operations within the framework of formed police units and civilian police officers. The ongoing recruitments must be continued in order to replace the numerous officers who have retired, and officer training and specialisation in the field of anti-terrorism must be enhanced.

Challenges and lessons from the crisis in Casamance

This crisis, which is the main security issue in Senegal, involves various stakeholders. It provides valuable lessons about SSR, in particular with regard to the degree of democratic control of security forces and the nature of civil-military relations.

Who are the actors involved in resolving the crisis?

When the MFDC took up arms in 1982 to demand independence for the southern region of the country, thus undermining the project of building a Senegalese nation, the government of Senegal responded with a strategy that while using military force, has never been based on resolving the conflict by force of weapons. The MFDC is built on an ethnic foundation, mainly of the Diola[2] group and includes a political wing whose influence over the military wing varies according to circumstances and events. Experience has shown that apart from the common security activities, large scale operations that may be seen as actual war operations are generally planned and conducted in response to acts of violence perpetrated by armed groups of the MFDC either against the civilian population or against units of the armed forces. It could be said that the operations carried out by the Senegalese armed forces serve more to support attempts at political negotiations with the political wing of the MFDC than to reduce the rebel camps, which are deeply embedded in the geographical territory of neighbouring Gambia and Guinea-Bissau. All observers consider both these neighbouring states as stakeholders in the conflict either for geopolitical reasons, or simply due to the links that they maintain with the MFDC, which can sometimes be useful in the tumultuous relations between these two countries and their larger neighbour. As a result, the territories of both countries may shelter rebel bases or serve as a fall-back zone when the Senegalese military carries out targeted operations, as is the case in any geographic area where there is a rebellion.

Political and administrative authorities. By virtue of art. 45 of the constitution, the president of the republic is "responsible for national defence". He is the commander-in-chief of the armed forces and presides over the higher council on national defence and the national security council. The president of the republic is therefore in charge of defining and conducting the national policy to counter the activities of the MFDC. From this point of view, he has full authority over all those in charge of the operational and tactical implementation of this policy, namely the armed forces, as well as the gendarmerie and the police. The ministries of interior, the armed forces and justice make up the strategic levels of policy implementation.

Government action is carried out locally by the deconcentrated administrative authorities, that is, regional governors, departmental prefects and sub-prefects and heads of the different arrondissements. The national assembly has the power to control government activities. This power is exercised through the work of its standing committees or when the budget is approved in the plenary session. It may also take the form of inspection and fact-finding missions carried out in the field by the standing committee on defence. The economic, social and environmental council is in charge of approving draft bills and proposals, as well as draft decrees that concern economic and social affairs, with the exception of finance laws (some development projects that affect the Casamance region). Various control bodies situated at different levels within the administration also contribute to accountability, observance of the law and safeguarding human rights.

Where the military is concerned, the armed forces inspectorate general, which is headed by a flag officer, carries out field visits and detailed inspections of the major commands within the armed forces and the gendarmerie and reports on them to the president of the republic. The ministry of interior and the ministry of the armed forces both include departments in charge of inspecting the financial bodies that are under the responsibility of these ministries. Finally, any authority with hierarchical powers is obliged to oversee their subordinates, in particular those in charge of managing public funds.

Decentralised local authorities. As part of the decentralisation policy initiated in 1972, which culminated in the passing of law n° 96 – 06 of 22 March 1996, establishing the local authorities' code, these local administrative authorities, namely mayors and heads of rural communities, are granted certain attributions related to general safety and economic development, as well as education, social affairs, sanitation, culture and science. Act III of the administrative decentralisation policy has now evolved considerably, with communes being granted full powers, which opens interesting prospects in the area of security. At the same time Act III also raises a number of difficulties for stakeholders.

Civil society. Essentially, civil society can be defined as the opposite of political society. It is based on an endeavour to ensure that the needs of citizens are met by the public authorities who have been entrusted with political power either legitimately, through universal suffrage, or legally by an administrative act. Civil society acts as an intermediary between the public authorities and citizens; on one hand, it expresses the needs of the population and seeks to make sure that they are met by these authorities and, on the other, it undertakes various initiatives aimed at substituting for the failures of the public authorities when they are derelict in carrying out their duties.

In the area of security, civil society aims to participate in defining public policy, but at the same time, in adopting the position of intermediary between government and citizens, it sets itself up as a guardian that evaluates government bodies and also plays a role as a facilitator and watchdog, while also sounding alerts and reporting incidents. Civil society is very active in Ziguinchor, where it is represented by various national and regional organisations. For example, an association known as the Platform of women for peace in Casamance, a grouping of women from Kolda, Ziguinchor and Sédhiou, travelled to Sao Domingo in the Republic of Guinea-Bissau on 24 July 2012 to initiate talks with MFDC representatives as part of the renewed dialogue between the independence movement and the government of Senegal (Senenews 2012).

The international community. ECOWAS has a number of peace and security mechanisms, including the following instruments in particular:

- The 1999 Protocol relating to the Mechanism for Conflict Prevention, Management, Resolution, Peacekeeping, and Security;
- The supplementary protocol to the protocol relating to the Mechanism for Conflict Prevention, Management, Resolution, Peacekeeping, and Security, on democracy and good governance;
- The ECOWAS Convention on small arms and light weapons, which is aimed at preventing the dissemination and accumulation of such weapons.

The West African Economic and Monetary Union is also in the course of establishing a peace and security architecture. It is however worth noting that international organisations, ECOWAS and the African Union have not had much involvement in the attempts to resolve the conflict in Casamance. This is no doubt due among other reasons to the fact that Senegal wishes to treat this matter as a purely internal problem.

Mediators and facilitators. Although the Senegalese political authorities have constantly sought to avoid internationalising the conflict in Casamance, the neighbouring states of The Gambia and Guinea-Bissau have always been involved as mediators or facilitators. The first two agreements signed within the framework of this conflict, for example, were signed in Cacheu in Guinea-Bissau in 1991 and 1993 respectively. The Gambia, for its part, was closely involved in the meetings held in Banjul in 2000 and participated actively in securing the freedom of five soldiers held by the MFDC in May 2012, who then travelled to Dakar from Banjul.

Some other foreign players have participated in mediation or facilitation efforts. One example is the Community of Sant'Egidio, a movement created in Rome in 1968 after the Second Vatican Council, which brings together lay persons from over 70 countries on different continents (Sant'Egidio [n.d.]). Sant'Egidio is particularly active in conflict mediation. It has been rather successful in Mozambique and in Guatemala and worked to ensure the participation of the MFDC hardliners in the negotiations held in January 2012. The movement is currently still active in Senegal and still working on the crisis in Casamance, as is Humanitarian Dialogue, a group based in Geneva.

Furthermore, a number of good offices missions have been carried out on the side lines and to varying degrees by certain Western embassies, in particular France and the United States, with the aim of bringing the parties together. The US has a special envoy on Casamance while for France, Ambassador André Lewin, among others, has devoted a great deal of his influence, energy and heart to this cause.

Where institutional players are concerned, certain personalities have served as 'Mr. Casamance'. One such person is Robert Sagna, mayor of Ziguinchor and former senior minister in the government of President Abdou Diouf, who played a role as an influential emissary and, for a time at least, was a central figure in this situation.

A wide range of other personalities have been involved in attempts at mediation and facilitation: political and traditional leaders, senior civilian and military officials who held these positions during the regime of President Abdoulaye Wade between 2000 and 2012 or prior to that. This variety has not made it possible to pursue a consistent national strategy.

What lessons can be drawn from the conflict in Casamance in terms of SSR?

The conflict in Casamance provides an extremely valuable opportunity to observe and assess the various aspects of the security sector in an African country that is consolidating its democracy and national unity. An analysis of the manner in which the conflict has been managed provides insights as to how civilian democratic control and the republican nature of the Senegalese armed forces have remained intact, despite the lengthy military operations carried out under often extremely trying conditions for both the units and the military command structure.

Officers in the armed forces are competent and well trained and have real authority over their troops. Commanders in charge of the various units are generally appointed solely on the basis of their professional qualifications and not according to regional, religious or ethnic criteria. This makes the Senegalese armed forces a truly national body.

Existence of true, combat-ready operational capacities. Fighting units can count on direct and in-depth fire support from the artillery as well as the air force, which despite its limited resources, is formidably effective against the armed groups. In manoeuvres, the command posts are generally properly sized to provide the main operational functions required in the engagement (artillery and aviation fire, logistics, intelligence, movements and communication).

An impersonal command chain, with combat-ready troops who are obedient to their chief and not to a particular individual. Most of the troops engaged are thus capable of containing any shock, that is, notwithstanding losses, they are able to continue carrying out the mission assigned them. This is the result of proper instruction and training, but above all the existence of a real esprit de corps within the units.

A command structure that is close to the troops, as demonstrated by regular visits and inspections by the high command. The armed forces chief of general staff makes it a point to visit the units in military zones 5 and 6 (Ziguinchor,

Kolda and Sédhiou) at least once every quarter. This enables him to constantly monitor the situation and find out about the state of the troops, the means at their disposal and their ability to carry out their mission. Generally speaking, these visits are organised systematically at all levels.

Financial advantages aimed at maintaining the morale of fighting units. Two types of incentives have been put in place. First of all, a daily intervention allowance that is paid to all soldiers in areas considered as operational zones. This allowance, which relates to their location, is paid to all soldiers garrisoned in military zones 5 and 6. In addition, a more substantial daily operations allowance is paid to units engaged in specific security operations throughout the duration of their engagement. These incentives are a supplement to their ordinary entitlements such as free meals for all categories of soldiers present in these zones.

What factors are relevant in maintaining discipline, dealing with complaints, guaranteeing the respect of human rights and establishing good relations with the local population?

Existence of general disciplinary regulations that are rigorously applied equally to all soldiers. Any misdeeds committed in the execution of missions are generally sanctioned by the commanding authority in the form of disciplinary action for the lower ranks or, in the case of higher officers, by a reconsideration of their career prospects.

Establishing rules of engagement and behaviour for units in operations. These rules define the conditions for opening fire, the gradual and measured use of arms and protection of places of worship, schools, etc.

Effective logistical support in the form of subsistence and combat resources delivered to all units, regardless of their geographical location. Thanks to this logistical capacity, the units are not dependent on the local population. On the contrary, the military barracks often serve as a 'canteen' for people living in the surrounding areas.

Bases are a reassuring presence for local inhabitants. Local inhabitants, who are often victims of acts of violence on the part of armed groups or simple criminals, are generally happy to have the military stationed in their villages. Indeed, they often do not hesitate to call on their political or traditional authorities to appeal to the military command in their favour for this purpose.

How has Senegal avoided a deterioration in civil-military relations in spite of the lack of adequate resources for the armed forces to carry out their mandate?

Because the Senegalese armed forces have a long-standing tradition of involvement in national development right from the time of independence, they have developed a deep understanding of civil-military relations. In the conflict affected regions, the armed forces quickly realised that it was essential to garner the support of the local population. They therefore included civil-military relations in their activities, from the highest levels of command, right down to the troops deployed on the ground. As a result, all the activities of the Senegalese armed forces in these security operations are based on a real concept of civil-military relations. These relations take different forms, but most often include:

- Providing medical services to the population through care, evacuating patients, supplying drugs and distributing mosquito nets;
- Permanent supply of food to village dwellers by sharing troops' food rations with them or by occasional gifts to the most affected communities;
- Educational assistance in the form of supply of school books or rehabilitation of classrooms;
- In certain specific situations, troops stationed in very remote areas actually step in as schoolteachers when the latter have fled the area as a result of the insecurity;
- Reconstruction of places of worship and rehabilitation of community infrastructure, as well as undertaking a major programme of reconstructing destroyed villages in order to facilitate the return of refugees and displaced persons;
- Strong communication with local inhabitants with a toll-free number that enables them to rapidly alert the troops when their safety is threatened;
- Putting doors in place, building bridges and rehabilitating rural roads to facilitate access, in particular in Casamance and in the Sindian arrondissement, close to The Gambia;
- Unit heads sponsor cultural and sporting activities for young people during the long school vacation.

Components of transformational change in the security sector

The way in which the approach adopted by the Senegalese authorities in dealing with the conflict in Casamance has evolved can be said to provide an example of transformational change in the area of security sector governance and reform. In more general terms, the changes in the security sector in Senegal are evident in several dimensions:

Personal commitment of the head of state

After his election in 2012, President Macky Sall immediately showed his interest in the security services and his desire to improve their working conditions by implementing certain measures.

During a visit to military zone 6 in April 2013, the head of state addressed the soldiers in the following terms: "Be assured that as commander in chief of the armed forces, I follow with keen interest the work that you carry out on a daily basis and I am even more determined to provide you with the means required to undertake the duties entrusted to you by the nation" (Le Soleil 2013). Such visits are extremely significant because they reassure the military command and have a positive effect on troop morale.

In addition, on armed forces day on 8 November 2013, President Macky Sall reaffirmed his decision to provide the armed forces with the necessary equipment to enable them to function efficiently.

High profile measures

Increasingly, members of the DSF are called to account for offences committed in executing their mission. In one instance, the director of the Central Office for the Control of Illicit Narcotics Trafficking (*Office central pour la répression du trafic illicite des stupéfiants*) and the director general of police were accused of drug trafficking. This case, which was the subject of broad media coverage even beyond the national borders, ended with the removal of the director of the Central Office for the Control of Illicit Narcotics Trafficking and the dismissal of the case against the director general of police.

Also, where accountability is concerned, the institutional arsenal in place for controlling the behaviour of members of the DSF covers all existing areas of control. These oversight measures are usually effective, at least for the implementing echelons. Public funds, be they individual entitlements such as wages and rations or miscellaneous general maintenance costs, do generally get to the departments for which they were disbursed. Some people however deplore the secrecy surrounding inspection and audit reports, which are not made public. Similarly, in the case of disciplinary sanctions, these remain confidential and only the senior authorities of the offender are informed. There is also the misuse of the 'defence secrecy' label in public procurement as a way of avoiding the procedures put in place to ensure more transparency in this area. This is why citizens and uninformed observers feel that there is no effective oversight of the defence sector. Nevertheless, the specific nature of the defence sector must not be overlooked, with certain aspects that cannot be dealt with in an open forum.

Organisational reform

President Sall initiated a reform of the intelligence services aimed at grouping the entire intelligence community within a single coordinating bodwy under the responsibility of the office of the president of the republic. The reform also takes account of the need to confer greater common law prerogatives on the intelligence services for the protection of individual liberties, in case of an imminent terrorist risk. It is worth noting that any decisions taken under this scheme may be subjected to subsequent control by a judge.

The head of state also launched a process to begin formalising the activities of the security forces with the drafting of a national defence and security concept aimed at clarifying the attributions and missions of each body. The purpose is to satisfy the requirements of human security and ensure proper strategic and operational coordination. This concept is to serve as the basis for defining the organisational structure and equipment required for the security forces in the years ahead.

In addition, an internal security orientation law that is currently under study is aimed at reforming the internal security system of Senegal by defining a programme of action to be implemented by government from 2015 to 2025. The greater part of this programme would be aimed at a more coherent and effective use of internal security forces to tackle new security requirements, in particular in the area of fighting crime, which is clearly on the increase, and to counter the relative inefficiency of the disaster forecast and management system. It will also clarify and harmonise the responsibilities of the various internal security actors, while clearly defining the scope of the latter. With regard to the question of whether there is a need to distinguish between the security sector and the defence sector, there is a debate about whether the gendarmerie should be placed at the disposal of the ministry of interior. In other words, both the police and the gendarmerie would be under this same ministry. While the experience of France could inform the decision to be made by the political authorities, there are for the moment divergent views on the issue.

With a view to instilling a culture of security within the elite of the republic, defence education has been initiated with the creation of a centre for higher studies on defence and security. The ambition of the centre is, among others, to conduct training seminars for the national elite.

Transformative action

Across the board, the educational level required for recruitment of security personnel has been raised. A reform of the requirements of the police force has led to raising the level of recruitment. To be recruited, aspiring police non-commissioned officers must hold a baccalaureate and those who wish to be policemen must be holders of an elementary school leaving certificate. The armed forces and the gendarmerie are also expected to follow the same trend and raise the level at which officers and non-commissioned officers are recruited. Indeed, non-commissioned officers will now be required to hold a baccalaureate, while officers must have a bachelor's degree.

The armed forces are beginning to benefit from some major equipment endowment programmes. The navy strengthened its fleet by commissioning a patrol vessel in 2013 and is awaiting delivery of other vessels very soon. Also, there have been reports in the press about a contract between Senegal and the Brazilian company *Embraer*, concerning the purchase of three Super Tucano fighter planes similar to those already supplied to Angola, Burkina Faso and Mauritania (SenewebNews 2013). A number of light armoured vehicles were also delivered at the Dakar port in April 2014 and a few examples were included in the Independence Day parade.

Where the gender dimension is concerned, female soldiers now participate in peace missions in external theatres of operation. For the first time, the armed forces contingent deployed to Guinea-Bissau under the auspices of ECOWAS included some female soldiers. The national police and gendarmerie units deployed in Darfur and in Haiti also include women. Above all, the army officers' corps now includes female lieutenants who for the moment work within the services units.

Lasting change

The vital question that now arises is to what extent can these positive changes in the area of security sector governance be sustainable? This part of the study takes a look at those changes that are well entrenched, as well as areas that remain more vulnerable.

Scope of government action

Given the scope of major reforms and the steps taken to increase the efficiency of security forces, it must be acknowledged that the government of President Macky Sall has demonstrated its desire to improve security sector governance. In addition to initiating the exercise of re-equipping the DSF with the purchase of major equipment, another welcome move has been the effort to rationalise the organisation and functioning of the security system. Where the conflict in Casamance is concerned, the overall management of the problem and the moderate use of force on the part of the DSF has made it possible to preserve the overall unity of the Senegalese nation. The fact that security forces personnel may be held criminally liable has made for greater respect of human rights, although human rights defence organisations still express some expectations that they consider not to have been met.

Well established achievements

The republican character of the DSF is one major achievement. It is demonstrated in the fact that they are not involved in politics and that no circles or lobbies interfere in the selection of flag officers to head major institutions by the president of the republic. Thus, there has always been continuity and stability in the handing over of authority over the major commands and this has never been officially called into question.

We must also acknowledge the respect of human rights; Senegal is recognised as one of the rare African countries where members of the security forces are subject to the law and do not benefit from any preferential treatment compared to the civilian population. Another point is that the armed forces are no longer needed to provide security during elections. Security coverage in the country must now be geared towards deploying only first and second category forces, namely the police and the gendarmerie. In reality, only the Ziguinchor, Kolda and Sédhiou regions, which are affected by the MFDC rebellion, could continue to require some specific security management.

Definition of the scope of internal security

The Senegalese authorities have never considered the conflict in Casamance as a war situation. The term generally used to describe the operations carried out in this region is 'securing'. These operations are mainly carried out by armed forces units, as already shown. This raises the question about whether the police and gendarmerie are capable of controlling an insurrectional situation within the national territory. For example, the Brazilian police carries out real armed operations to dislodge criminals and drug traffickers from the favelas of Rio de Janeiro.

When the armed forces have to carry out policing operations, military units often find themselves having to investigate suspects, search homes and carry out arrests, activities that are all responsibilities of criminal police officers. The right solution might be to set up a specific legal service for the armed forces, with sworn personnel fully capable of drawing up any legal acts needed. This is the solution adopted by Burkina Faso, which has a corps of military judges who are capable of providing advice to unit chiefs right up to battalion level, both in the garrison and in the field. (Twenty years ago, the armed forces chief of general staff of Senegal also had a judge detached part-time to him, to act as a legal advisor). Also, in order to comply with the framework for the use of each force, the gendarmerie and police units need to be structured to take into account this type of armed threat within the national territory.

Matching administrative constituencies and territorial command sectors of the security forces

Within the framework of decentralisation, the objective of act III is to organise Senegal into viable territories that will ensure sustainable development by

2022. The aim is to enhance the decentralisation and territorialisation of public policy, in order to boost local development.

In the area of territorial coherence, decentralisation really needs to take into account not only local sociological specificities, but also the coherence of territorial command sectors. Under the terms of art. 3 of the new decentralisation law, Senegal is now divided into administrative constituencies comprising 14 regions, 45 *départements* and 125 arrondissements, as well as local authorities with 42 *départements* and 557 communes.

Although the administrative and security concerns are not exactly identical, it may be useful to consider whether the administrative division and the functional relations described in act III on decentralisation need to match the territorial command sectors of the armed forces and the gendarmerie (military zones and gendarmerie legions). The command structure of the gendarmerie in particular is considering establishing one legion per region and one company per *département*.

Improving parliamentary control

Parliamentary control needs to be improved through enhanced capacity building and improving the knowledge of members about security and defence. In addition, field visits should be organised. It is rather significant that the national assembly has never summoned the armed forces chief of general staff nor the high commander of the national gendarmerie before it to answer questions on defence or specific operations directly. Indeed, the only hearings to involve the minister in charge of the armed forces are during the budget sessions. Furthermore, the procedures for auditing equipment procurement programmes need to be defined, while observing strict secrecy and confidentiality concerning national defence. The security forces could take more initiative in this area and invite representatives of parliament to participate in some of their activities. Another way of helping parliamentarians familiarise themselves with the forces would be to give them an opportunity to visit military barracks or even units in operations inside and outside the national territory, a practice that used to be common some years ago. Furthermore, it would be valuable for the national assembly to be aware of the opinion of senior commanders regarding certain aspects of security policy implementation. This could take the form of oral presentations in a solemn session and would supplement and broaden their knowledge of the subjects discussed during question time in plenary or in budget sessions. Generally speaking, it must be acknowledged that parliament tends to show a certain natural reserve concerning investigations of any issues that are labelled 'defence secret' and indeed of any issues related to national defence. To enhance the culture of oversight of this institution, this attitude will have to change.

Organisation of the private military and security companies sector

Companies providing security services are responding to a demand that is not satisfied by the national police force. There are 257 such private security companies on the Senegalese market today and they are characterised by an inadequate legal framework, in particular in the area of social protection for their workers. Also, because the sector is doing well financially some multinational security companies are now showing an interest and increasing their presence on this market. This compelled the president of the republic to urge government to sign a collective bargaining agreement to provide the sector with a stable regulatory framework, in line with its current size and its future development.

Certain religious leaders have also set up their own private guards who provide security services during the public events that they organise. This is an infringement of a government duty, although the latter does not have sufficient resources to adequately carry out this duty.

Implementing the concept of community security

The concept of community security was unprecedented in Senegal. The mission of the Community Security Agency (*Agence pour la sécurité de proximité*), which was created in August 2013, is to "participate, together with the police authorities and security forces (police and gendarmerie), in implementing community policing based on prevention and active partnership among government, local authorities and the actors of social life". The Community Security Agency began its activities by recruiting a total of 10,000 young people in one year. After undergoing technical training, they were deployed to the local authorities. Some of these young people were also detached to the police and the gendarmerie.

To a certain extent, the Community Security Agency can be seen as a contribution to fighting against youth unemployment. This new agency could also be supplemented by the revitalisation of the municipal police service, which was created by decree, according to the terms of law n° 96-06 of 22 March 1996, establishing the local authorities' code. Police auxiliaries could also be recruited once again, if necessary. For the Community Security Agency, these measures could guarantee its long term existence and avoid a situation where the concept is abandoned when President Macky Sall leaves power.

Conclusion and recommendations

In conclusion, despite its political and social stability, Senegal cannot claim that a reform of the security sector is irrelevant for this country. Indeed, the country faces real external threats related to its geopolitical situation, in an environment characterised by fragile states to the south and the upsurge of jihadist terrorism to the north and east. The institutional and legal environment also needs to evolve to adapt to the concept of human security, which mobilises new stakeholders.

The initiatives taken by the regime that assumed power after the last presidential and parliamentary elections in 2012 are thus very welcome. They have sought to reform existing institutions to ensure that the powers of the executive branch in the area of defence and security are shared, that control is enhanced and more formal and that public security policies are rationalised. The moves to organise and equip the forces must continue because a secure environment is a prerequisite for any development policy. We must not lose sight of the fact that years of investment and sacrifices can be swept away in just a few days. The examples of Mali and, more recently, the Central African Republic are a rather eloquent confirmation of the fact that security should be a priority investment sector.

All that is needed now is for these good intentions to be translated into concrete action. This would require a more formal structure for an overall security sector reform process, which would make it possible for all the initiatives undertaken to be coordinated within a framework that includes all sectors. Thus, oversight institutions, parliamentary representatives, the legal system and policy makers, as well as other stakeholders will be able to contribute in a coordinated manner to meeting the security needs of the population, in compliance with existing laws and regulations. In practical terms, a number of texts will need to be adopted to structure national defence and security in a way that allows for broad participation of new players in defining, implementing and controlling public security policy. There is a need for improved coordination of implementing bodies, through the establishment of frameworks for planning and conducting operational activities. In a sub-region that is characterised by long-standing conflictual relations between the armed forces and political authorities, Senegal is the exception. The republican nature of the armed forces is grounded on legal principles and embodied by officers of all ranks. Far from being a simple slogan, it is amply demonstrated through numerous daily acts.

Nevertheless, while Senegal may not need to officially engage in a security sector reform programme, it still faces major challenges in security sector governance. These challenges must be openly acknowledged in order to generate synergy among the various initiatives undertaken in different sectors and identify those areas that have not yet been tackled.

Notes

[1] 'Benno Book Yaakar' is Wolof for 'United in the same hope'. This coalition was made up mainly of Moustapha Niasse's Alliance des Forces de Progrès

Macky Sall's Alliance pour la République and the Socialist Party led by Ousmane Tanor Dieng.

2 An ethnic group representing 9% of the Senegalese population and made up of various sub-groups (Diouf 1994).

CHAPTER 8

Conclusion: Learning the Lessons from West African Experiences of Security Sector Governance

Alan Bryden* and Fairlie Chappuis†

*Assistant Director and Head of Public-Private Partnerships Division at the Geneva Centre for the Democratic Control of Armed Forces (DCAF)

†Programme Manager within the Research Division at the Geneva Centre for the Democratic Control of Armed Forces (DCAF)

Introduction

Security sector reform (SSR) in Africa has been accompanied by both a strong critique and an uncomfortable reality. The critique characterizes internationally-supported SSR as externally generated and driven, dislocated from African realities and needs (Donais, Halden and Egnell). The uncomfortable reality is that an agenda to promote greater oversight and accountability of the security sector is not and has not been attractive to many African political and security elites (Bryden and Olonisakin 9 – 10). Arguably, exogenous and endogenous concerns over SSR in Africa are two sides of the same coin; they reflect the costs of approaches that pay only lip service to democratic security sector governance. While legitimate critiques need to be taken seriously, there is a risk of doing more harm than good if the central insight that underpins the SSR discourse is obscured: good governance of the security sector is a key enabler for wider progress. Indeed, the key message emerging from this volume is that a failure to understand, acknowledge and address dysfunctional security sector governance not only undermines SSR (whether labeled as such or not) but generates wider, negative impacts on prospects for security, development and democracy.

How to cite this book chapter:

Bryden, A and Chappuis, F. 2015. Conclusion: Learning the Lessons from West African Experiences of Security Sector Governance. In: Bryden, A and Chappuis, F (eds.) *Learning from West African Experiences in Security Sector Governance*, Pp. 139–156. London: Ubiquity Press. DOI: http://dx.doi.org/10.5334/bau.h. License: CC-BY 4.0.

In each of the six narratives collected in this volume, national experts examine the micro-dynamics behind specific moments that make up larger reform processes, shedding light on the enabling or constraining factors that shape specific efforts to alter the landscape of security sector governance. The accounts provided by the authors represent a balancing act between contextual layering and detailed process analysis. Both elements are important. An appreciation of historical and political framing conditions is essential to understanding opportunities and constraints on reform. At the same time, the focus on specific reform moments and key actors generates practical lessons through considering reform processes from the inside out.

This concluding chapter considers the lessons that can be drawn from these selected African experiences in security sector governance. It begins by offering an analysis based on a comparative reading of the six narratives, seeking to identify typical structural conditions and patterns that have conditioned reform efforts. Drawing on this analysis, a number of key lessons for the promotion of democratic security sector governance are identified, including specific implications for international support to SSR. Finally, potential opportunities are considered for national actors to lead governance-focused reform processes in West Africa.

Unpacking the micro-dynamics of security sector governance

The six examples of reform recounted in this volume are not directly comparable in the sense of conventional comparative analysis. They focus on different historical periods and vary in scope from broader perspectives on national SSR processes over a given period (Guinea, Mali and Senegal) to more specific analyses of change processes in security sector institutions and what this tells us about wider security sector governance dynamics (Ghana, Liberia, Nigeria).

Beyond the structural differences that tend to distinguish Anglophone and Francophone governance structures,[1] each context has experienced its own distinct trajectory of social, economic and political development. Today, Ghana, Nigeria and Senegal are regional power houses while Guinea, Liberia and Mali deal with the consequences of recent conflict and political upheaval. This diversity masks the similarities these narratives share and it is only in looking through the lens of iterative and gradual governance reform that these commonalities become clear. In particular, reform in all these accounts took place in the context of legacies of security governance that had established security as a reserved domain for elite political and security actors and perpetuated adversarial relations between security services and the executive; between the executive and other branches of government, including the opposition; and between government and the wider public, and their representatives in civil society. Thus, despite the variety of political and institutional configurations across the six examples, all share similar problems: an institutional landscape of reserved domains in the security services, strong executives, weak legislatures, co-opted judiciaries, and confrontational relationships between the state and civil society. This section explores the implications of these pathologies of dysfunctional security sector governance from the perspective of reform as an iterative and gradual process.

Security as a reserved domain

Across the variety of national experiences evoked in these six chapters, treatment of security affairs has traditionally been restricted to the highest ranks of the security services and elite civilian governance actors. Since this trait is most directly associated with autocratic or dictatorial rule, it is all the more remarkable to find that the tendency to reserve security for elite control figures so prominently whether in the transition context of Guinea, democratizing contexts of Nigeria or post-war Liberia, the consolidating democracies of Ghana or Mali, and even the established democracy of Senegal. Reserved domains had three distinct effects on the wider security sector governance environment: first, the political class beyond the presidential circle found little interest in discussing, or attempting to influence security decision-making; second, it created a wall between the security services and popular concerns over security; and third, it generated a climate of suspicion among security 'insiders' over any role for perceived domestic 'outsiders' in security sector governance. These deeply entrenched attitudes created barriers to change because privileged elites failed to recognize the need for or possible benefits of reform, while potential reform constituencies were disenfranchised through the absence of entry points for engagement.

In terms of the structural conditions of security sector governance, the immediate implication was that the margin for action in favour of reform was highly restricted in each case. This demonstrates that if security institutions principally serve the interests of regime security, little political space will be ceded for other stakeholders to fulfil legitimate roles and responsibilities regardless of their constitutional or otherwise formal authority to do so. In these circumstances, the security sector is not responsive to public security needs, nor inclusive of representative voices from across the population, and fails to win trust and legitimacy through practices of participation or transparency. Thus in Mali, Moulaye tellingly points out that no public documents on security were issued prior to 2009. Even in Senegal, with a history of republican armed and security forces, defence secrecy is a common argument deployed to stop discussion of security matters in its tracks. This culture of secrecy, deeply entrenched in all the contexts, can be linked to the tradition of treating security as a sovereign imperative, by the state and for the state, instead of a matter of public service provision in the interests of the population. Institutionally, this tendency frequently expresses itself in the dominance of the President's office in security affairs, and the exclusion of oversight actors and institutions regardless of their formal roles and responsibilities.

Across all six narratives a common theme resulting from the dynamic of reserved domains was the fact that political and security elites failed to recognise the roles, responsibilities and rights of other stakeholders in security sector governance. By the same token, public governance actors displayed little sense of their own relevance in ensuring effective management and oversight of the security sector. Weak parliamentary and judicial branches thus failed to provide a counterbalance to the executive. On the one hand, informal influences prevented the exercise of authority as it was formally distributed: the real power brokers were not necessarily those assigned power by the 'rules on paper' that defined the formal arrangements of security sector governance. On the other hand, it is also relevant that populations as well as security and political elites themselves had no experience of any other type of political culture on which to imagine a different way of doing things. This lack of an alternative vision for security helps to explain how opportunities for change could be neglected, overlooked or easily missed even when structural conditions might allow the exercise of formal authority in favour of better security sector governance.

Complex power dynamics shape the relationships between political and security elites. Regime security imperatives lead to inter- and intra-institutional distortions in the security sector. This is a result of executive authorities seeking to protect themselves through balancing different actors and interests. As examples of the former, in Ghana the police was reinforced as a counter-balance to the military whereas in Guinea the police was subordinate to and under-resourced in comparison with the military. Intra-institutional meddling by the executive in the form of promotions and preferment along ethnic or regional lines in order to preserve authority figures at different times in all of these national narratives except Senegal. Yet in this jockeying for position, opportunities for reform could also be created when occasionally an imbalance of power or a moment of shift softened structural constraints on reform. At such moments, reform-minded individuals could exercise influence in favour of better governance. If not resulting in an instant transformation, such small steps held at least the potential to become significant in a chain of events that might lead ultimately to substantive improvements. For example, in Liberia, apparently modest efforts by new parliamentarians to exercise their powers of oversight and control in the face of a traditionally dominant executive over time helped to create a new precedent in executive-legislative relations over security matters. This shift was marked by many small firsts, each of which alone might appear insignificant but which developed into a pattern of improved security sector governance: for the first time security officials were summoned to account before the responsible legislative committees; for the first time the bill for a major new piece of the national security architecture was put to public hearing before being signed into law; for the first time civil society input on the legislative draft was sought; for the first time legislators sought access to and input on the executive's plans for defence reform. Whether or not these moments of potential change become missed opportunities or small evolutions depends at once on the individuals involved and the specific configuration of the power balance which they sought to change, again emphasizing the importance of understanding the micro-dynamics of security sector governance.

Civil-military relations characterized by exclusion and mistrust create incentives for powerful actors to stall reform agendas. As Moulaye demonstrates, in Mali, these dynamics permitted security sector elites undue influence on policy decisions, demonstrated by the fact that vested interests in the defence services were able to stall and eventually halt completely the defence reform process in 2005. While in principle the executive held all the cards in determining security policy (and the shape of SSR), in practice the security sector could exercise an indirect veto on reform agendas. Yet at the same time, as evident in the narratives where change was brought about by reform-minded security officials in the context of pacted military transitions, this indirect veto could also be turned to the purposes of reform. Bangoura describes how General Konaté in Guinea could guide the transition because he was able to use his vested interests in the defence sector to push the institution towards a withdrawal from politics. Similarly, in Nigeria, Obasanjo as both a military insider but also an elected president made use of his vested interests as a resource for reform.

If it is evident that the nature of reserved domains means that individuals within the security and political elite wield undue influence sometimes in favour of reform but most often in their own interest, then another manifestation of this dynamic is that security sector reform can become captive to other, unrelated political agendas. Under the Obasanjo administration in Nigeria, momentum for reform of the military was lost when the President tried to overturn the constitution by seeking a 3rd term in office. The resulting tensions between the executive and legislative meant that pressure for military reform waned and many hard-fought gains were lost when the wrangling over the presidential terms stymied efforts to enact relevant new legislation and constitutional amendments. As Aiyede notes, subsequent heads of state confined their role to controlling the appointment of senior positions until Boko Haram forced SSR back onto the national agenda. A similar dynamic was perhaps narrowly avoided in the transition from single to multi-party democracy in Senegal, when Wade's desire to remain in office threatened unprecedented instability. If ultimately this fate was avoided with the peaceful transition to new leadership under Macky Sall, this only reinforces the point that where security is treated as a reserved domain it is captive to the vagaries of political competition, which can work both against and in favour of better security sector governance.

Executive dominance in security matters

A further commonality among each of the narratives is that support for reform at the level of the executive has been a determining factor (or at least disproportionately important) in how far and how fast reforms progressed in practice. Examples where progress was made quickly over a short period were characterized by strong leadership from reform champions who either enjoyed delegated authority from the head of state or were able to fill a power vacuum resulting from transition to advance their agenda. This was the case with Guinea, under the leadership of the transitional government; in Senegal, when the new president threw his political weight behind policy development; and in Mali, when the responsible minister moved quickly to allay criticisms of police behaviour by initiating reforms. The influence of support at the executive level showed that change could come suddenly and reach surprisingly far where the full weight of a dominant executive was bent on achieving change.

Naturally the inverse is also true: thus the importance of top level political will is confirmed by the fact that reform processes stalled or suffered reversals when executive support was withdrawn. If it may seem obvious that SSR is unlikely to succeed where the executive is not prepared to stake its political capital, it should be noted that subtleties of resistance emerged, taking the form of more nuanced forms than the straight-forward rejection of the SSR agenda. Tactics for back-tracking on commitments included linking reform in one area to reform in another, effectively making the whole process hostage to particular interests (as the analysis of stalled defence reform in Mali shows); declining to translate pronouncements and political commitments in favour of SSR into concrete reform projects (as in Senegal since 2013); or implementing a strategic slow-down in reform such that progress is held back to the point of stalling altogether (for example, in Guinea in the face of a volatile political environment after the 2010 transition was completed).

A qualitatively different but no less real problem of executive dominance lies in the reliance on key individuals. Thus, the commitment of President Sirleaf to the Liberian reform process needs to be backed up by the establishment of strong institutions that can sustain this process beyond her term in office. Even in Liberia, where unprecedented efforts have been made to reinforce institutions, the culture of strong presidential rule can be found in the extra-budgetary authority utilised by the President and the reticence to give up the practice of presidential appointments which extends networks of patronage deep into the operative levels of security sector management. The influence of strong reformist figures is also evident in the examples of Kofi Abrefa Busia in Ghana whose leadership and advocacy was the determining factor behind the creation of meaningful control and oversight of the police through the initial establishment of the Police Council. Similarly during his early terms in office, Obasanjo proved that extensive changes could be made quickly in Nigeria. Yet in both Ghana and Nigeria the problem of the reliance on key individuals is aptly demonstrated. In both cases, once these key actors were removed from political office (Busia) or withdrew their support (Obasanjo), reform momentum faltered immediately.

The withdrawal of executive support may also reflect a failure to appreciate the gravity of what is at stake. In Mali during the period under study, it is possible that executive authorities simply did not fully appreciate the danger to which an unaccountable and ineffective security sector left the state exposed. This demonstrates that if reform is least challenging during periods of stability and peace, it also less pressing. Building momentum for reform in the face of a hypothetical threat is more difficult than when presented with a clear and present danger to the security of the state. Clearly articulating the threat to national security posed by dysfunctional security sector governance could thus offer opportunities to reinforce political will: events in Mali since 2012, and in northern Nigeria since the resurgence of Boko Haram, amply illustrate the dangers that exist and in both countries have led to renewed calls for security sector reform.

Inadequate security sector oversight and accountability

Each of the narratives presented in this volume emphasize the limited space available for democratic oversight of the security sector. It is also clear that there is little or no culture of challenging the pre-eminent role played by political and security elites. It is therefore essential to manage expectations around change processes. As Sayndee points out, efforts to promote democratic security sector governance in Liberia over the past decade need to be set against a culture of regime-focused security that stretches back to the origins of the Liberian state. If this trend goes back longer in Liberia than elsewhere in the region, the same could still be said for the other states addressed in this volume.

Weak parliaments failed to offer an effective counter-balance to the influence of the executive. In Guinea and Mali, the parliament is characterised as a "rubber stamp" institution, offering unconditional and uncritical support to executive initiatives, failing to perform its oversight function, and not making use of legal authority to review, amend and initiate legislation. Without a credible parliament, reforms are vulnerable to retrenchment in the event of a change in political leadership. For this reason, according to Cissé, in Senegal despite some improvements in parliamentary capacity, a parliament that is inexperienced in security matters is still considered vulnerable to executive influence. Yet at the same time, the inverse is also true: Liberia's experience demonstrates that a parliament that can improve its performance even in a piecemeal fashion can nevertheless make substantive contributions to improving security sector governance.

Civil society has been the strongest and most vocal advocate for security sector reforms. The essential operative role played by civil society in giving voice to and channelling public discontent underlines their importance as change agents in reform processes. Beyond the pressure generated through advocacy, a significant role has been played by civil society in injecting new thinking into security debates. In Senegal, Guinea and Mali, progress was achieved when the non-governmental sector was able to come together in a structured platform to lobby constructively, creating essential pressure to make SSR a priority. The fact that civil society was able to play this role on security issues was new to each context. In Guinea, the consultation of civil society on security matters was unprecedented in the history of the country and played an important role in introducing new ideas and perspectives. In Mali, SSR was in part a response to popular criticism of the performance of the security services, with civil society framing the security debate for the first time from a human security perspective. In Senegal, Cissé argues that civil society pressure for improved security provision, in conjunction with wider agendas for political and economic change, represented a contributing factor to only the second democratic transition in the 54 years since Senegal's independence.

The potentially determinant role that civil society can play in promoting reform is demonstrated in their contribution to national dialogues in Mali, Liberia and Guinea. Through these national dialogue processes, civil society became a resource for the reform agenda. This included providing direct feedback on people's security needs; constituting a de facto accountability mechanism holding governments to deliver on reform promises they had openly and publicly committed to; and finally as a public relations measure, enhancing state legitimacy and trust through public consultation but also managing expectations by sharing information.

Violence and conflict as reform 'triggers'

Some of the narratives emphasise crucial reform moments as a result of the status quo being upended by incidents involving violent abuse or repression by the security services. In these examples, a strong public reaction catalysed the political agenda for reform. Such events constitute moments that can soften structural constraints on reform, making change not only possible but occasionally politically necessary. At such junctures, the availability, attitude and ability of specific actors can have a determinant effect on whether a moment of crisis translates into momentum for reform or only a brief rupture in the status quo. In Guinea, abuse by security services provoked public demand for change that contributed directly to making SSR a political priority during the 2010 transition. In Mali, the violent reaction of the security services to riots following a 2005 football match created public demand for improved security provision that was not satisfied by the replacement of senior security officials. In Senegal, incidents of repression by the security services during operations in the Casamance led to changes to the overall approach taken by the military in the region. While the primary objective of SSR should be understood from the perspective of preventing conflict, the opportunity offered by such catalytic moments to garner political will for reforms needs to be recognised. As discussed above, where civil society is well organised, a moment that galvanizes public demand for reform is more likely to become a platform for change.

Threats to state integrity and national security can also act as trigger events or catalytic moments. In the first instance, such threats can create barriers to reform. Armed challenges to state authority, originating either internally or from beyond national borders, provide increased political room for manoeuvre to argue that reforms re-orienting security management and oversight could compromise national security. Security threats can make it easier to co-opt reform agendas, including by exaggerating the risks and underselling the benefits of SSR. The scope for SSR in the context of threats to national security is therefore linked directly to the problem of reserved domains. At the same time, threats to national security may also sap public demand for reform by mobilizing fear of change at a moment when populations may feel vulnerable. The same dynamic can occur in the face of increased crime whereby a population may prefer a heavy-handed approach to policing even at the cost of political, civil and human rights because they perceive it to be countering a legitimate threat that requires a tough response. Yet at the same time, a threat to national security may lay bare deficiencies in national security and thus security sector governance and in this way can become a catalytic influence on reform. Considering Boko Haram in Nigeria sheds further light on these important dynamics because the threat to national security posed by this insurgent group was used by vested interests in the military to demand budget increases and to resist reform. However, as public frustration with the ineffective response to this threat grew, countering Boko Haram came to be seen as a major reason for the military to submit to reform with an increasingly vocal public constituency mobilizing on this issue. A similar dynamic is also illustrated in Mali as the state security forces struggled to respond to the threat from insurgents in the North of the country.

Enabling governance-driven reform processes

What do the micro-dynamics of security sector governance tell us about an enabling environment for reform processes? Drawing on the rich narratives of these six chapters, this section considers approaches that can contribute to effective, sustainable SSR and proposes 'signposts' for their implementation.

Fostering dialogue on security sector governance

The roles, responsibilities and rights of different stakeholders are often unclear or disputed throughout the reform process, and as a result, every step is unnecessarily contentious. For security services reform may appear as a threat to their position, status and expertise, to say nothing of their livelihood or even their freedom where they face the prospect of transitional justice. The generalised lack of trust between different stakeholders in the contexts considered in this volume underlines the importance of building a shared understanding of what reform means, addressing the potential benefits and dangers it holds. This point is reinforced by the fact that failed attempts at SSR can be found in the history of every country covered in this volume: the experience of failure only increases the need for a shared vision of realistic and feasible change in the terms of security sector governance.

Histories of adversarial relations between the state, security services and citizens makes constructive engagement difficult and can lead to cycles of escalation. In each account, changes that occurred in the context of controlled democratic openings stalled when cardinal interests felt threatened, suggesting that security services and political elites did not share an understanding of their own interests in reform but saw change as a threat. Certainly moves towards more democratic security sector governance often require culture change within the security sector. Discussing new ideas in order to allay fears and build support is essential groundwork in order to carry a change process forward. Support to SSR should therefore focus on creating strategic opportunities for trust-building and engagement. Dialogue reduces the uncertainty associated with change and eases the way for reform-minded actors to seek out compromise solutions.

Engagement with civil society on security matters is an essential part of a meaningful dialogue around security sector governance. Indeed, the singular importance of civil society actors in promoting SSR and contributing to its momentum suggests the role of these actors in early stages of SSR is not sufficiently integrated into national political strategies or international support. However, this is not without risk, since civil society is not always or only a constructive partner in reform. From the perspective of security 'insiders', it is easy to characterise civil society advocacy as motivated by a desire to control or restrain security services, highlighting alleged abuses and seeking to limit their resources and operational remit. Certainly, in Nigeria the military rejected opportunities to engage with civil society both because this would result in 'humiliation' and because of a deeply rooted conviction that only the military is equipped to deal with military affairs. Again, from an 'insider' perspective, resistance is exacerbated by the apparently disproportionate significance of civil society 'outsiders' in promoting SSR.

These factors point to the need for bridge-building that can situate the respective roles of government and non-state actors, as well as intra-security sector relationships within a coherent approach to state and human security. This problem reflects the fact that attempted reforms did not take into account the rights of security personnel or emphasise the benefits that accrue to security institutions through improved effectiveness and accountability. Instead, SSR was perceived as placing new and sometimes controversial obligations on security services. Attempts to make these links in SSR initiatives were either incomplete or unsuccessful, suggesting a need for a deeper contextual understanding of inter- and intra-institutional dynamics.

Signposts for successful dialogue-driven interventions include:

- Security is 'demystified': there is increased public dialogue / debate on security, reducing fear and mistrust;
- A broad constituency of actors is engaged, creating bridges across different branches of government, the security sector as well as civil society and media;
- Discussion does not start with pre-conceptions about the objectives of reform but rather focuses on the vision and norms of the security sector, before addressing actual reform propositions;
- Communication is an integral part of the reform process: a public relations strategy should raise awareness and improve public understanding, while carefully managing expectations;
- Dialogue is not a one off but is sustained over an extended period, giving time for ideas to be shared and considered in depth, and for knowledge to spread.

Creating a shared understanding of risks and benefits

It is unrealistic to ask individuals to stake their personal future and well-being on a process that only vaguely defines what it aims to achieve and how. Strategic policies need to be translated into operational plans that lay bare the new direction of the security sector and allow each actor to understand their roles in concrete terms. This requires a long process of confidence-building based simply on talking through concepts and reform possibilities in pursuit of common understandings.

Supporting initiatives that emphasise the rights as well as the obligations of security services in an atmosphere of mutual respect is a first step towards correcting these tendencies, which have otherwise proved so damaging to reform efforts. Such approaches involve managing expectations. Emphasising the increased legitimacy for the security services which higher standards of professionalism and service delivery can generate, should be an integral element of SSR. At the same time, it is often the case that the public has unrealistic expectations both of SSR as a process, and the roles and responsibilities of security sector actors. Managing expectations and raising awareness about the respective roles, responsibilities and rights of actors on all sides will help to overcome and correct the imbalances that mistrust and unequal power relations breed.

Lack of resources is a common grievance within security institutions, leading to strong claims for force modernization, new equipment and improved conditions of service as evidenced in the accounts of security sector demands in Guinea, Mali, Nigeria and Senegal. Measures to support the effectiveness of security providers can incentivize wider reforms. Opportunities to contextualize improvements in effectiveness with improvements in accountability can be realised if the means and ends of modernisation are made the subject of public discussion. During the transition in Guinea, technical measures to improve conditions for the defence and security forces were an important first step in drawing them into a wider reform process. A similar dynamic unfolded in Nigeria, becoming a key link between reformist elements in the military leadership and the wider government. The subject of force modernization also offers the opportunity to initiate a public discussion on the vision for security and the means for achieving it. Consultative processes linked to national security policy development were effective at contextualising these types of discussions in Guinea, Liberia and Mali. Such dialogues can also be effective in ensuring that force modernization becomes part of a larger SSR process that tackles accountability as well as effectiveness: making this link is essential to ensuring that force modernization contributes to improved security sector governance.

One of the reasons that force modernization issues may stand at odds with better security sector governance is that security institutions often fail to recognise how SSR can serve their own interests. Fear of increased accountability and democratic civilian control can generate resistance and opposition within security institutions. This resistance may be based on an assessment of personal and corporatist interest, or instead reflect a truly different vision of the role of the security sector in a state. In either case, dialogue about the form, function and motivations for better security sector governance is essential to ensuring that security institutions become productive champions of the reform process instead of spoilers.

Signposts that can show the development of common understandings include:

- Inclusive national security policy processes create shared understandings of the roles and responsibilities of different security sector actors;
- Civil society engages with security services in a non-adversarial manner, creating a positive dynamic towards more openness and better service provision;
- SSR processes address the rights as well as the obligations of security sector personnel;
- Activities that address force modernization needs are linked to initiatives that reinforce oversight and accountability.

Binding constituencies into reform processes

In each narrative the most promising moments for reform provided for more inclusive public dialogue processes, either as one-off initiatives (the *Etats généraux de la Sécurité et de la Paix* held in Mali in 2005); as part of a political process (the election of a new president in Senegal); or through transitional institutions (the engagement of the *Conseil national de Transition* on SSR in Guinea or the Governance Reform Commission in Liberia). Reform faltered when consensus around a shared vision broke down, or the path to reform was too vague to follow with adequate accountability.

Broadening the shared vision of what reform is and what it should achieve is helpful even if discussions include only elite actors as a first step – for example, parliamentarians, executive staff and security services. Reforms will be better sustained if entry points can go beyond the usual SSR constituencies: extending from core security oversight bodies, to include other actors such as state finance authorities and independent oversight institutions with broad responsibilities in anti-corruption or defence of human rights, for example. The engagement of human rights advocates has often been catalytic at different junctures of the process.

The importance of civil society as a potential change agent is magnified by the relative weakness of other institutionalized systems of oversight (especially the parliament and the judiciary). Because these formal institutions are often under-capacitated and dominated by executive influence, the informal and public oversight that civil society can offer becomes disproportionately important compared to their formal role. In an example that is both significant and rare, Aiyede describes how a human rights lawyer, Festus Keyamo, obtained a high court judgement challenging the unconstitutional practice of the President appointing service chiefs without the approval of the National Assembly. This led to the President referring the 2014 appointments back to the Senate, showing how formal and informal oversight functions can be mutually reinforcing. Tensions between this process of formalisation and the continued existence of reserved domains can also be seen in the horse trading around the 2008 National Defence Act in Liberia, or in the stalling of defence reform in Mali. The contested nature of these processes illustrates that a constitutional or legal basis provides an important reference point for security sector roles and responsibilities.

The different ways that political will can be withdrawn points to the need for clear and public reform plans against which executive authorities can be held publicly accountable for lack of progress. In the best-case scenario, this shared vision of security sector governance should be articulated in a public statement of reform goals, and if possible, steps to be taken over a specified time-frame. Creating and sharing such a joint vision of change may also prevent reversals and backsliding, by providing a clear benchmark against which progress – and the lack of it – can be clearly measured.

Signposts that show constituencies being bound into reform processes include:

- Conversations around security sector governance extend beyond the usual suspects, who may be seen as opponents or allies of the status quo, to include different political parties, unions, and professional organisations, including private and commercial security interests; this also makes room for input from marginalised constituencies, such as youth, women's groups, and the poor;
- Structured groupings of civil society actors, such as working groups or national coalitions, allow civil society from diverse interests and backgrounds to speak with a unified voice, gaining influence through speaking from a legitimate platform;
- Parliament visibly assumes its prerogatives in the area of security sector oversight;
- A national dialogue on SSR is grounded through being directly linked to the revision or development of security policy and legislation.

Calibrating international SSR support

As discussed in the introductory chapter to this volume, the SSR approach has been frequently accompanied by large claims and unrealistic expectations. In contexts where state capacity has failed to address a resurgence of internal and cross-border conflicts, there is an increasing tendency to prescribe SSR as a stabilization tool. The narratives explored in this volume should caution against such overloading of the SSR agenda. The trust that is required in order to coax security actors to commit to reform is difficult to achieve even in stable political environments, let alone during conflict. The factors that lead to destabilisation and conflict are central to the dynamics that SSR aspires to transform, including the nature of public service provision and the legitimacy of state authority. This underlines the essentially prevention oriented nature of SSR. Ensuring that the security sector is both effective and accountable within a framework of democratic governance, rule of law and respect for human rights, provides a legitimate basis for SSR that unites both national stakeholders and international partners.

This section draws from the narratives of security sector governance set out in this volume to consider implications for international SSR support. It focuses on two key dimensions: donor approaches from a process perspective and under-emphasised vectors of SSR engagement.

Re-orienting donor approaches

A shared understanding of SSR and its potential benefits needs to be established in order to build support for reforms among constituencies that might otherwise perceive such a process as threatening. However, supporting governance-focussed SSR that can help create this kind of consensus poses a challenge for current international approaches to SSR. In the absence of actual reform activities, a defined reform agenda is frequently seen as a required sign of political commitment and good intentions. Putting aside time to talk does not offer tangible results against which donors can measure their own effectiveness and is therefore systematically undervalued. The value of confidence-building through dialogue is underrated. Simply talking about reform, without making any concrete plans, can also be seen as a way for reform spoilers to hijack reform programmes and divert reform away from a more transformative agenda. While there is some danger of this, it is also clear that discussion is the only means by which a broad-based and shared vision of change can be constructed and that without this the risk of failure increases dramatically. It is well known that SSR is controversial because it seeks to change the dynamics of power relations in the security sector. In short, it risks creating winners and losers. Translating this tension into an operational policy response means seeking out opportunities to build trust among stakeholders and foster a shared vision.

It is inherently difficult for international partners to avoid doing more harm than good when contributing to sensitive national discussions. The programme delivery mechanisms used by donors will influence the likelihood of success. Thus, sensitivity within the Nigerian military over assistance in the area of civil military relations is not only a result of the message but also the (US) messenger. Similarly, the outsourcing of the military reform process in Liberia to a private military and security company created significant problems in terms of the credibility of nascent Liberian governance institutions. In this respect, South-South cooperation in promoting reform offers a much more promising route since states that have already traversed the challenges of the reform process have both pragmatic expertise to offer and a moral authority from which to speak.

Donors often apply great pressure to make visible and early progress. A tendency exists to confuse the value of an SSR programme with its cost, meaning that more is expected of expensive SSR interventions than of comparatively less costly governance-focussed activities. This diverts focus away from identifying progress in governance, while directing more attention and much greater resources to infrastructure, training and equipment activities that privilege effectiveness over security sector governance. Based on the perspectives presented in this volume, a focus on the 'technical' elements of reform appears especially wrong-headed. The nature and scale of structural change implied in transformational SSR means that reforms focused on force capacity and equipment – often the most visible signs of change – are unlikely in isolation to herald significant shifts in the structural conditions of security governance within a state.

While the claim that "SSR is about politics" is a common-place statement in SSR policy discussions, the norms and values governing who has a say in security provision, management and oversight remain under-analysed. One aspect of this problem is the automatic linkage of buy-in from political elites to donor funding decisions. To cite just one example, in Mali, UN funding for PGPSP was cut when executive support waned. This was arguably the time when efforts should have been increased. Because power moves through deeper social structures, the reasons why formal roles and responsibilities are unheeded remain unrecognised (van Veen and Price, 2014, Hills, 2014, Schroeder and Chappuis, 2014). The emphasis on visible, tangible, outward signs of change (things that can be counted, measured, bought and paid for) exacerbates this tendency to overlook shifts in expectations, attitudes and values surrounding security provision, management and oversight. Yet these intangibles are essential elements without which there will be no change in the way that force is used and controlled by state and non-state actors.

If the preference for technical over governance-focused reform reflects the fact that what we consider success in SSR is often measured by the wrong metric, then a further example of this approach is the continuing tendency to focus on top-down aspects of institutional reform instead of starting from bottom-up experiences of security. While a nuanced understanding of elite politics is important to revealing the conduits of power within a state, the ultimate measure of success in SSR should be the subjective experience of security at the level of the population. Methodologies have not yet adequately integrated the fact that security is a subjective, inter-personal experience that interacts with political judgments about legitimacy and power as well as institutional configurations of coercive force.

Overcoming these problems requires innovative approaches that can offer new interpretations of progress and impact. Longer term engagement is needed based on a flexible SSR methodology. In terms of measurement and evaluation, much conceptual and methodological work remains to be done to develop tools that aptly capture the real value of governance-driven reform agendas. Cutting-edge qualitative methods could be applied with greater effectiveness in fragile contexts to capture changes in the indicators that actually matter such as organisational culture, modes of service delivery and public legitimacy.

Valorising 'Soft' SSR

The importance of a shared vision of security among reform constituents suggests that apparently 'soft' measures that focus on discussion, transparency and consultation may be crucial in creating openings for SSR. Creating the trust that is necessary to carry the reform process forward will require raising awareness of reform concepts, building networks among reform constituencies, and sensitizing actors on all sides to different perspectives and security needs.

Support for improved security sector oversight remains under-emphasised and under-resourced. Parliamentary capacity development remains a priority area of SSR activity that could benefit from a stronger institutional focus: in concrete terms this suggests focussing on parliamentary support, including staff development and committee functions, as well as individual representatives and engagement with civil society and the media. Training for media and government staff on security issues is essential. This could mean involving media in the process of discussion as well as providing training on responsible reporting for government and media.

The reform processes considered in this volume often failed to translate rhetorical commitments to SSR into concrete improvements in institutional governance arrangements or improvements in security service provision. While on the surface this may look like a case of too much talk and not enough action, in fact the reverse is true. Reform faltered at junctures where key constituencies within the security sector felt their interests were threatened. The sense of threat was in part based on flawed understandings of how SSR could affect their interests. A shared vision of how the security services stand to benefit from improved accountability and professionalism needs to be established early on in order to defuse a confrontation of interests before it arises.

Creating a shared vision for security sector governance needs to be based on a nuanced understanding of security threats and reform priorities. As evident across the national narratives, state-centric approaches are out of touch with the reality of security provision since the state is not the only, nor in many cases the most important security provider, nor is it the most trusted. A realistic assessment of reform needs is impossible without an understanding of how non-state security providers are meeting generalised needs for security in the absence of a people-centred state security sector.

At least two different facets to the privatisation of security are directly relevant to SSR: on the one hand, community-based non-state security and justice providers organise themselves in various ways to meet the self-protection needs of the communities they stem from; while on the other hand, commercial security providers, of both national and international origin, supply security on a market basis to those with the means to pay for it. These two groups represent different facets of the privatisation phenomenon but both are essential in understanding how to reform the security sector because they exist at least in part as a result of the state's failure to provide sufficient security for the population. Their activities in turn have a direct effect on the nature of public security provision and the relative legitimacy of the state as security provider. No SSR programme can realistically aspire to improve human security without accounting for both types of non-state security actor.

Conclusion

SSR is no longer a new agenda; it is necessary to reflect on shortcomings and to identify innovations in the approach and its application. While the results of reform efforts may be judged underwhelming, the fault may lie less with the results themselves than the analytical tools at our disposal for understanding and interpreting them. While no one would claim that West Africa's nations no longer suffer the dysfunctions that first made SSR relevant to the region, it would also be a mistake to claim that no progress has been made. Instead an analysis based on a revaluation of what matters in SSR and what it looks like in practice, yields a distinctly more nuanced picture. This collection of local narratives has sought to provide such a perspective through the lens of six unique moments in long and uncertain trajectories of change.

The time is right to critically evaluate current approaches to SSR in order to maximize its contribution to wider security, development and democracy promotion discourses. Indeed, good governance of all aspects of public service delivery is a cross-cutting theme of the post-2015 agenda for development. Through emphasising the need to build peaceful inclusive societies based on access to justice and effective, accountable institutions, the framework of the Sustainable Development Goals offers an important opportunity to promote a holistic SSR approach. Although the goals are universal, the pathways to achieving them are not: success will be defined by whether we are able to understand the specific realities of distinct reform contexts. It will depend on collectively maintaining a commitment to good governance, human rights and democracy.

As this volume has sought to demonstrate, unpacking the micro-dynamics of security sector governance is essential if national actors and international partners are to develop partnerships that are context-sensitive, based on trust and respectful of local ownership. These realities need to be recognized in order to seize reform opportunities and understand constraints. Despite the challenges described throughout this volume, the overall message emerging from these narratives is by no means negative. If it is clear that the political space for reform is limited, under-exploited channels do exist to create such space. We hope that these narratives of security sector governance in West Africa provide a basis to reflect, learn and seize such opportunities.

Notes

1 For more on these distinctions, see Bagayoko (2010: 279–298).

Reference List

Accra Agenda For Action 2008 Third High Level Forum on Aid Effectiveness. Accra: Ghana.

Acemoglu, D and **Robinson, J** 2012 *Why nations fail: the origins of power, prosperity, and poverty. Crown Business.*

Adejumobi, S *1999 Demilitarisation and the Search for Democratic Stability in Nigeria. Nigeria: The Republic of Nigeria.* Available at http://unpan1.un.org/intradoc/groups/public/documents/CAFRAD/UNPAN009003.PDF [Last accessed 12 August 2015].

Adejuwon, L 2014 Emergency rule extension and politics of 2015. National Mirror, 6 December.

Adekanye, J B 1997 The military in transition. In: Diamond, J L, Kirk-Greene, A H M and Oyediran, O (eds.) *Transition without End: Nigerian politics and civil society under Babangida.* Ibadan: Vantage Publishers. pp. 33–66.

Adekson, J B 1979 Dilemma of military disengagement. In: Oyediran, O (ed.) *Nigerian Government and politics under military rule, 1966–1979.* London: Macmillan.

Adeniyi, O 2011 *Power, politics and death: A front-row account of Nigeria under the late President Yar' Adua.* Lagos: Kachifo Limited.

Adesina, J 1995 *Labour in the Explanation of an African Crisis.* Dakar: CODESRIA.

Adu-Amanfo, F 2014 *The Roles of Peace and Security, Political Leadership, and Entrepreneurship in the Socio-Economic Development of Emerging Countries: A Compendium of Lessons Learnt from Sub-Saharan Africa.* Bloomington: AuthorHouse.

African Union Commission 2013 African Union Policy Framework on Security Sector Reform. Addis Ababa: African Union.

Agbambu, C 2014. Criticism dampening soldiers morale. *Nigerian Tribune,* 14 August, p. 8.

Aiyede, E R 2013 Parliament, Civil Society and Military Reform in Nigeria. In: Rüland, J, Manea, M, Born, H (eds.) *The Politics of Military Reform: Experiences from Indonesia and Nigeria.* New York: Springer. pp. 161–184.

Akinlotan, I 2014 Desertion, Boko Haram: Nigeria's fragility underscored. The Nation, 31 August, p. 80.

Akinloye, B 2014 Nigerian military uncooperative, slow to learn-US hearing. The Punch, 13 July, p. 1.

Alaga, E and **Akum, R** 2013 Civil-Military Relations and Democratic Consolidation in Nigeria: Issues and Challenges. In: Blair, D (ed.) 2013 *Military Engagement: Influencing Armed Forces Worldwide to Support Democratic Transitions (Volume Two: Regional and Country Studies).* Washington, DC: Brookings Institution Press. pp. 215–235.

Albrecht, P and **Jackson, P** 2009 Security System Transformation in Sierra Leone 1997–2007. Report commissioned for the UK Government Global Conflict Prevention Pool.

Altbeker, A 2005 The dirty work of democracy: A year on the streets with the SAPS. Jonathan Ball Publishers,

Amnesty International 2012 *Nigeria: Trapped in the cycle of violence.* London: Amnesty International. London: Amnesty International.

Amnesty International 2014 Nigeria: Gruesome footage implicates military in war crimes. *Amnesty International,* 5 August. Available at http://www.amnesty.org/en/news/nigeria-gruesome-footage-implicates-military-war-crimes-2014-08-05 [Last accessed 12 August 2015].

Anderson, L 2006 *Post-Conflict security sector reform and the challenge of ownership-the case of Liberia.* DIIS Brief. Copenhagen, Denmark: Danish Institute for International Studies (DIIS).

Aning, K and **Lartey, E** 2008 Parliamentary Oversight of the Security Sector: Lessons from Ghana. Available at http://www.agora-parl.org/sites/default/files/lessons_from_ghana.pdf [Last accessed 13 August 2015].

Aning, K 2004 Investing in peace and security in Africa: the case of ECOWAS. Conflict, Security & Development, 4.

Aning, K 2008a Ghana. In: Adedeji, E and N'Diaye, B (eds.) *Parliamentary Oversight of the Security Sector in West Africa: Opportunities and Challenges.* Geneva: Geneva Centre for the Democratic Control of Armed (DCAF). pp. 117–121.

Aning, K 2008b Managing the security sector in Ghana. In: Agyeman-Duah, B and Fawundu, A S (eds.) *Understanding Good Governance in Ghana.* Accra: Digi Publications.

Aning, K, Birikorang, E and **Lartey, E** 2013 The Processes and Mechanisms of Developing a Democratic Intelligence Culture in Ghana. In: Davies, P H and Gustafson, K C (eds.) *Intelligence Elsewhere: Spies and Espionage outside the Anglosphere.* Washington, DC: Georgetown University Press. pp. 199–218.

Aning, K. 2002 An historical overview of the Ghana Police Service. In: Karikari K (ed.) *The Faces and Phases of the Ghana Police Service.* Accra: Media Foundation for West Africa.

Asamoah, O Y 2014 The Political History of Ghana (1950–2013): The Experience of a Non-Conformist. Bloomington: AuthorHouse.

Assistant Staff Officer of Ghana Police 1990 'The Year 1990 – An Overview' Memorandum from Assistant Staff Officer to Inspector-General of Police, 15 January 1990.

Atuguba, R 2007 The Ghana Police Service (GPS): A practical agenda for reform. *IEA Policy Analysis*, 3(1), January.

Avuyi, P 1995 Ghana Police is Sick. *Chronicle*, 10–13 August.

Bagayoko, N 2010 Similarités et differences entre les systems de de sécurité francophone et Anglophone. In: Agokla, K, Bagoyoko, N and N'Diaye, B (eds.) *La réforme des systems de sécurité et de justice en Afrique francophone*. Paris : Organisation de la Francophonie. pp. 279–298.

Bah, T 2009 *Trente ans de violence politique en Guinée (1954-1984)*. Paris: Editions L'Harmattan.

Bali, D Y 1989 The Defence of the nation. In: Tamuno, T N and Ukpabi, S C (eds.) *Nigeria Since Independence: The Civil War Years v. 6: The First 25 Years*. Ibadan: Heinemann Educational Books.

Ball, N 2001 Transforming Security Sectors: The IMF and World Bank Approaches. *Conflict, Security and Development*, 1: 45–66.

Bangoura M T 2007 Comment obtenir une véritable CENI? In: Bangoura, D, Bangoura, M T and Diop, M (eds.) *Enjeux et défis démocratiques en Guinée (février 2007–décembre 2010)*. Paris: Editions L' Harmattan.

Bangoura, M T, Bangoura, D and **Diop M** 2006 *Quelle Transition politique pour la Guinée?* Paris: Editions L'Harmattan.

Baker, J 2015 Professionalism without reform: The security sector under Yudhoyono. In: The Yudhoyono Presidency, Institute of Southeast Asian Studies, pp. 114–135.

Barker, B 1979 *Operation cold chop: A coup that toppled Nkrumah*. Tema: Ghana Publishing Corporation.

Barnes, W K G 2013 *The Flipside of Governance: Evaluation of the Authenticity of Public Administration in Liberia*. Accra: Paxi Systems.

BBC 2015 Nigeria's Boko Haram unrest: African leaders urged to act. BBC, 26 January.

Bendix, D and **Stanley, R** 2008 Security Sector Reform in Africa: The Promise and the Practice of a New Donor Approach. *ACCORD Occasional Papers Series, 3(2)*. Durban, South Africa: African Centre for the Constructive Resolution of Disputes (ACCORD).

Bojie, P J O 2011 Transformation experiences and joint-service imperatives: Nigerian army perspective. Paper presented at the workshop re-positioning the Nigerian Navy for greater effectiveness, 4–7 April. Abuja, Nigeria.

Boyes, R P A 1971 *Report on the Ghana Police Service*. Accra: Government Press.

Bright, N O 2002 Liberia: America's Stepchild. USA/Liberia: documentary film.

Bryden, A and **Hänggi, H** (eds.) 2004 *Reform and Reconstruction of the Security Sector*. Münster: Lit Verlag.

Bryden, A and **N'Diaye, B** (eds.) 2011 *Security Sector Governance in Francophone West Africa: Realities and Opportunities*. Münster: Lit Verlag.

Bryden, A and **Olonisakin, F** 2010 Conceptualising Security Sector Transformation in Africa. In: Bryden, A and Olonisakin, F (eds.) *Security Sector Transformation in Africa*. 8 ed. Münster: Lit Verlag. pp. 3–26.

Bryden, A, Olonisakin, F and **N'Diaye, B** (eds.) 2008 *Challenges of Security Sector Governance in West Africa*. Münster: Lit Verlag.

Brzoska, M 2002 *Development donors and the concept of security sector reform*. Occasional Paper No. 4. Geneva: Geneva Centre for the Democratic Control of Armed (DCAF).

Busan Partnership For Effective Development Co-Operation 2011 Fourth High Level Forum on Aid and Effectiveness. Busan: Republic of Korea.

Busia, K A 1951 *The position of the chief in the modern political system of Ashanti*. London: International African Institute.

Camara, K 1998 *Dans la Guinée de Sékou Touré: cela a bien eu lieu*. Paris: Editions L'Harmattan.

Cawthra, G and **Luckham, R** (eds.) 2003 *Governing Insecurity: Democratic Control of Military and Security Establishments in Transitional Democracies*. London: Zed Books.

Cenap/Credess-Bdi 2012 Etude en besoins de sécurité au Burundi. Bujumbura: Centre d'Alerte et de Prévention des Conflits (CENAP) et le Centre de Recherche, d'Etudes et de Documentation en Sciences Sociales (CREDESS-Bdi).

Chappuis, F and **Hänggi, H** 2009 The Interplay between Security and Legitimacy: Security Sector Reform and State-building. In: Raue, J and Sutter, P (eds.) *Facets and Practices of State-building*. Leiden: Martinus Nijhoff.

Chappuis, F and **Hänggi, H** 2013 Statebuilding through Security Sector Reform. In: Chandler, D and Sisk, T D (eds.) *Routledge Handbook of International Statebuilding*. London and New York: Routledge.

Chappuis, F and **Siegle, J** 2015 Security Sector Reform in Times of Democratic Reversal. *S+F: Sicherheit und Frieden / Security and Peace*, 33.

Collier, P 2007 *The Bottom Billion: Why the Poorest Countries are Failing and What Can be Done About It*. Oxford: Oxford University Press.

Collier, P 2010 Wars, Guns, and Votes: Democracy in Dangerous Places. New York: Harper Perennial.

Commission Africaine des Droits de l'Homme et des Peuples (CADHP) 2015 Institutions nationales des droits de l'homme. Available at http://www.achpr.org/fr/network/nhri/ [Last accessed on 13 August 2015].

Conakryka 2010 Politique – Mamadou Aliou Barry , Président de l'ONDH: «Alpha Condé est à mon avis un danger pour l'unité nationale. Blog by Ibrahima Ahmed Bah, 3 November 2010. Available at http://unbah.over-blog.com/article-politique-mamadou-aliou-barry-president-de-l-ondh-alpha-conde-est-a-mon-avis-un-danger-pour-l-unite-nationale-60216706.html [Last accessed on 13 August 2015].

Council of the European Union 2005 *EU Concept for ESDP support to Security Sector Reform (SSR)*. Brussels: Council of the European Union.

Council of the European Union 2006 *Council Conclusions on a Policy framework for Security sector reform.* Luxembourg: Council of the European Union.

Daily Graphic 2015a Police recruitment scam: 2 cops, and 3 others arrested, *Daily Graphic*, 6 March, pp. 1, 3.

Daily Graphic 2015b Police recruitment scam: Commissioner of Police interdicted. *Daily Graphic*, 7 March, pp. 1, 13.

Daily Graphic 2015c We are surprised at sophistication of recruitment scam, says police administration. *Daily Graphic*, 9 March, pp. 1, 3.

Délégation de l'Union européenne en Guinée 2013 European Union delegation in Guinea: L'UE débloque 5,24 millions d'euros pour appuyer le renforcement de la capacité de la police nationale et la réconciliation avec la population. *Communiqué de presse*, 5 June.

Diallo, S 1986 Les relations entre l'Armée, l'État et le Parti, et le problème des forces civiles (Milice, Parti). In: Bangoura, D (ed.) *Les Armées africaines.* Paris: Economica. pp. 111–117.

Diouf, M 1994 *Sénégal: Les ethnies et la nation.* Paris: Editions L'Harmattan, 1994.

Direction générale de la police nationale (DGPN) 2001 Rapport des Journées de réflexion de la police nationale, 21, 22, 23 février 2001. Bamako: DGPN, February.

Donais, T (ed.) 2008 *Local Ownership and Security Sector Reform.* Münster: Lit Verlag.

Donais, T 2009 Inclusion or Exclusion? Local Ownership and Security Sector Reform. *Studies in Social Justice*, 3: 117-131.

Halden, P and **Egnell, R** 2009 Laudable, ahistorical and overambitious: security sector reform meets state formation theory. *Conflict, Security & Development*, 9(1): 27–54. DOI: 10.1080/14678800802704903

Dudley, B J 1973 *Instability and political order: Politics and crisis in Nigeria.* Ibadan: Ibadan University Press.

Ebo, A 2005 *The Challenge and opportunities of security sector reform in post-conflict Liberia.* DCAF Occasional Paper No. 9. Geneva, Switzerland: Geneva Centre for the Democratic Control of Armed (DCAF)

Ebo, A 2008 Local Ownership and Emerging Trends in SSR: A Case Study of Outsourcing in Liberia. In: Donais, T. (ed) *Local Ownership and Security Sector Reform.* Münster: Lit Verlag.

ECOWAS 1999 *Protocol relating to the Mechanism for Conflict Prevention, Management, Resolution, Peacekeeping and Security.* Abuja: Economic Community Of West African States.

ECOWAS 2001 *Supplementary Protocol on Democracy and Good Governance.* Abuja: Economic Community Of West African States.

ECOWAS 2011 *Supplementary Act on the Code of Conduct for Armed Forces and Security Services.* Abuja: Economic Community Of West African States.

ECOWAS 2014 *Regional Framework on Security Sector Reform and Governance.* Abuja: Economic Community Of West African States.

Eghaghe, E 2014 Obanikoro advocates reforms in military. *National Mirror*, 30 May, p. 1.

Esambo Kangashe, J L 2013 *Le droit constitutionnel.* Louvain-la-Neuve, Belgique: Academia-l'Harmattan.

Falana, F 2014 Soldiers have No Business in Policing Polls. *The Punch*, 23 July.

Fall, I M 2012 *Sénégal, une démocratie « ancienne » en mal de réforme.* Dakar: AfriMAP and OSIWA.

Freunda, C and **Jaud, M** 2013 On the Determinants of Democratic Transitions, Middle East Development Journal, Volume 5, Issue 1

Fukuyama, F 2013 What Is Governance? *CGD Working Paper 314.* Washington, DC: Center for Global Development.

Galtung, J 1964 An Editorial: what is peace research? *Journal of Peace Research*, 1(1): 1–4. DOI: 10.1177/002234336400100101.

Gbelewala, K 2013 Liberia: Over 200 Retired AFL Soldiers Thrown Out of Civil Law Court. *Heritage*, 14 November.

Geneva Centre for the Democratic Control of Armed (DCAF) 2005 Summary Report of the Liberia National Dialogue on Security Sector Reform, 3–4 August 2005. Monrovia, Liberia: DCAF.

Geneva Centre for the Democratic Control of Armed Forces (DCAF) 2015 *The SSR Backgrounder Series.* Geneva, Switzerland: DCAF.

Ghana 1963 Security Service Act (Act 202).

Ghana 1965 Police Service Act (Act 284).

Ghana 1969 Constitution of the Republic of Ghana 1969.

Ghana 1970 Police Service Act (Act 350).

Ghana 1974 Police Force (Amendment) Decree (NRCD 303).

Ghana 1979 Constitution of the Republic of Ghana1979.

Ghana 1992 Constitution of the Republic of Ghana 1992.

Ghana 2012 Police Service Regulations, 2012 (C. I. 76).

Ghana Web 2013 Prez Mahama swears in new Police Council. *Ghana Web*, 12 November.

Glencourse, B 2013 Liberia: Corruption and Accountability Remain Biggest Challenges. African Arguments Blog, 16 August 2013. Available at http://africanarguments.org/2013/08/16/liberia-ten-years-on-corruption-and-accountability-remain-countrys-biggest-challenges-by-blair-glencorse/ [Last accessed 13 August 2015].

Gompert, D C, Davis, R C and **Sterns Lawson, B** 2009 *Oversight of the Liberian National Police.* Santa Monica, CA: National Defense Research Institute, RAND Corporation.

Gompert, D C, Oliker, O, Stearns Lawson, B, Crane, K and **Riley, K J** 2007 *Making Liberia Safe: Transformation of the National Security Sector.* Santa Monica, CA: National Defense Research Institute, RAND Corporation.

Greene, O and **Rynn, S** 2008 Linking and Co-ordinating DDR and SSR for Human Security after Conflict: Issues, Experience and Priorities. *Thematic Working Paper 2.* Centre for International Cooperation and Security, University of Bradford.

Guinea 2009 Décret (D/2009/001/SG/PRG/CNDD).

Guinea 2010a Constitution of the Republic of Guinea.

Guinea 2010b Décret (n°014/PRG/CNDD/SGPRG/2010).

Haggard, S and **Kaufman, R R** 1995 *The Political Economy of Democratic Transition.* Princeton NJ: Princeton University Press.

Hall, P A and **Taylor R C R** 1996 Political science and the three new institutionalisms, Political studies, 44(5), 936–957.

Halperin, M, Siegle, J and **Weinstein, M** 2010 *The Democracy Advantage: How Democracies Promote Prosperity and Peace.* London and New York: Routledge.

Hänggi, H 2003 Making Sense of Security Sector Governance. In: Hänggi, H and Winkler, T (eds.) *Challenges of Security Sector Governance.* Münster: Lit Verlag. pp. 3–23.

Hänggi, H 2004 Conceptualising Security Sector Reform and Reconstruction. In: Bryden, A and Hänggi, H (eds.) *Reform and Reconstruction of the Security Sector.* Münster: Lit Verlag. pp.3–20.

Hills, A 2014 Security Sector or Security Arena? The Evidence from Somalia. *International Peacekeeping*, 21: 165–180.

Horoya 1993a Aperçu historique sur les Forces armées guinéennes. *Horoya*, 3790, 20 December.

Horoya 1993b Aperçu historique sur les Forces armées guinéennes. *Horoya*, 3892, 31 December.

Human Rights Watch (HRW) 2013 No Money, No Justice. Police Corruption and Abuse in Liberia, 22 August. Available at http://www.hrw.org/reports/2013/08/22/no-money-no-justice-0 [Last accessed 17 August 2015].

Hutchful, E 1999 Peacekeeping under conditions of resource stringency: Ghana's army in Liberia. In: Cilliers, J and Mills, G (eds.) *From Peacekeeping to Complex Emergencies: Peace support missions in Africa.* Johannesburg and Pretoria: SAIIA and ISS. pp. 97–118.

Hutchful, E 2004 Security sector governance: Institutions, processes and challenges. Unpublished paper presented at DCAF Workshop, April 19-20. Abuja, Nigeria.

International Center for Transitional Justice (ICTJ) 2015 Liberia. Available at https://www.ictj.org/our-work/regions-and-countries/liberia [Last accessed 13 August 2015].

International Crisis Group (ICG) 2009 Liberia: Uneven progress in security sector reform. Africa Report, no.148, 13 January 2009. Available at http://www.crisisgroup.org/~/media/Files/africa/west-africa/liberia/Liberia%20

Uneven%20Progress%20in%20Security%20Sector%20Reform.pdf [Last accessed 17 August 2015].

International Crisis Group (ICG) 2014 *Curbing Violence in Nigeria (II): The Boko Haram Insurgency*. Brussels: ICG.

International Dialogue on Peacebuilding and Statebuilding 2011 A New Deal for Engagement in Fragile States. Busan, South Korea.

IRIN 2013 Despite Reforms, corruption rife among Liberian police. *IRIN News*, 11 October.

Iroegbu, M O and **Adinoyi, S** 2014 Army Begins to Take Delivery of Critical Assets in War Against Boko Haram. *This Day*, 15 July, p. 1.

Jaye, T 2006 An Assessment Report on SSR in Liberia. Report submitted to the Governance Reform Commission (GRC) of Liberia, 23 September.

Jaye, T 2008 *Liberia's Security Sector Legislation*. Münster: Lit Verlag.

Jaye, T 2009 Liberia: Parliamentary Oversight and Lessons Learned from International Security Sector Reform. Available at http://issat.dcaf.ch/content/download/10645/106742/file/Liberia_SSR.pdf [Last accessed 17 August 2015].

Joy Online 2013a Police Council to consider new procedure to appoint IGP. *Joy Online*, 12 November.

Joy Online 2013b Extending IGP's tenure could threaten internal security – Dr Aning. *Joy Online*, 13 November.

Kaba, A T 2007 Les dossiers brûlants de la Justice. In: Bangoura, D, Bangoura, M T and Diop, M (eds.) *Enjeux et défis démocratiques en Guinée (février 2007–décembre 2010)*. Paris: Editions L' Harmattan.

Kieh, G K 2008 *The first Liberian civil war*. New York: Peter Lang Publishing.

Konaté, D (ed.) 2013 *Le Mali entre doutes et espoirs: réflexions sur la nation à l'épreuve de la crise du Nord*. Bamako: Éditions Tombouctou.

Krause, K 2006 *Towards a Practical Human Security Agenda*. DCAF Policy Paper 26. Geneva: Geneva Centre for the Democratic Control of Armed Forces.

L'Observateur 2010 Discours de son Excellence le Général Sékouba Konaté, Président de la transition, Président de la République par intérim à l'occasion de l'installation solennelle du CNT. *L'Observateur*, no. 484, 15 March, p. 2.

Lesoleil 2013 Zone militaire 6: Le chef de l'Etat va renforcer les moyens des militaires. *Seneweb.com*, 20 April.

Liberia 2006 Executive Order No. 2: Repositioning of the Governance Reform Commission, 6 March. Liberia: Government of Liberia. Available at http://www.emansion.gov.lr/doc/EXECUTIVE%20ORDER%20_%202%20-%20Repositioning%20of%20the%20GRC.pdf [Last accessed 17 August 2015].

Liberia 2008 National Defense Act.

Liberia 2011 National Security, Reform and Intelligence Act.

Liberia 2013 An Act to Repeal and Amend Sections 1, 2, and Section 6(IV) of the National Security and Intelligence Act of 2011.

Loden, A 2007 Civil society and security sector reform in post-conflict Liberia: painting a moving train without brushes. *International journal of transitional justice* 1(2): 297–307. DOI: 10.1093/ ijtj/ijm022.

Luckham, R and **Hutchful, E** 2010 Democratic and War-to-Peace Transitions and Security Sector Transformation in Africa. In: Bryden, A and Olonisakin, A (eds.) *Security Sector Transfomation in Africa.* 8 ed. Münster: Lit Verlag. pp. 27–54.

Malan, M 2008 *Security Sector Reform in Liberia. Mixed Results from Humble Beginnings.* Carlisle, Pennsylvania: Strategic Studies Institute, US Army War College.

Malan, M 2008 *Security Sector Reform in Liberia: Mixed Results from Humble Beginnings.* Carlisle, PA: Strategic Studies Institute United States Army War College.

Mali 1992 Constitution of the Republic of Mali.

Manea, M and **Rüland, J** 2013 Taking Stock of Military Reform on Nigeria. In: Rüland, J, Manea, M, Born, H (eds.) *The Politics of Military Reform: Experiences from Indonesia and Nigeria.* New York: Springer. pp. 57–76.

March, J G and **Olsen J P** 1983 The new institutionalism: organizational factors in political life. *American political science review*, 78(03), 734–749.

McGregor, A 2015 Conflict at a Crossroads: Can Nigeria Sustain Its Military Campaign Against Boko Haram? *Terrorism Monitor*, 13(13): 7-11. Available at http://www.jamestown.org/programs/tm/single/?tx_ttnews-%5Btt_news%5D=44084&cHash=93b4e15e1e02c9c2570b02b1bab1421b#.VafZuFWqpBc [Last accessed 12 August 2015].

Ministère de la sécurité intérieure et de la protection civile (MSIPC) 2003a Exposé sur la politique de sécurité du Mali. Bamako: Secrétariat général du MSIPC, August.

Ministère de la sécurité intérieure et de la protection civile (MSIPC) 2003b Discours d'orientation de Monsieur le Ministre de la Sécurité Intérieure et de la Protection Civile à l'occasion de sa prise de contact avec les responsables des services de sécurité et de protection civile. Bamako: MSIPC.

Ministère de la sécurité intérieure et de la protection civile (MSIPC) 2005 Rapport général des États généraux de la sécurité et de la paix. Bamako: MSIPC, November.

Ministry of Defence (MOD) 2008a *Report of the Armed Forces Transformation Committee, Main Report.* Abuja: MOD.

Ministry of Defence (MOD) 2008b *Report of the Armed Forces Transformation Committee, Joint Doctrine for the Armed Forces of Nigeria*, Vols 1&2.Abuja: MOD.

Moulaye, Z (ed.) 2008 *Société civile et gouvernance de la sécurité au Mali.* Bamako: Éditions Coopération Technique Belge, January.

Moulaye, Z 2014 *La problématique de la criminalité transnationale et le contrôle démocratique du secteur de la sécurité*. Bamako: Friedrich Ebert Stiftung, February.

Moulaye, Z and **Niakaté, M** 2011 *Shared gouvernance of peace and security: The Malian experience*. Abuja: Friedrich Ebert Stiftung, December.

Nathan, L 2007 *No Ownership, No Committment: A Guide to Local Ownership of Security Sector Reform*. Birmingham, UK: University of Birmingham.

Nigeria 1979 Constitution of the Federal Republic of Nigeria.

Nigeria 1982 Economic Stabilization (Temporary Provisions) Act.

Nigeria 1999 Constitution of the Federal Republic of Nigeria.

Nigeria 2004 Armed Forces Act (CAP. A20 L.F.N).

Nigeria 2006 *National Defence Policy*. Abuja: Government Printer.

Nigerian National Planning Commission (NNPC) 2004 *Meeting Everyone's Needs: National Economic Empowerment and Development Strategy*. Abuja, Nigeria: NNPC.

Nigeria National Planning Commission (NNPC) 2009 *Nigeria Vision 20: 2020. Economic Transformation Blueprint*. Abuja: NNPC.

North, D C 1990 *Institutions, Institutional Change and Economic Performance*. New York, Cambridge University Press.

Nossiter, A 2014 Nigeria's Army Hampers Hunt for Abducted Schoolgirls. *New York Times*, 23 May.

OECD-DAC 2007 *The OECD DAC Handbook on Security System Reform (SSR): Supporting Security and Justice*. Paris: OECD.

Ojiabor, O 2014 Senate confirms new Service Chiefs. *The Nation*, 30 January, p. 6.

Oloja, M and **Onuorah, M** 2011 National security reform agenda coming, says Azazi. *The Guardian*, 31 July. p. 1.

Olukoshi, A O (ed.) 1993 *The politics of structural adjustment in Nigeria*. Ibadan: Heinemann.

Omitoogun, W and **Oduntan, T** 2006 Nigeria. In: Omitoogun, W and Hutchful, E (eds.) *Budgeting for the Military Sector in Africa: The Processes and Mechanisms of Control*. Oxford: Oxford University Press. pp. 154–179.

Onoma, A K 2014 Transition regimes and security sector reforms in Sierra Leone and Liberia. *WIDER Working Paper, No. 2014/012*. Available at http://www.wider.unu.edu/publications/working-papers/2014/en_GB/wp2014-012/ [Last accessed 17 August 2015].

Onuoh, Felix 2014 Nigeria Islamists better armed, motivated than army: governor. *Reuters*, 17 Feb.

Onuorah, M 2011 Army begins new structure for better security. *The Guardian*, April 10, p.4.

Onuorah, M 2014 Nigeria: Military Denies Report on Soldiers' Defection to Cameroun. *The Guardian*, 25 August, p. 4.

Onwudiwe, E and **Osaghae, E** 2010 *Winning hearts and minds: A community relations approach for the Nigerian military*. Ibadan: John Archers.

Osaghae, E E 1998 *Crippled Giant: Nigeria Since Independence*. London: C. Hurst & Co. Publishers.

Oyegbile, O 2014 Why the fight against Boko Haram is stunted. *The Nation on Sunday*, 31 August, p. 9.

Panter-Brick, S K 1970 From military coup to civil war, January 1966 to May 1967. In: Panter-Brick, S K (ed.) *Nigerian Politics and Military Rule: Prelude to the Civil War*. London: University of London. pp. 14–57.

Parley, W W 2013 Lawyers Fail Ex-Soldiers. *The New Dawn*, 20 November.

Peters, B G 2011 *Institutional theory in political science: the new institutionalism*. Bloomsbury Publishing USA.

Post, K and **Vickers, M** 1973 *Structure and Conflict in Nigeria, 1960-65*. London: Heinemann.

Przeworski, A, Alvarez, M E, Cheibub, J A and **Limongi, F** 2000 *Democracy and Development: Political Institutions and Well-Being in the world, 1950–1990*. Cambridge: Cambridge University Press.

Quantson, K B 2000 *Peace and Stability: Chapters from the Intelligence Sector*. Accra: Napascom Publishers.

Salia, A 2015 Police Council backs efforts to unravel recruitment scam. *Daily Graphic*, 10 March, pp. 32–33.

Sant'Egidio [n.d.] La Communauté. Available at http://www.santegidio.org/pageID/2/langID/fr/LA_COMMUNAUT.html [Last accessed 13 August 2015].

Sawyer, A 2002 Liberating Liberia. In: *The Emergence of Autocracy in Liberia. Tragedy and Challenge*. San Francisco, CA: Institute for Contemporary Studies.

Schmitt, E and **Knowlton, B** 2014 U.S. Officials Question Ability of Nigeria to Rescue Hostages. *New York Times*, 15 May.

Schnabel, A 2009 Ideal Requirements versus Real Environments in Security Sector Reform. In: Born, H and Schnabel, A (eds.) *Security Sector Reform in Challenging Environments*. Münster: Lit Verlag.

Schnabel, A and **Born, H** 2011 *Security Sector Reform Narrowing the Gap between Theory and Practice*. SSR Papers. Geneva: Geneva Centre for the Democratic Control of Armed Forces.

Schroeder, U C and **Chappuis, F** 2014 New Perspectives on Security Sector Reform: The Role of Local Agency and Domestic Politics. *International Peacekeeping*, 21: 133–148.

Schroeder, U C, Chappuis, F and **Kocak, D** 2013 Security Sector Reform from a Policy Transfer Perspective: A Comparative Study of International Interventions in the Palestinian Territories, Liberia and Timor-Leste. *Journal of Intervention and Statebuilding*, 7: 381–401.

Senenews 2012 Paix en Casamance: Les femmes sur le pied de guerre. *Senenews.com*, 29 July.

SenewebNews 2013 Exclusif – Vente de 3 avions de combat au Sénégal : Les assurances du fournisseur et milliardaire Luiz Carlos Aguiar. *Seneweb.com*, 15 April.

Shabbir Cheema, G 2005 *Buiding Democratic Institutions: Governance Reform in Developing Countries.* West Hartford, C T: Kumarian Press.

Siollun, M 2013 *Soldiers of fortune: Nigerian politics from Buhari to Babangida, 1983–1993.* Abuja: Cassava Republic Press.

Soumah, M 2004 *Guinée, de Sékou Touré à Lansana Conté.* Paris: Editions L'Harmattan.

Stroehlein, A 2013 'The guns may be silent now, but Liberia is going nowhere': After a decade of peace, country is still suffering under a corrupt police force. *The Independent,* 20 December.

Sustainable Development Goals 2015 Transforming our world: the 2030 Agenda for Sustainable Development. In: United Nations (ed.) *Agreed Outcome Draft as of August 2015.*

Sy, D 2003 La condition du juge en Afrique : l'exemple du Sénégal. Afrilex, 3, June. Available at http://afrilex.u-bordeaux4.fr/la-condition-du-juge-en-afrique-l.html [Last accessed 13 August 2015].

The Paris Declaration On Aid Effectiveness 2005 *Second High Level Forum on Aid Effectiveness.* Paris: France.

UN SSR Taskforce 2012 *Security Sector Reform Integrated Technical Guidance Notes.* United Nations.

United Nations 2000 *United Nations Millenium Declaration.* A/RES/55/2. United Nations General Assembly, 18 September.

United Nations 2008 *Securing Peace and Development: The Role of the United Nations in Supporting Security Sector Reform. Report of the Secretary-General.* A/62/659–S/2008/39. United Nations General Assembly, 23 January.

United Nations 2013 *Securing States and societies: strengthening the United Nations comprehensive support to security sector reform. Report of the Secretary-General.* S/2013/480. United Nations General Assembly, 13 August.

United Nations Peacebuilding Commission (PBC) 2012 *Report of the first review of the Statement of Mutual Commitments between the Government of Guinea and the Peacebuilding Commission (September 2011 to March 2012).* PBC/6/GUI/3. United Nations General Assembly and Security Council, 19 June.

United Nations Peacebuilding Commission (PBC) 2012 *Review of progress in the implementation of the statement of mutual commitments on peacebuilding in Liberia.* PBC/6/LBR1. United Nations General Assembly and Security Council, 13 March.

United Nations Security Council 2005a *Progress report of the Secretary-General on ways to combat subregional and cross-border problems in West Africa.* S/2005/86. United Nations Security Council, 11 February.

United Nations Security Council 2005b *Eighth progress report of the Secretary-General on the United Nation Mission in Liberia.* S/2005/60. United Nations Security Council, 1 September.

United Nations Security Council 2006 *Eleventh Progress Report of the Secretary-General on the United Mission in Liberia*. S/2006/376. United Nations Security Council, 9 June.

United Nations Security Council 2007 *Letter Dated 5 December 2007 from the Chairman of the Security Council Committee Established Pursuant to Resolution 1521 (2003) Concerning Liberia Addressed to the President of the Security Council*. S/2007/689. United Nations Security Council, 5 December.

United Nations Security Council 2009 *Eighteenth progress report of the Secretary-General on the United Nation Mission in Liberia*. S/2009/86. United Nations Security Council, 10 February.

United Nations Security Council 2014 *The maintenance of international peace and security: Security sector reform: challenges and opportunities*. S/RES/2151 (2014). United Nations Security Council, 28 April.

Uvin, P 2009 *Life After Violence: A People's Story of Burundi*. London: Zed Books.

Uzoechina, O 2014 *Security Sector Reform and Governance Processes in West Africa: From Concepts to Reality*. DCAF Policy Paper. Geneva: Geneva Centre for the Democratic Control of Armed Forces.

Van Veen, E and **Price,** 2014 *Securing its success, justifying its relevance: Mapping a way forward for Security Sector Reform*. CRU Policy Brief. Clingendael: Netherlands Institute of International Relations.

World Development Report 2011 *Conflict, Security, and Development. World Development Report 2011*. Washington D C: The World Bank.

About the Geneva Centre for the Democratic Control of Armed Forces (DCAF)

The Geneva Centre for the Democratic Control of Armed Forces (DCAF) is an international foundation whose mission is to assist the international community in pursuing good governance and reform of the security sector. To this end, the Centre develops and promotes appropriate norms at the international and national levels, determines good practices and relevant policy recommendations for effective governance of the security sector, and provides in-country advisory support and practical assistance programmes to all interested actors. Detailed information is available at **www.dcaf.ch**

Geneva Centre for the Democratic Control of Armed Forces (DCAF):
Chemin Eugène-Rigot 2E
1202 Geneva, Switzerland

P.O.Box 1360
CH-1211 Geneva 1, Switzerland

Tel: +41 (0) 22 730 9400
Fax: +41 (0) 22 730 9405
E-mail: info@dcaf.ch

www.ingramcontent.com/pod-product-compliance
Lightning Source LLC
Chambersburg PA
CBHW071126280326
41935CB00010B/1131

* 9 7 8 1 9 0 9 1 8 8 6 7 9 *